W9-AVG-395

THE SHAPE OF THE NEW EUROPE

THE SHAPE OF
THE NEW EUROPE

Edited by Gregory F. Treverton

COUNCIL ON FOREIGN RELATIONS PRESS

NEW YORK

COUNCIL ON FOREIGN RELATIONS BOOKS

The Council on Foreign Relations, Inc., is a nonprofit and nonpartisan organization devoted to promoting improved understanding of international affairs through the free exchange of ideas. The Council does not take any position on questions of foreign policy and has no affiliation with, and receives no funding from, the United States government.

From time to time, books and monographs written by members of the Council's research staff or visiting fellows, or commissioned by the Council, or written by an independent author with critical review contributed by a Council study or working group are published with the designation "Council on Foreign Relations Book." Any book or monograph bearing that designation is, in the judgment of the Committee on Studies of the Council's Board of Directors, a responsible treatment of a significant international topic worthy of presentation to the public. All statements of fact and expressions of opinion contained in Council books are, however, the sole responsibility of the author.

If you would like more information on Council publications, please write the Council on Foreign Relations, 58 East 68th Street, New York, NY 10021, or call the Publications Office at (212) 734-0400.

Library of Congress Cataloguing-in-Publication Data

The shape of the new Europe / edited by Gregory F. Treverton.
p.   cm.
A project of the Council on Foreign Relations.
Includes index.
ISBN 0-87609-107-9 : $16.95
1. Europe—Economic integration. 2. Europe—Politics and government—1989– 3. European federation. 4. International economic relations. I. Treverton, Gregory F. II. Council on Foreign Relations.

HC241.s515   1991
337.1'4—dc20

91-23295
CIP

92 93 94 95 96 97 PB 10 9 8 7 6 5 4 3 2 1

Cover Design: Whit Vye

CONTENTS

ACKNOWLEDGMENTS

The chapters in this volume were presented to a Study Group, "1992: Political and Strategic Implications," which met at the Council on Foreign Relations during 1989–91, chaired by Stanley Hoffmann. The editor would like to express his appreciation to the members of that Study Group, whose comments enriched the book, and to William Diebold and Tony Smith, who reviewed it. His thanks go also to Robert Goldsmith, Suzanne Hooper, Judith Train, David Kellogg, and, especially, Steven Spiegel, who saw it through to publication. Appreciation of another sort is owed to the Ford Foundation, whose generous financial support made the project possible.

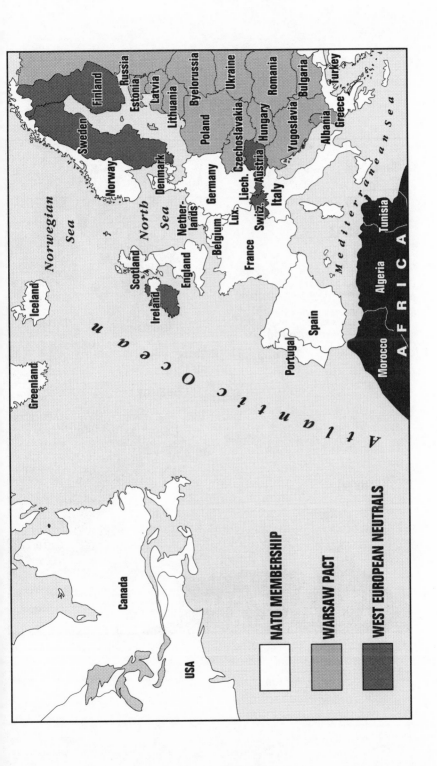

NATO MEMBERSHIP

WARSAW PACT

WEST EUROPEAN NEUTRALS

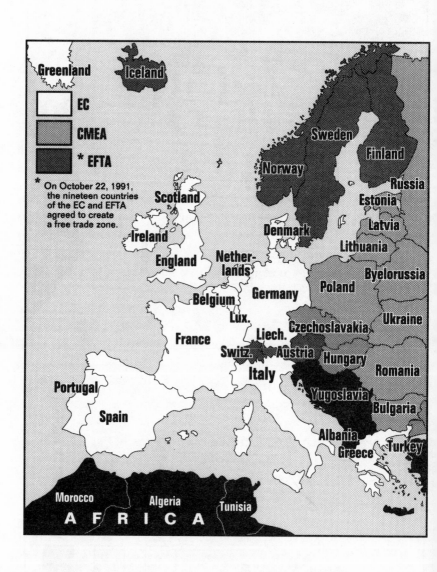

Greenland

Iceland

EC

CMEA

* EFTA

* On October 22, 1991,
the nineteen countries
of the EC and EFTA
agreed to create
a free trade zone.

Sweden

Finland

Norway

Russia

Scotland

Estonia

Latvia

Ireland

Denmark

Lithuania

England

Nether-
lands

Byelorussia

Belgium

Germany

Poland

Lux.

Ukraine

France

Liech.

Czechoslavakia

Switz.

Austria

Hungary

Romania

Italy

Yugoslavia

Portugal

Bulgaria

Spain

Albania

Greece

Turkey

Morocco

Algeria

Tunisia

A F R I C A

INTRODUCTION

Gregory F. Treverton

This book, and the Council on Foreign Relations project from which it emerged, was conceived before the fall of the Berlin Wall in 1989. Yet, the project's purpose from the start was to look at the set of events labeled in shorthand "1992" in their broader political setting. The European Community's (EC) plans for the next steps in economic integration were then and are now important in themselves—and a parallel portion of the project under the direction of my colleague C. Michael Aho will address their economic effects in *The European Challenge*. But 1992 was also a window into broader currents in Europe's construction, and so it provided a vantage point from which to think about Europe's future.

We were looking through that window when the Wall fell—as the project's chair, Stanley Hoffmann, nicely put it. I visualized that image as a book cover: eager students looking through a window for glimpses of reality while the wall around the window was coming down. That metaphor was too obscure for a cover, but it does evoke the book's task. What would have been speculations about a future within relatively fixed boundaries became an inquiry about boundaries. Then, "Europe" was western Europe; now, the question "What is Europe?" is at the center of the inquiry.

WHICH EUROPE?

Because events since 1989 are so absorbing, it is worth pausing to remember how Europe came to our starting point, the Single European Act of 1986, which initiated the 1992 program. Surely, if the Wall had not come down, we would be thinking of

1

1992 in a quite different light. The driving force behind the Single European Act of 1986 was more economic than political, more the urging of the private sector than the leading of the public. The mid-1980s were the years of "Eurosclerosis," of abiding doubts about whether Europe could compete with Japan and the United States.

European business argued that if Europe did not move ahead, it would fall behind. Both diagnosis and prescription derived from classic integration economics: internal barriers within Europe raised costs for governments and firms, and denied Europe the benefits of economies of scale; European firms would stand a better chance of competing if they could enjoy the advantage of a continental market.

A second strand of motivation for 1992 was more political, illustrative of the half-intended consequences of political acts. EC leaders had been through years of wrangling over the EC budget, especially Britain's contribution. By the mid-1980s, they were looking for something to put a more positive face on Europe. The EC Commission's 1985 white paper on the internal market was at hand, assembled by Britain's commissioner, Lord Cockfield, from ideas long languishing in file drawers; it was a blueprint for moving forward.

When EC heads of state a few months later approved the blueprint in its entirety as the Single European Act of 1986, it is not that those leaders did not know what they were doing. But no doubt none of them quite imagined the full sweep of what they had set in motion. History often seems to move at a creep, with the accumulated change apparent only later, when some event or action demarcates it. Here, though, the action came first, setting loose a process that ran beyond what almost all of those taking it had intended.

And so by the late 1980s Eurosclerosis had given way to "Europhoria" over Europe's future. The fall of the Wall and the realization of the immense tasks that lay behind it were a dash of cold water, yet Helen Wallace's interpretation of Europe's mood remains upbeat. She, like François Heisbourg, imagines a foul weather scenario: Europe could turn inward—the EC not a fortress but a regional bloc; Germany not a leader, but an introspective and parochial state; and the interest in collective foreign and security policies a way not to take responsibility, but to opt out of it.

The inward turn is possible, yet Wallace does not think it likely. Hers is a vision of Europe for the Europeans, one that again underscores the central role of the EC: "the EC does radiate magnetic impulses that are pulling other Europeans into its gravitational field." Sentimental pan-Europeanism motivates some in Europe's east but few in its west; nevertheless, the rediscovery of half a continent, known for a half century only at a distance, provides a challenge.

That challenge is more economic than military, and it concerns the Europeans in the first instance. Will the EC be able to deliver on all that is expected of it? Can it do so through its continued development along now orthodox lines, or is a distinct shift in Europe's integration called for? And can Europe bear the weight of adjustments alone, or will it need the active engagement of others, notably the United States?

Wallace's answers are more confident for the first two questions than for the last. Rhetoric surely will outstrip reality. Demands will go unmet; if that is true from within Europe, it will be more true of demands made from outside. The EC's reluctant grappling with Yugoslavia's agony demonstrated both. The EC will sometimes make and sometimes avoid hard choices; sometimes the process will be explicit, and sometimes it will reflect the interplay of pressures across domestic politics. In any event, it would be foolish to think the EC itself will not be changed in the process. A Community twice the size of the current twelve-member EC could hardly be only an enlargement.

Will building the new Europe require a new transatlantic bargain? Here, the answer is perhaps. Certainly, western Europeans would like the United States to stay engaged, even militarily so. But any new bargain would have to be very different from the original postwar one, when Europe needed the United States much more than it does now. Then, in Wallace's words, "the levers of influence in U.S. hands were powerful." Now, Europe wants America "not to spearhead . . . a recovery program, but to be an active partner in conserving and reinforcing a multilateral order."

Europe's postwar order, founded on its division, was based on a transatlantic security partnership, NATO, plus a European economic zone, the EC. Now the division is gone and, with it, the postwar order. François Heisbourg's chapter begins by outlining how sharp the change is—from a European order centered on defense, clear-cut and comprehensive, to one in which defense is subordinate, but with confusion and flux aplenty.

Only the incautious would call Europe's changes irreversible except in one area, eastern Europe. For all that region's turmoil, nothing short of a massive military adventure would reestablish communism or, especially, Soviet or Russian dominance. Western Europe would thus have literally years of warning of a renewed Cold War–style military threat to it. The Soviet threat that animated the Cold War security structure has disappeared as irreversibly as history permits to be foreseen.

Indeed, while the Soviet Union's future is as uncertain as eastern Europe's, its turmoil will not lead to increasing influence beyond its borders; quite the contrary. The one terrifying exception is difficult to address through western policy—nuclear madness ensuing from civil war and the resulting loss of control over the thousands of Soviet nuclear weapons. Over the long run, Europe cannot be stable if Soviet territory is in turmoil or if the states on that territory, Russia in particular, feel alienated from Europe.

Europe's uncertainty makes architecture fool's play, but Heisbourg hazards his own institutional collage, based on fair weather assumptions—both America's troops in some number and its European commitment will be sustained, and so will the momentum of EC integration. In those conditions, the collage would overlay the Conference on Security and Cooperation in Europe (CSCE) as the embryo of a pan-European order with the institutions of a democratic Europe (like the EC, the Council of Europe, and the Western European Union (WEU)), and with the transatlantic connection (in the near term, embodied in NATO).

Over the longer term, if the weather held fair, the WEU might converge with the EC as the latter moved into the security realm. That could eventually mean a new European-American connection, even a reshaped alliance, one whose European weight would be greater. Instead of NATO's sixteen nations, with the United States first among ostensible equals, the new connection would be based on the WEU-cum-EC and the United States.

The high drama of eastern Europe has obscured the real development in the core of the EC; 1992 was not a fluke, as Peter Ludlow's chapter reminds us. Yet the program presumed that "*deepening* the community of existing members was to be given frank precedence over *widening* it to include new members," in Stanley Hoffmann's words. The fall of the Wall made that priority awkward, and the Gulf war put pressure on European cooperation where it always had been most fragile—military cooperation outside Europe.

Implementing a monetary union, not to mention a political union, will be difficult. Ludlow is optimistic, however, a committed deepener. The role of a unified Germany looms but, so far, the Bonn-Brussels axis has been more important to the EC's success than the Bonn-Paris connection. Under Prime Minister Margaret Thatcher, Britain was the odd country out; yet, it could not afford to be left entirely behind, and Thatcher's successor, John Major, has changed the tone, if not always the substance, of Britain's relations with its EC partners.

Economic and Monetary Union (EMU) is the benchmark at hand. Bonn had reassured its partners that unification would not deflect it from its European vocation, and in December 1990, EC intergovernmental conferences agreed on an ambitious timetable for creating a common currency and a single central bank, or Eurofed. Ludlow is surely right: EMU is a matter of when, not if.

Yet, Germany will be preoccupied with the costs of unification, which escalated daily. That preoccupation will make the government more inflation-phobic and the Bundesbank still less willing to share authority over a Eurofed with countries, such as Italy, which are running large budget deficits. In March 1991 Karl-Otto Pöhl, then Bundesbank president, took his concerns on that score public. He criticized his government for its haste in creating a *German* monetary union the previous summer, thereby implicitly calling for caution in moving to a Eurofed.

The EC's institutional changes over the last decade and a half are often interpreted as a victory for "intergovernmentalism" (that is, the Council of Ministers representing the member states) over "supranationalism" (the Commission and European Parliament). Ludlow argues that this view is too black and white; rather, the Council itself now operates within a supranational framework in which it depends on the Commission and vice versa. In the short run, the EC's political agenda is modest, aimed at making the Community work better and democratizing its institutions by conceding more authority to the parliament and making greater use of majority voting in the Council of Ministers; the difficult issues of social policy and of financial transfers from richer north to poorer south are left to be resolved.

In the long run, the most difficult issues facing the EC political union are foreign policy and defense. The Single European Act brings European political consultation more firmly into the EC, and as Europeans frame common foreign economic policies—for instance, toward eastern Europe—they also necessarily edge toward common foreign policies; foreign economic policy *is* foreign policy.

The timing of the Gulf war, however, could not have been worse, especially for Germany. Preoccupied internally, Germany was slow to recognize the importance of its allies' stakes, especially those of the United States, and to draw the appropriate conclusions. Its own debate over altering its constitution to permit the deployment of soldiers beyond NATO territory, contentious enough, was only just beginning. "Europe" was left in some disarray, especially on the military side, the war underscoring the imbalance between Germany's economic weight and its constrained military role, particularly outside Europe. The Yugoslav crisis made the same point about the EC as a whole: its political consultation was impressive, if not always effective, but it lacked any military instruments.

In his chapter, Stanley Hoffmann concludes that both "a common EC foreign policy which would be more than a series of declarations and deplorations" and "a common security policy with its own effective institutions" are as far away as ever—not because the major European states disagree about the dangers, but because in the absence of a single overriding threat, their approaches go in different directions: witness France and Germany over Yugoslavia. Ludlow is more hopeful for the EC. He sees the disarray as a powerful stimulus to do better, though he believes progress toward a common foreign policy will be faster than progress on security issues.

EUROPE FOR WHICH EUROPEANS?

F. Stephen Larrabee looks through the window to the other side of the erstwhile Wall, at what we used to call eastern Europe. Events in eastern Europe denied western Europe the luxury of taking the next steps in its own integration—the 1992 program and beyond—before thinking about expanding. The fall of the Wall raised the question of new members and new associations, and with it, the larger issue of what kind of EC in what kind of Europe. As Hoffmann notes, widening and deepening are not entirely opposed, for the Community would have to reinforce its core institutions before it could widen. Still, the result of a rapid widening would inevitably be a looser federation of more diverse states with more special provisions in their adhesions to the Community.

It is not easy to be optimistic about an eastern Europe that faces not one transition but two, toward both democracy and free markets. Czechoslovakia aside, eastern Europe is a region where democratic experience is thin but ethnic identities are strong among groups not sorted neatly into separate territories. Larrabee foresees uneven progress and the reemergence of an "east central Europe"—Hungary, Czechoslovakia, and Poland—which will move faster toward democracy and free markets than a still uncertain southeastern Europe.

The collapse of the Warsaw Pact and Comecon has left the eastern European states to cast about for new connections in the west even as it leaves them skeptical about banding together lest they be consigned to a ghetto in their part of Europe. That casting about is apparent in the security realm, and it has induced many in east central Europe to look favorably on NATO and the presence of American troops on the continent.

The search is more urgent in the economic realm. The breakup of Comecon disrupted trade eastward, and the eastern Europeans were twice hit by higher oil prices—first as Moscow began to require hard currency payment for its oil at the beginning of 1991, and then as the Gulf war pushed prices higher. At the same time, their energy dependence on the Soviet Union will not quickly decline.

Eastern Europe has embraced almost anything with the label "Europe"—that is, western Europe—from the Council of Europe to subregional groupings like the Pentagonal of Hungary, Czechoslovakia, Yugoslavia, Austria, and Italy. EC membership, however, remains the key, even though no eastern European state expects to become a full member soon. The EC can offer the region some money and more access for its exports to EC markets; the EC's Common Agricultural Policy (CAP), however, has so far been no more generous in affording access to eastern European products than those from any other part of the globe. The EC has, in Hoffmann's words, "deliberately or passively, put deepening ahead of widening."

Wolfgang Danspeckgruber's focus is one circle nearer the core of the EC—the European Free Trade Association (EFTA), the set of industrialized European states that have not joined the EC. With the exception of Norway and Iceland, they are all postwar neutrals—Austria, Switzerland, Sweden, and Finland. Traditional neutrality, however, seems less and less relevant, while the possibility of new "neutrals"—eastern European members of the now defunct Warsaw Pact—adds another dimension to European politics.

EFTA is the EC's most important trading partner, and the two reached an agreement in 1991 on a European Economic Area (EEA). Especially to an American, the EC offer of the EEA looks like an offer that cannot be accepted: it imposes taxation without representation and EC rules without much say in constructing them. That first Austria and then Sweden indicated a desire for full EC membership is hardly a surprise. The others, save perhaps Switzerland, will not be far behind, and so the EEA will be important mostly as a stepping-stone to full membership.

That will make the EFTA attractive to eastern Europe, but will not make eastern Europe very attractive to the EFTA. EFTA countries are richer than all but the richest EC states; therefore, for the EFTA to try to form a free trade area with eastern Europe would be a diversion from its members' goal of joining the EC and an almost impossible adjustment for the eastern Europeans.

The fall of the Wall is robbing the traditional neutrality of most EFTA members of meaning. As one small indication, the UN embargo against Iraq was the first such action in which Switzerland participated. The waning of the East-West conflict may, for example, mute previous objections to Austria's EC membership on grounds that its neutrality would complicate EC foreign policy. At the same time, however, a vaguer concept of neutrality is appealing to eastern Europe.

In the long run, with luck, pan-European arrangements like the Conference on Security and Cooperation in Europe would amount, in Danspeckgruber's phrase, to a kind of "global neutralization." NATO or the WEU might remain as an alliance of subgroups of states, but such an alliance would be devoid of ideological content, if not entirely of meaning. Europe's states might be joined by the "Europeanness" of their foreign and security policy more than they were divided by their separate memberships. But this is a long-term vision.

It is plain that Europe's future will be less orderly than the vision of concentric circles around the EC that EC Commission President Jacques Delors harbors. It will be an institutional collage—different and overlapping institutions for different but overlapping purposes. In any event, though it remains in doubt how soon, or even whether, the EC will become the guiding institution for all of Europe, there is no doubt it will be fundamental.

It is equally plain that Germany will be at the center of that core, a theme that runs through the chapters of this volume. Larrabee notes the shift in attitudes toward Germany on the part of east central Europe. Old anxieties about German dominance in a new *Mitteleuropa* have not disappeared but have ceded place to their opposite: concern not that Germany will loom too large, but that in its preoccupation with unification, it will be too small an economic partner. The line making the rounds in eastern Europe is, "How far east will east central Europe extend? As far as German taxpayers want."

Over time, those eastern European areas adjacent to Germany where old connections remain, in Poland and Czechoslovakia, seem likely to develop the same relation to Germany as northern Mexico bears to the United States—another country by sovereignty but economically of a piece with the other. German fears of new waves of migrants will abet that process. At what point that German role in eastern Europe might become a source of tension between Germany and the Soviet Union or Russia is another question posed by Danspeckgruber.

JAPAN'S PUSH AND AMERICA'S RESPONSE

Without the drama of the Wall's fall and the opening in eastern Europe, we would be more impressed by the EC 1992 process than we are. We probably would also be less Eurocentric in our assessment of it: the chapter by Michael Borrus and John Zysman reminds us just how much Japan influenced both the fact and shape of 1992. If the desire to stay competitive in a fast-moving world was the motivation for 1992, the specific target was Japan; cynically put, Europeans hoped to prevent Japan from doing to Europe what it had done to the United States.

Yet policies aimed at Japan also hit others, the United States in particular. When the EC insisted on reciprocity in banking, in an effort to open access to Japanese financial institutions, the resulting directive was, as wags had it, "the missile launched at Tokyo that landed on New York and exploded in Washington." By the same token, questions have arisen about whether Europe will consider Hondas made in Tennessee as American or Japanese if it places quotas on Japanese imports. Europe will impose local-content rules in an attempt to hold on to component and subsystem production even if final assembly in Europe passes into Japanese hands. But American experience casts doubt on whether Europe will succeed in doing so.

The world's major firms are becoming increasingly global, but at the same time, three roughly equal regional economies are emerging—Europe, East Asia, and North America. In the words of Borrus and Zysman, they "are not autonomous, but they are separable." The emergence of an Asian zone around Japan is the most striking recent development, but trade within the EC has been growing faster than EC trade with others since the Community's establishment. Europe's position is not weak; it has a skilled work force and a strong basis of wealth, and its industry has been more successful than its American counterpart at remaining competitive in traditional industries.

The EC remains committed to open markets, but just as plainly, it is not integrating its market as a favor to non-Europeans. A world broken into autonomous regions would be in no one's interest, but in such a world, Europe would have significant advantages. Will Europe's preoccupation with itself—first 1992 and then the unexpected task of dealing with eastern Europe—make its regional emphasis more pronounced? And what would that imply for security arrangements in Europe and beyond? These questions lie at the edges of this book's inquiry.

Undeniably, Europe needs America less than it did just after World War II. For forty years, NATO and the presence of U.S. forces have been the anchor of that American engagement. The United States grew accustomed to a privileged position, one it will have no more. Stanley Hoffmann, in his chapter, is more concerned with Europe than the United States, but he is relatively comfortable with the loss of American privilege—if not, perhaps, with the political task of accommodating to it.

On the economic side, he foresees the EC becoming as ambiguous externally as it is in its relations to the sovereignty of its member-states. It will be both a regional bloc, often irritating—as it was to the United States during the argument over CAP in the Uruguay Round of the General Agreement on Tariffs and Trade (GATT) negotiations—and an international actor, one that invites in American and Japanese capital.

On the security side, Hoffmann implicitly agrees with Wallace that the business at hand is primarily European, but Europe's business requires a "drastic turnaround by Washington."

Repeated warnings from the United States in 1991 that EC discussions of common security policy must not undercut NATO demonstrated the old ambivalence: "Washington would like its partners to speak in a single voice, as long as they repeat what the United States tells them." Cheerleading for NATO smacked of clinging to the institution that embodies American dominance, a point Ludlow also touches.

Instead, the United States should eagerly support European cooperation in defense. For one, that cooperation will not go very far, precisely because Britain, France, and Germany are so divided over what to do; neither the first nor the last wants to upset the status quo, though for different reasons, while France can express its European vision confident that it will not have to make good on it. Moreover, Hoffmann believes that Europeans themselves will best handle many of the security threats the continent will confront, from refugees to the spillovers of conflict in Europe's east. On that score, as on issues beyond Europe, the alternative to a common western European policy is not NATO. Rather, it is "paralysis or fractured reactions," perhaps even the renationalization of defense policies.

For Hoffmann, the question mark for Europe is not whether the nation-state will survive (it will), but whether the European Community can be made strong enough to be effective in defense and diplomacy, where national autonomy has continued but policies based on it have "produced more illusions than results," and to engage and then absorb east central Europe. America's task is to manage, "at last, a shift from primacy to world order," recognizing that, globally, yearnings for a unipolar moment are unfounded, and that in Europe, Washington's veto is no longer justified.

Hoffmann's argument hints at a conclusion that runs against the last forty years of history, not to mention the internationalist inclinations of the American Europeanists and Europeans writing in this book. Might this not be the time for seeking to avoid new transatlantic projects, rather than for seeking them? This approach would not be disengagement, let alone isolationism in whatever "neo" incarnation. American troops would remain in Europe in some numbers. Plenty of business would remain to be done. But this does not seem the time to try to conceive projects comparable to the Marshall Plan and NATO for reconstructing western Europe and containing the Soviet Union.

No such comparable project is at hand. For instance, reconstructing eastern Europe and the Soviet Union is a tempting candidate. However, aside from the technical reasons why eastern Europe, let alone the Soviet Union, is not postwar western Europe, Europe's east seems destined to be Europe's responsibility, for better or worse. The United States, having convinced itself it is poor, has also convinced itself that talk alone can rebuild eastern Europe. A grand new bargain over issues beyond Europe seems an unpromising venture on which to hang the future of the transatlantic connection, while a dramatic initiative in tripartite management—United States, EC, Japan—of the global economy seems premature, perhaps unwise.

A better approach might be to try to make facts into virtues, letting nature take its course, but thinking of the course as one to welcome rather than bemoan. It would mean limiting the claims we make on our European partners and, in so doing, on ourselves. It would mean trying to invest particular policies with less political capital, and so to run less risk that every particular incident will become a litmus test of cooperation and every failed test an occasion for handwringing or recrimination.

Such a tack would rest on the assumptions that security threats are not pressing, but domestic business is—for both the United States and Europe. America will confront no shortage of international problems, but no mortal threats of the sort that animated it for the last forty years. The Soviet Union or Russia, its threat to the United States overstated in the past, may be underestimated now, but does not pose a direct threat to territorial integrity, sovereignty, or political institutions—not for western Europe and surely not for the United States. The same seems the case for threats from the Third World, the Gulf war notwithstanding.

The names of the more serious "threats"—competitiveness and Japan—call attention to the judgment on which the alternative approach rests: if the world will permit limiting claims,

American interests will require it. America's pressing business now lies at home, not abroad; the tails of those problems stretch across borders, but their roots are at home. For instance, no amount of beating on Japan to open its markets, however appropriate, will help American industry as much as competing better with Japanese products in the United States.

If America's urgent business is at home, the same is the case for Europe, and perhaps for Japan, as well. Europe's business is constructing itself, moving through the 1992 project and beyond while opening to eastern Europe. That is plenty to do. Like America's business, its international tails are long, but its roots are in Europe; for example, nothing the United States might do for eastern Europe would help as much as more open access to western Europe's markets.

This call to demand less and expect less is a far cry from the staple of transatlantic rhetoric over the last two generations. It can be criticized as an invitation to those who want to disengage, even newly isolate, the United States, not refocus its energies at home. The criticism is apt. Yet, the question is whether it is wise to try to sustain, in general, the level of American internationalism of the Cold War and, in particular, the intensity of the American engagement in Europe. Might it not be better to recognize that the ending of the main enemy is a momentous change, and to try to refocus energies accordingly?

November 1991

1

WHAT EUROPE FOR WHICH EUROPEANS?

Helen Wallace

The events of the last two years have turned Europe topsy-turvy. The old order has been overturned and the old certainties, however much they were disliked, have been shattered. As the liberal democratic and market-based model of west European society has prevailed peacefully over the shadows and threats of a now discredited alternative to the East, the consequences have in large part been greeted with relief and rejoicing. Yet, the task remains of creating a stable and solid version of west European society across the rest of the continent. It is this task that now necessarily bears down heavily on the politicians, policymakers, and entrepreneurs of western Europe. They come to the task with optimism, but their recognition of just how much needs to be done and how many resources will be needed to achieve success increasingly tempers that optimism.

In one sense, the task seems simple, since the events of the last two years appear so obviously to vindicate the politics, economics, and policies pursued in western Europe over the past 45 years. In particular, one could argue, the beacon of west European integration seems to be shining brightly as an example for the rest of the continent. Yet, this is too simple an analysis. The European Community (EC) has indeed achieved much since its creation, but it is an incomplete construction, as the current intergovernmental conferences (IGCs) bear witness with their twin agendas of reinforcing, respectively, economic and political integration. Thus, simultaneously, the leaders of the EC find themselves immersed in a process of improving the way they manage their own affairs and irretrievably engaged in piloting the transition of their eastern neighbors. To do both at once is a pretty tall order. The temptation to introversion was already a strand of intra-EC debate; the pull of responsibility for the other Europeans adds to the pressures to concentrate on Europe. The uncertainties about the future of the former Soviet Union, as a fragmenting neighbor with both new political units and many potential migrants, can only add to the anxieties of Europeans.

Thus, for most Europeans, Europe dominates the international agenda. The key issues are to do with securing European stability, security, and economic health, and with a daunting balancing act to be performed between consolidation at home and responsibilities toward neighbors. The requirements of both are considerable in terms of political attention and energy and of economic resources. Beside these important preoccupations, all other international issues pale in significance. This is not to suggest that Europeans will or should opt out of the international system or abandon their responsibilities toward the rest of the world. But it is to recognize that intra-European preoccupations heavily shape attitudes toward the rest of the world, and that faced with stark choices, Europeans are likely instinctively to avoid prejudicing the European construction.

However, one central element of that European construction, or the (west) Europeans' understanding of its potential impact, has always been the perception of a Europe that played an important and influential part in world affairs, of a Europe with several windows open to non-European neighbors, and of a Europe with strong extra-European interests. So to neglect the rest of the world would be to deny a crucial purpose of the European integration process and to remove a critical, sometimes primary, reason for establishing a robust European identity. Hence the persistent talk of the drive to establish a common foreign policy and a common security or defense policy as necessary corollaries of further (west) European integration.

Specifically, therefore, the leaders of the EC and its member-countries, necessarily the predominant focus for elaborating European policies, have four core tasks on their agenda: to consolidate the EC; to assist their east European cousins' transition to market economies and functioning democracies; to find some means of responding to the economic, social, and political

1eeds of the former USSR; and to enhance their capabilities in 1nternational relations more generally. One should perhaps add 1 fifth task to this list—namely, to develop a new approach to heir Mediterranean neighbors, both the Europeans still outside the EC and the non-Europeans tied by geography, economics, 1nd politics to the fortunes of Europe.

That Europe must be made safe for democracy is thus the leitmotiv of the west European agenda. That a democratic Europe must be made safe for the world is recognized as the concomitant goal of Europeans, though it may not always be so insistently pursued. Yet, it is just as much an interest of partners outside Europe as it is of the Europeans that these two objectives be congruent, not conflicting. This requires that the transatlantic relationship be resilient, but also that it adjust to the consequences of change in Europe and the refocusing of American interests.

The relationship faced severe tests at the end of 1990—in the domain of political economy because of the turbulence of the final phases of the Uruguay Round of the General Agreement on Tariffs and Trade (GATT), and in the security sphere because of the Gulf crisis. Each risked becoming the litmus test Americans would use to determine the new Europe's external identity, and on both counts, the Americans have legitimate grounds for concern over the continued evidence of European introversion. Europeans, however, though acknowledging the importance of each, would generally not attribute the same level of salience to them.

The Uruguay Round has a lower political profile in Europe than in the United States, with no active parliamentary scrutiny and much less orchestrated lobbying by interest groups. In any case, the Europeans deduced (rightly or wrongly) that in Brussels, the Americans were engaged more in histrionics than in substantive negotiation, not least with their apparent refusal to recognize that the trade consequences alone could not drive agricultural reform within Europe. This led to considerable irritation in the EC at American unwillingness to move on the other issues in the Round. Very few Europeans understood the adverse impact on U.S. opinion of what the Americans viewed as European obduracy.

As for the Gulf crisis, European opinion was divided. Those who saw the Iraqi occupation of Kuwait as a critical test for the civilized international community regretted, and in the British case publicly castigated, the weak European response. A strong current of European opinion favored sanctions but not intervention, a reflection perhaps of the limited military ambitions of some west European countries. But both hawks and doves agreed that no European organization had the authority to produce a collective response that would cover the span from military action to financial aid. Whether the EC or the Western European Union (WEU) should have such responsibility is a matter for future decisions.

This chapter addresses the shifting debate inside Europe, particularly within the EC, and its central preoccupation with sorting out Europe. It argues that this is of real importance for the transatlantic relationship, since a stable and healthy Europe is in the American and wider international interest. Indeed, the European instinct is to regard these European tasks as qualitatively different from much of the old transatlantic agenda because they mark part of a historic shift of paradigm. Europeans thus see them as being in a quite different category from either the important but more mundane issues in the GATT Round or, for somewhat different reasons, the Gulf crisis, which few Europeans considered a test of the transatlantic relationship. But the notion of a shift of paradigm does bear heavily on the debate about Europeanizing the defense of Europe. None of this should be taken to exonerate Europeans from the need to make a responsible contribution to wider international regimes or extra-European problems. But that contribution would be impaired if it were not to be based on the emergence of the new Europe as a stable and robust regional system. Much of this will depend in any case on what happens within the EC politically and economically.

THE INHERITANCE

The year 1992 symbolizes the regaining of a sense of economic and political purpose for the EC as such. Its establishment as a feasible objective with concrete commitments attached gave the

EC a renewed confidence in itself and greatly enhanced external credibility. Whatever the mix of market-led and policy-led factors (on which views differ) that made the 1992 goal feasible, its result was to reinforce the political identity of the EC and to make it emerge more explicitly as the center of gravity of Europe.

That sense of identity is apparent among the political classes in most EC member-states, though in the United Kingdom, Greece, and Portugal some reticence persists. It is matched by a sense of west European identity among the economic actors— that is, spreading wider than the EC, but not much wider— though some service providers see themselves as global players (as distinct from most industrial players, who want global markets from a European base). Members of the European Free Trade Association (EFTA) have reinforced this sense of EC identity by the avid desire to share it. At first they saw this only in partial form through the European Economic Area (EEA), but the race to deposit applications for full membership now seems to be on.

The drive toward Economic and Monetary Union (EMU) is a successor EC preoccupation and aimed at keeping the train of economic integration steaming ahead. It has little to do with the rest of Europe or the rest of the world. There would have been calls for a reinforcement of the EC institutions even if nothing had changed to the East, because of the need to deliver effectively on the promises of 1992 and EMU. For this sense of European identity to be durable and positive, 1992 will have to be delivered in tangible "currencies" of growth and fair outturns across the EC. The same will be true of EMU, which cannot solidly bind all EC members without delivering something on economic convergence. Even if a fence could be thrown around the EC economy (which it cannot), the internal adjustments would be difficult and controversial. Much of this work remains to be done.

Simultaneously with these economic drivers, an increasing frustration with and concern about the old balance of the transatlantic relationship had begun to emerge in the minds of some politicians and policymakers in western Europe. Niggles about

the role of the North Atlantic Treaty Organization (NATO) are
not new. NATO has been a persistent French preoccupation that
some other Europeans had begun to echo, and the revival of the
WEU was a reflection of this. It is easy to forget the old constellation of anxieties, but the Reykjavik dog that almost barked when
Ronald Reagan seemed ready to ignore the Europeans in his
rush for an agreement with Gorbachev sent waves of anxiety
around western Europe, which have left a mark. Even if the
Soviet empire had not crumbled, the west Europeans would have
been now firmly on course to make greater provision for their
own security and to rebalance the Atlantic Alliance.

REGAINED CONFIDENCE

If 1992 has come to symbolize the new mood of confidence in the
EC, the dramas of change in eastern Europe appear to catalyze
the opportunities for the EC to establish primacy as the framework for reshaping the old continent. Looked at from the eastern side of the Atlantic, the challenge of the next decade is
seductively absorbing. The unification of Germany has removed
one of the most sensitive scars of the division of Europe. Reinvigorated economically and released from the long shadow of
East-West confrontation, Europeans face with some relish the
tasks of further reconstruction and enhanced collective identity.
This is not to say that those tasks will be straightforward or that
the problems of adjustment will not be legion. It will take time,
patience, and resources to rebuild the economies and polities of
central and eastern Europe.

Viewed from the western shores of the Atlantic, the picture
is not quite so rosy. Many Americans regard the jury as still out
on the 1992 process. Though early and over-simplified images
of a "fortress Europe" in the making have given way to a more
nuanced appreciation of the potential benefits of intra-European liberalization, Europeans still seem longer on promises
than on delivery of improved market access. Of course, Americans welcome the thaw in East-West relations, but they remain
concerned lest this lead to a jettisoning of the Atlantic Alliance.
However heartening they may find the relaxed mood of the new

Germany, their most important European partner, Americans worry about an introverted Europe, too preoccupied with its own concerns to play an active global role, and they fret about the consequences of a more confident Europe that will defer less readily to American leadership.

West Europeans may be in an upbeat mood, but the shape and implications of their collective endeavors still lack focus. The IGCs on political union and on EMU have interesting agendas, but their ambitions may prove elusive. Real uncertainty surrounds the recasting of the relationship between the EC and the other west Europeans in EFTA. A new partnership with central and eastern Europe is easy to promise but difficult to consummate. In the final travails of the Uruguay Round of the GATT, the continued indigestion of the EC caused by the effort to swallow reform of agricultural support has not reassured the rest of the world that the EC is a globally responsible partner. The debate on a new security order for Europe, though actively engaged, has not yet generated clarity or coherence on the question of how west Europeans will pursue their collective defense polices, nor did events in the Gulf find west Europeans, let alone the EC, united on the goals or the details of policy.

Thus, the signals from western Europe are confused and confusing. The much heralded Atlantic Declaration, which the U.S. administration and the EC signed in November 1990, might have provided reassurance that the transatlantic relationship was alive and well and the gateway to a new partnership. Yet, according to the irreverent murmurings of some of those involved, it could turn out to be as meaningful as the declarations of undying friendship signed in former times between, say, East Germany and Algeria. In these circumstances it is all too tempting for Americans to believe their own worst fears. The worst-case analysis of the first phase of the 1992 process could be repeated in American judgments of the new European agenda.

What would the skeptic emphasize? First, 1992 may not turn the EC into a fortress, but it could turn the Community into a regional economic bloc using aggressive and uncompromising strategies to pursue its interests. The possible "absorption" of the EFTA nations into an EEA might confirm this strategy rather than demonstrate an openness to other partners. Second, EMU still only a fragile embryo, might turn out to be equally intro verted, with its protagonists concentrating on European mone tary unification and paying too little attention to internationa responsibilities. Third, eastern Europe could become an arena for a new phase of colonialism for the west Europeans, leaving at least parts of the former USSR exposed and beleaguered Fourth, Germany might eschew the opportunity to blossom as a major global player and become bogged down in its own paro chial and central European preoccupations, leaving a destabiliz ing competition for primacy among the larger European states. Fifth, all the talk about a collective west European foreign policy and security policy may add up only to an opting out of global responsibilities. And so the pessimistic projections could all too easily proliferate.

"Europe for the Europeans" and the excitement that it might conjure up within Europe risks becoming a slogan that hits all the sensitive buttons in terms of the transatlantic relation- ship. For the EC to privilege its relationships with other Euro- peans could mean discrimination against the United States. To argue that EFTA partners, other Mediterraneans, or the central and east Europeans need special attention and preferential ar- rangements that distract from wider international engagements could be taken to imply disregard for the webbings of transatlan- tic solidarity. To refashion defense and security arrangements in Europe separate from NATO would be blatant and inflamma- tory ingratitude. To spend time sorting out intra-European dis- agreements on, say, agriculture would be to show a declining commitment to multilateralism.

Yet, analyses of this kind (and they have been deliberately overstated here) would misunderstand what is happening in Europe and misread badly the kinds of policies and political underpinnings being created within the EC and between the EC and its immediate neighbors. This chapter seeks to argue that a fundamental process of transformation is already under way in Europe and that it is engaging Europeans across the continent. Sentimental pan-Europeanism is almost certainly not the driv- ing force for west Europeans, though it may be for some in the

East. But the EC does radiate magnetic impulses that are pulling other Europeans into its gravitational field, and these are in turn exercising a powerful impact on the debate within the EC. The parallel Europeans often draw is with Marshall aid from the United States to Europe after World War II. The Americans judged at the time that they had a special responsibility and an immediate opportunity to underpin European economic reconstruction for a mix of political and economic purposes. Many west Europeans argue that the case for an analogous effort on their part to underpin east European reconstruction is immediate and unavoidable.

SCENARIOS FOR THE EC

What kind of EC is likely to emerge over the next few years, in terms of its economic policies, its political attributes, and its membership? And how will it position itself in relation to other European organizations or vis-à-vis the rest of the world?

The conventional Brussels scenario has been that the EC of twelve will steam full speed ahead toward full union. In this view, the purpose of the IGCs is to reinforce economic and political integration in an EC with an essentially stable membership over the short to medium term. The Community must embrace commitments to EMU with a timetable and specific goals, to which most member-states would subscribe at least in principle, though the British government and, indeed, some of the southern Europeans may not be full participants at the outset. EC institutions must be reinforced sufficiently—that is, given clearer and more authoritatitive powers—to make political union as a goal irreversible, even if that makes it harder for some (most?) potential applicants to pursue membership. The EC must develop a common foreign and security policy (CFSP, in the new and very current acronym), and over the rest of the decade must merge with the WEU to provide a single and collective expression of both policy goals and policy implementation. Thus, the EC would also become a defense community. The result would be more supranationalism now and talk of more to follow, with the language of political integration remaining ambitious and from time to time bolstered by the vocabulary of Community preference.

The relationships of the EC with its neighbors should, if the Community orthodoxy can be maintained, remain in a partnership mode rather than lead to absorption. This was always the strong argument for building up the EEA concept and stopping short of enlargement, in the process necessarily giving the EFTA members a more intimate and intensive dialogue with the EC to accompany their continuing dependency. The heady rhetoric about the new Europe would best be turned into practice by constructing a form of "super" association with the EC and the emerging liberal market democracies of central and eastern Europe through the new "Europe" agreements, accompanied by phrases but not promises about eventual membership. The EC would then be forced also to make some corollary adjustments of its policies toward and links with Mediterranean neighbors, both European and non-European. Turkey would not become an EC member in the short term. Enlargement would be on the distant, but not the immediate, agenda, though this would probably increase, not decrease, other Europeans' concerns to force the EC to be more open to them.

The difficulty with this tidy and logical approach is that the untidiness of events, the differences of opinion among Europeans over the details, and the inertia of disjointed incrementalism are fast overtaking it. The two IGCs will make some real changes, but they may achieve little more than to reaffirm the continuing goals of economic and political integration—that is, prove long on promises and short on substance. Disagreements on policy content and the acceptable level of institutional commitment could prevent the emergence of a consensus on how to strengthen the EC. The interesting question would then be whether the ambitions to do more than this would simply be put on ice or be consigned to the wastepaper bin. Some would argue that such an outcome could produce a viable steady state, which rested on the firmness of the *acquis*. Others would contend that to freeze integration at its current level would in effect be to loosen the compact among the member-states. Depending on whether a limited outcome from the IGCs was the result of ıcrimonious conflict or widely shared reticences, the climate would be more or less favorable to continued gradual accretions of EC policy powers.

Under this scenario, the threshold of commitment for any new would-be members from western Europe would look readily attainable, but still quite difficult for the new European democracies. The EC would find it hard to resist the pressures for gradual enlargement, and it could well succumb, but individually, case by case. It would not, however, in the meantime have adopted the tighter constitutional rules that would be required to enable a larger Community to perform effectively. The EC would thus risk reversion to its model of the late 1970s, when the Community proved both frustrating to its members and irritating to its external partners. EC members and their European partners could well therefore conclude that the result was suboptimal, and much time would go to discussing how to rekindle ambitions.

Some would argue that a loosened and more interstate framework would then be inevitable—something more like a mixture of the Council of Europe and a European version of the Organization for Economic Cooperation and Development in new policy areas. So stark an analysis of what may emerge from the IGCs is, however, beyond the current probabilities and, in any case, rests on a misunderstanding of what is afoot. On the traditional EC issues, the IGCs seem likely to produce a modest, but serious, extension of policy and political powers at the EC level on the conventional issue agenda. However, the concept of European union is beginning to be fleshed out and, in some quite novel ways, as the umbrella for Europeanizing, but not (yet?) "communitarizing", new areas of collaboration, notably internal and external security policies.

One constituency supports the view that the EC has achieved its original goals and should accept the lessons of the new European history, which requires new thinking in the western half of the continent, as well as in the East. The new challenge, some say, is to build pan-European structures and thus rapidly to bring the rest of Europe into a refashioned Community. This logically implies acceptance of all the EFTA six (seven with Liechtenstein) pretty quickly and of the central and east Europeans as soon as they reach approximate levels of functioning democracy and market economy. Community membership would thus quite rapidly reach 20 or so, and the arguments against southern enlargement would at that point wear thin.

However, each of three distinct versions of this proposition has quite different implications. The soft version rests on advocacy of a much looser concept of integration and an unpicking of some of the *acquis communautaire*. Its most powerful and determined proponent, Margaret Thatcher, is no longer in office to run the argument, but the assumption that the proposition has definitively fallen with her may be premature. The hard version has as yet been barely articulated, but essentially would aim simultaneously to widen and to narrow. The argument is simple: the EC cannot and should not resist the tide of history, and must therefore accept enlargement as the corollary; but this would be workable only if an inner core of really committed, economically robust, and serious defense players ran the new European system. Ideas of this kind can be found in the Mertes and Prill articles[1] or in the discourse of the Italian foreign minister, and they are an old theme of French debate. It is a version of the two-speed Europe scenario, adapted for post-1989 Europe. An intermediate and more fluid approach may emerge as more favored, especially if the IGC produces a loose union umbrella with different pillars of cooperation and integration, which would perhaps allow other Europeans to be members of some but not all parts of the union.

Lurking in the debate as a possible worst-case outcome is the notion that Europe, if left untended and without serious investments of political capital, could revert to one or other model extracted from "bad" history. Allusions to the Congress of Vienna, the Treaty of Versailles, Balkanization, Rapallo, and so on send contemporary commentators scurrying for their history books, mostly to be depressed by the pessimism of the precedents. While the notion of historical replay is almost certainly misplaced, the persistence of such comparisons as relevant symbols for however small a minority of commentators and politicians is striking. The point perhaps serves a purpose as a straw man.

The most plausible choice for the IGC negotiators is between the orthodox integration agenda, predicated on current membership, and a shift over the next decade to a larger, but in some respects remodeled, EC. Each would have different implications both for the rest of Europe and for the rest of the world. If orthodoxy prevails, then eastern Europe will be taken under the wing of but not integrated within the EC, while the EFTA members will be left with a very much second-best position as close but excluded partners. However, this would make it much easier for the arguments to run strongly in favor of giving the EC twelve (*pace* Ireland) a strong foreign and security policy personality. If the more flexible approach to a larger EC is adopted, with a blurring of the lines between the Union and the Community, then foreign and security issues would probably be developed in a more compact grouping alongside but not within the EC as such. The first appears to offer a crisper foreign policy profile, but defers the question of accommodation with eastern Europe. The second looks more open to the east Europeans, but would be untidy vis-à-vis the rest of the world because of the diffuse approach to external policies.

THE NEW INGREDIENTS

Everything that has happened since mid-1989 has made the notion of greater European self-reliance more plausible, as well as more attractive. The diminution of the Soviet threat has led to a relaxation of the pressures for strong defense capabilities, with or without a continued American military presence. European public opinion will need much more convincing that high levels of defense expenditure continue to be justified. West European governments (at least the WEU and NATO members) may continue to prefer policies of prudently maintained defense capabilities, but they differ in their views as to how best to achieve this. The British and Dutch, for example, argue vigorously that while Europeans must be ready to carry more of the weight in the Alliance than hitherto, the Alliance must still be a cornerstone and NATO a player, albeit flanked by a WEU that would enhance the European dimension. The Belgians (much influenced by their historical experience as temporarily a neutral country) and Italians, however, argue that the European label must be the primary justification for domestic opinion of a collective defense and security policy, and the European label connotes an EC involvement progressively. Here, then, are two routes to Europeanization in the IGC debate about a CFSP, in which the French and Germans veer between the two positions. Neither is intended to exclude the Americans, but they imply rather different ways of recasting the transatlantic relationship.

Then there are the new questions about Germany. The unification of Germany may have healed one of the most gaping wounds of European history, but at the same time conjures up for some the specter of other European wounds inflicted by that same history. Of course, that makes many Europeans in many countries deeply concerned to ensure that the transition and the consequences of the process produce a widely accepted and acceptable pattern of intra-European stabilizers, in terms of economics, politics, and security. And, of course, it matters that the largest European country (excluding Russia for the moment) should be able to mobilize its considerable economic power benignly and to exercise its newfound political personality constructively. The rest of Europe needs Germany to thrive, and Germans need to be sure of the confidence of their European neighbors. Whatever the part that the United States may play in helping to shepherd the transition, the Europeans have no exit option—they have to make German unification work in European terms. In this respect, the achievement of German unification via the enlargement of the Federal Republic, and thereby the automatic geographic extension of the EC, is a very important stabilizer of a delicate situation.

Then there is the challenge of rediscovery of the rest of the European continent, of countries known only at a distance or via emigrés for nearly half a century. The west Europeans have to shift from often complacent pity for inaccessible neighbors and fear that those neighbors could at Soviet instigation become adversaries to acceptance that they are after all European cousins. The question that follows is how far in current circumstances family obligations extend.

The answers look clearer from the East than from the West. Irrespective of the extent to which the individual countries of central and eastern Europe accept the need for self-reliance, all share the determination to ensure that the ties of kinship are acknowledged in principle and reflected in practice. The extent to which references to a shared European heritage and culture permeate the political discourse of their politicians is striking. The symbolism of Europeanism is of high salience for these countries' domestic politics and their external policies.

From the west European side, the picture is much more differentiated. Kinship ties are acknowledged, but the warmth with which they are expressed varies, except where it is based on old historical and geographic ties with particular central and eastern European countries. On the other hand, the sense of obligation to be helpful in concrete ways is evident. The quick commitment to aid packages (Phare program, etc.) and the immediate recognition of the need to improve the trade and economic relationship reflect this sense. Indeed, the latter explains the EC's willing to sign "European" (and the label is significant) association agreements with central and east European countries as soon as they meet basic conditions of economic and political transformation.

The EC developed this new offer in autumn 1990, and negotiations opened in early 1991, with the aim of quickly signing agreements to take effect from 1992 or 1993. Its novelty lay in the clear distinction it drew between the projected intimacy of this specially constructed form of association and the more distant and cautious partnership arrangements with other associates, even in Europe. Or at least so the argument runs, even though the Greek and Turkish agreements contained similar elements in their "eventual membership" clauses. Curiously, the EC initially resisted this provision, but has conceded it more or less as a result of Polish pressure in particular. As important is the Community's underlying commitment to use association as a vehicle for fostering political and economic reforms in the new democracies. Hence negotiations were started quickly with the

Polish, Hungarian, and Czechoslovak governments, in the expectation that the other east Europeans would follow in due course.

Yet, "real" support on a sustained basis would require much more than has been offered so far, not least some sacrifice of vested interests within the EC to permit *effective* market access into the Community, including in agriculture and "sensitive" products. The jury will be out on this question until the negotiations are completed in all their detail. Much will also depend on whether the gloom that has followed the initial euphoria of late 1989 is replaced by a more positive atmosphere, thus encouraging sustained investment in the new European economies and even justifying lower levels of increase in the material prosperity of west Europeans. What may tip the balance is the fear of the disenchanted on the march as migrants move to western Europe in search of better prospects and a welcoming shelter. Even without giving credence to the most dramatic estimates (or guesstimates) of population movements beyond the scale of those at the end of World War II, it would be reasonable to expect some displacement. It may be cheaper politically, if not economically, to pay people to stay in central and eastern Europe and even in the former USSR.

However, the east Europeans have another call on the west Europeans, namely, for some form of security guarantee. Here, the west Europeans are in a real quandary. Their sympathy and willingness to respond are clear, but they have not yet found the means to do so effectively, as their evident reluctance to sign actual military pledges demonstrates. The east Europeans have canvassed associate membership of NATO or of the WEU, so far unsuccessfully. The conventional west European position for the moment is talk of the Conference on Security and Cooperation in Europe and the "security shadow" that close association with the EC casts over central and eastern Europe.

Whatever the specifics in terms of policy and resources, the west Europeans are destined to spend a lot of their time dealing with east Europeans, and probably also with people from the USSR. The inevitable intensity and growing intimacy of dialogue will both convey the appearance of substantive dialogue and egin to embed new special relationships. This is already a ource of serious concern to the west Europeans from the ranks f EFTA.

Some of the same issues also arise in the relationships of the C with the Mediterranean countries. The bids for enlargement o the south and southeast will continue. The claims will prolif-rate for compensating and functionally equivalent arrange-ments with Mediterranean noncandidates. North Africans produce agricultural goods that compete with production in the Mediterranean parts of the EC, as well as with Florida and California. They produce simple manufactures that compete vith east Europeans. They have large, young, increasingly well-educated, and highly mobile populations. The fact that they are slamic countries is inconvenient and worrisome: to absorb a arger Islamic population within the EC's borders would not be easy; to contemplate rising fundamentalism in North Africa or Turkey would be deeply disturbing.

Population and migration issues are likely to preoccupy Europeans greatly, and the issues are probably rather more complex than those Mexico presents to the United States. The case for trying to find substantial resources for economic devel-opment in the other Mediterranean countries is strong, though the willingness to deliver the relevant level of resources will be much weaker. At a minimum, there will be pressures to rework the trade and aid relationships with the Mediterranean: the EFTA countries will be asked to shoulder some of the burden and there will have to be some consequential reflection of this in trade with the rest of the world, as there was at the time of the Iberian enlargement of the EC.

THE COMMUNITY UNDER TEST

So three big questions remain. First, will the EC wish or be able to deliver the political and economic resources and attention ap-parently needed to underpin the new European configuration and to make it stable, secure, and prosperous? Second, will the new demands require a redefinition of the process and priorities of European integration, or can the continued development of the EC on orthodox lines satisfy them? Third, can the Europeans bear the weight of adjustment on their own, or will they need the active engagement of other partners, notably the United States, in this new phase of European integration?

First, on the issues of resources and attention, all realistic estimates suggest that the rebuilding and refashioning of Europe to the east and to the south will be a long-term process. There are indeed risks that rhetoric will outstrip reality. EC leadership, not least in the context of the IGCs and the new association agreements, is using strategic language, but lacks the instruments to pursue the logic of the strategy. The Community will perhaps have scope for graduated engagement vis-à-vis those Europeans who remain outside the EC, though perhaps only at the cost of piling up frustrations. The chickens would come home to roost earlier if the EC were to proceed fast to enlarge. Whichever side of the membership line the new Europeans fall on, much will depend on how buoyant the EC economy turns out to be. Even in the most optimistic of scenarios, it will be hard to satisfy the mix of demands from within Europe, let alone also respond to demands from countries outside the continent. In practice, the EC will make distinctions about levels of need and irresistibility of pressures, whether ad hoc or on the basis of conscious priorities, thus touching the interstices of domestic policies and politics, external economic policies, and foreign policy.

Second, will the processes of economic and political integration demand redefinition? The prevailing orthodoxy in the EC is that they will not, but that the need to persist on the same route has become more compelling. In this context, the multifaceted agenda of the IGC on political union offers too convenient a formula for the "deepening" panacea. This is almost certainly an illusion. Deepening may be desirable for other reasons and may help to equip the EC better to manage the wider European adjustment process. EFTA countries can perhaps be asked to choose whether or not to endorse the strong, traditional variant of EC integration. Such premature rigor may not make so much sense for southern and eastern Europeans.

Yet, it would seem imprudent to assume that what could be a doubling in the size of the EC could take place without influencing *both* the pace *and* the character of integration. It would be rash to expect the EC to maintain the rhythm of economic and political integration *à douze* (whatever the formal outcomes of the IGCs) while simultaneously accepting extensive new responsibilities. The harder test may come on security and defense policies, long regarded as the pinnacle of ambition of European integration. Even an EC of the original six countries only would have been hard-pressed to produce a single policy on the Gulf crisis. Some of the suggestions as to how to respond to the new European agenda imply a case for decoupling political from economic integration. To do so would be to reverse the lessons of EC experience to date.

Third, can or should the west Europeans try to find a way through on their own? Or do they need to renew the postwar transatlantic bargain to deal effectively with the new European agenda? Here, one must take great care to distinguish among factors in the discussion. The prevalent, and sincere, belief in western Europe is that the EC and its members share with the United States a common interest in a close, harmonious, and multidimensional transatlantic partnership. Most west Europeans would prefer the Americans to retain a strong stake and engagement in Europe. However, the context in which such affirmations are made is quite different from the period immediately following World War II. Then, the degree of European dependence on the United States was high; now, the relationship is much more independent. Then, the levers of influence in U.S. hands were powerful, and those in west European hands persuasive. Then, the west Europeans had their own identities and political and economic fabric to reconstruct; now, they operate from robust and resilient foundations.

Thus, the west Europeans need to shift the transatlantic relationship on to a more symmetrical and more balanced basis, across the political, economic, and security issue areas. On this point, the challenge of adjustment for the United States may be as great as the challenge of active responsibility to west Europeans. Forty-five years on, the Europeans look to the United

States not to spearhead a new European recovery program but to be an active partner in conserving and reinforcing a multilateral order; that would provide a benign context for a more self-reliant process of European reconstruction. But this objective is easier to state than to achieve. The hard work will be in establishing the new ground rules of a more balanced transatlantic relationship.

NOTE

1. See Michael Mertes and Norbert J. Prill, "L'Allemagne unifiée et L'Europe," *Politique Etrangère*, no. 3 (Autumn 1990), pp. 559–574. Also— *Frankfurter Allgemeine Zeitung*, July 19, 1989, p. 8.

2

FROM A COMMON EUROPEAN HOME TO A EUROPEAN SECURITY SYSTEM

François Heisbourg

The notion of a "common European home" has a rather loaded history. One of its first significant public expressions goes back to January 18, 1983, when Andrei Gromyko stated in Bonn that "both the FRG and the Soviet Union live in one European house, under one roof."[1] Gromyko's remarks came at a time when the Soviet campaign against the deployment of Pershing IIs and ground-launched cruise missiles was reaching fever pitch, only a few weeks before the fateful West German elections of March 1983, whose outcome ensured that the issue was resolved in conformity with NATO's decisions.

It is an understatement to say that times have changed. The "Second Cold War" of the late seventies to mid-eighties eventually gave way to "Gorbymania"—at least in the West—and increasingly benign assessments of the strategic situation have supplanted ominous threat evaluations. Similarly, the idea of the common European home, which initially conjured up the specter of collectivized overcrowding in a Moscow-supervised communal tenement—or barracks—eventually took on a somewhat warmer and more congenial glow, notwithstanding the numerous uncertainties surrounding its architecture, materials, and management. But whereas a common home for Gromyko was the wrong answer to the wrong questions, its more recent invocation during the first years of Mikhail Gorbachev's tenure can at least serve as the prelude to an honest attempt to answer the right set of questions. Notable among these questions is the one that will be at the center of this chapter: how to organize a new system in Europe from the debris of the old order.

The first step toward answering this question is to contrast

the characteristics of the postwar order with the emerging traits
resulting from the eastern European revolutions of 1989. After
that, we can look at the alternative types of European systems that
may evolve as a consequence of this leap from old disciplines to new
freedoms, with a particular emphasis on the future roles of the
Conference on Security and Cooperation in Europe (CSCE), the
Atlantic Alliance, and the European Community (EC).

THE HARSH AND REASSURING VERITIES
OF THE OLD ORDER

A simple description of the pre-1989 order conveys the extent to
which Europe's situation has actually changed. The statement
attributed to a courtesan of Louis XVI applies here: "Sire, ce
n'est pas une révolte, c'est une révolution." Four phrases sum up
the old order: it was defense-centered, clear-cut, comprehensive, and rigidly stable.

The *defense-centered* nature of postwar Europe requires little
elaboration. Until the buildup in the Persian Gulf, central Europe remained the most heavily militarized piece of real estate
ever encountered in peacetime; the arsenals of the two superpowers remain awesome. The military requirements of the East-
West confrontation were the driving factor, to which all other
considerations were ultimately subordinate: political and economic reconstruction in western Europe and the birth and
growth of the EC would have been impossible in the absence of
the robust defense epitomized and organized by the North Atlantic Treaty Organization (NATO).

Even less in need of elaboration is the *clear-cut* quality of the
order. The Iron Curtain—the ideological, societal, economic
and military division of Europe—was plain enough to see: on
one side lay the Soviet Union and its satellites; on the other, the
West, including the neutral states.

Comprehensiveness is a less-obvious feature of the old order.
In effect, the postwar order was very much akin to the "seamless
robe" image used to portray escalation theory and flexible response. On paper, and in practical experience, bipolarity was
sufficiently strong to maintain a set of structures that lasted for

40 years, in the West as in the East, covering all relevant aspects of security policy in Europe. In architectural terms, the European home had foundations, walls—indeed too many walls—and a roof with reasonably few holes in it. (In the East, it also had an appalling lack of doors and windows.)

Although this European estate, with its eastern and western wings, was designed to fulfill its role in adverse circumstances and proved to be immensely stable during the worst Cold War crises, it had the fragility associated with excessively *rigid* structures: when earthquakes occur, the least-flexible buildings collapse first.[2] The lack of flexibility in the eastern wing ensured its breakdown in the face of generalized societal pressure. Within a few weeks, this downfall erased the dividing line between the halves of Europe, even if the more flexible west wing has swayed (but not—as yet— toppled).

In other words, the old order had the advantages of simplicity and of great stability in all but earthquake-type circumstances. However, for the eastern peoples, the price was high indeed: they could buy peace only at the expense of basic freedoms and economic performance. West of the Iron Curtain—where liberty, security and prosperity were the norm—the situation was less uncomfortable, but maintaining those norms had a high cost in terms of coping with the Soviet threat and, more fundamentally, entailed the mutilation of Europe as a whole and the division of Germany in particular. West Europeans bore these burdens with a fair amount of equanimity before 1989, notwithstanding West German angst and broader western European fears.

The West, meanwhile, had never formally agreed to legitimize the postwar order,[3] but was more intent on making containment succeed than eager to roll back Soviet power. As events demonstrated, this was an appropriate policy. Indeed, the example of the West's political and economic success and the growing effectiveness of the modern media in bringing the West's messages to the East helped determine the manner in which the old order was overthrown. That upheaval was entirely the work of the peoples in the East, reacting to both the glaring failure of the Leninist mode of governance and the release of traditional Soviet controls under Gorbachev; nevertheless, the values those peoples embraced, and the overwhelmingly peaceful nature of change, must have been influenced by "real pluralism" as practiced in the West, notably in the EC.

NEW HOUSE RULES

Whereas Europe had a defense-centered order, *defense is becoming a subordinate variable* there. The manner in which a united Germany fits into a future European system, the extent to which eastern European countries succeed in their transition to political and economic pluralism, the way in which a disintegrating USSR manages its internal decolonization and reform processes, the degree of future western European political and economic integration, the political and economic evolution of the Maghreb and Near East—all of these issues are clearly more important in determining the shape and nature of Europe's security than are the traditional measure of the military balance of forces and the requirements that flowed from the East-West confrontation. This is not to say that defense, including its transatlantic dimensions, will cease to be important; clearly, reasonable forces will continue to be required, for the USSR (or Russia) will remain the largest of European powers, even after completion of the Conventional Forces in Europe (CFE) treaty, even after a total Soviet withdrawal from central Europe, even if the Soviet Union is reduced to an essentially Russian core. Nor is Moscow the only potential threat: the Third World is the seat of a number of active conflicts with increasing levels of ever more destructive armaments, as the Gulf crisis brutally demonstrated. But defense—and the organizations that accompany it, not least the military aspects of NATO—will no longer be pivotal in Europe. Its role will be that of an insurance policy—important, indeed indispensable, but not the heart of family life.

The clear-cut strategic situation of postwar Europe has given way to great strategic *confusion and complexity.* How will the eastern Europeans, who are now effectively in a state of strategic limbo, ensure their security? What type of security relationship (or absence of relationship) will the western countries have with each of these states?

Furthermore, "eastern Europe" is no longer a discrete geostrategic entity; each of its parts now has to be dealt with separately. How will the West factor the diverse territory between the Baltic and the Black seas into NATO and western Europe's strategic planning and military doctrine? These questions will have to be addressed down the road. Is Europe's current array of principles, institutions, and concepts in a position to provide an appropriate set of answers?

Lastly, *a generalized state of flux* has at least temporarily replaced rigidity. Consider the growing turmoil in a possibly disintegrating USSR, the uncertainties confronting central and southeastern Europe after the overthrow of Leninist governments, the prospect of civil war in Yugoslavia, not to mention western European integration. From this depolarized situation, new lines of force will emerge, most quickly in the case of German unity, which became a fact of life on October 3, 1990; questions relating to the area between the Rhine and the Oder are now of a domestic nature. Whatever the turn of events, the most unlikely outcome is a return to stable bipolarity and its strict disciplines.

Numerous variables will help determine the future European scene and should play a role in the decision-making process. The following warrant close analysis here: the security implications of the resolution of the German question; the consequences of eastern Europe's revolution; and the effects of Soviet uncertainties on the evolution of Europe.

Consequences of Resolution of the German Question

The immediate security ramifications of German reunification have been the object of considerable discussion between governments. Literature abounds on the bilateral West German–Soviet agreement of July 1990 and the "two-plus-four" accord of September 1990. It is therefore unnecessary to detail here the security regime accompanying unification—especially since united Germany's membership in NATO, the Western European Union (WEU), and the EC has resolved some of the fundamental uncertainties initially involved. However, a Germany anchored in Western institutions can nonetheless be tempted into neutrality such as by refusing to participate in military contingencies outside of the territory of NATO's members; the Gulf crisis witnessed such a refusal, notwithstanding the active involvement of European and NATO partners in a conflict sanctioned by the United Nations. The very strong antiwar sentiments evinced in German opinion polls reinforce this feeling that Germany may become, in defense terms, the equivalent of a larger Austria. If this became a permanent pattern, possibly confirmed by an explicit and restrictive amendment of the German constitution, the prospects for Euro-American coupling, and for western European political (and even economic) union, would become poor; an "Austrianized" Germany's partners could have difficulty consenting to the major transfers of sovereignty European political and security union implies.

Another aspect of the resolved German question deserves attention: With unity and a peace settlement, Germany will have become an entirely "ordinary" country. Its partners will simply not be able to take for granted hitherto accepted situations rooted in the consequences of World War II, whether those situations are de jure (as in Berlin, or in terms of residual rights) or de facto (as in the case of stationed forces). Germany will have to expect, even more than it did in the past, that what is good for the goose is good for the gander, notably in terms of stationed forces, conventional or nuclear. To use a theological comparison, in a fully sovereign Germany, the strategic situation and its military manifestations will move from predestination to fully free will.

Irreversibility of the Revolution

The word *irreversibility* is best used sparingly. However, it does apply to eastern Europe, to the extent that in practically all countries no significant constituency has the means to reestablish the Leninist model in domestic affairs along with the acceptance of Soviet, or Russian, overlordship in external relations. The only way Moscow could reestablish lost positions would be through large-scale military operations, which would greatly exceed the scope of the 1956 and 1968 interventions. With the disappearance of the Iron Curtain, the implicit "each takes care of his own" rule which the West respected vis-à-vis Soviet military intervention in the past, is ceasing to be applicable. Yet, irreversibility does not necessarily mean that reform will succeed in eastern Europe: Romanian-style instability and Yugoslav tensions are not encouraging developments. Nor will Moscow cease to be a powerful interlocutor, a reality noncommunist Poland was not slow to recognize in the face of German unification. Whatever the trends, they will at worst resemble pre-1914 practices, and at best, follow a post-Franco-type road. But they will not lead to a return to the historical parentheses which the Cold War represented from 1947 to 1989.

Entirely open, then, is the question of what strategic regime will apply east of the Oder. Finlandization (armed neutrality with a special relationship with Moscow) would be one course, but it would hardly be appealing to countries that feel compelled to reduce defense spending. Austrianization would be more likely, but it still raises the issue of whether outside states should recognize and eventually guarantee this neutrality, and whether it would appeal to countries that want to join a European Community which increasingly frowns upon neutrality. Membership in NATO may tempt some, but Moscow would probably not greet this with pleasure, and the Soviet Union's direct neighbors would be imprudent to discount that state's opinions. Geography will not change. Nor would NATO or the WEU have an obvious interest in extending binding security guarantees to countries that have their own neighborhood quarrels: one Greek-Turkish relationship is more than enough for NATO. However, NATO or the WEU could intensify relations with the eastern European countries at the diplomatic and parliamentary levels, in effect providing an institutionalized framework for dialogue. Furthermore, the western countries could consider providing negative security guarantees if the eastern European countries seek these from partners to both the East and the West. (For example, France could promise not to seek to use Hungarian territory for the stationing of military forces, provided no other country uses Hungarian territory in such a manner.)

Soviet Domestic Uncertainties

The outcomes of internal Soviet problems will have important, but limited, effects on the evolution of a European security system. Short of risking World War III, the USSR was not in a position to stop German unity once the Germans had decided to go ahead with it. Nor could Moscow dictate a united Germany's security choices, or directly prevent western European integration, or forcibly break the Euro-American bond. Furthermore, were Moscow to shift from its current policy of accommodation toward one of tension, Soviet influence itself would probably diminish rather than increase. For instance, Moscow could decide to renege on the withdrawal of its forces from eastern Germany by the end of 1994. However great the difficulties this about-face would create, it would virtually ensure western Europe's evolution in a fashion particularly hostile to the USSR, or Russia, with long-term penalties for Moscow—not to mention the impossible situation this would create for Soviet forces plunged into an environment made doubly corrosive by ambient rejection and the growing contrast between a capitalist society and the austerity of Soviet garrisons.

In addition, foreign affairs as such are likely to lose priority on Moscow's agenda. Redefining the union, coping with the collapse of the economy, managing the administrative and political consequences of the disappearance of the Communist Party of the Soviet Union (CPSU)—all of these will capture Moscow's attention more and more; the armed forces are naturally also concerned by this process. International relations will matter only insofar as they will directly affect domestic issues. The postunification European security environment, the U.S.-Soviet relationship, and force reductions may be relevant in this respect. But even these considerable issues are slipping down Moscow's agenda as the Soviet system disintegrates.

Civil war or catastrophic breakup or breakdown could lead to irrational flare-ups of external aggressiveness or border disputes between ex-Soviet Republics and their western neighbors as a spin-off from internal turmoil. The real risks are of a very different nature than those of the 1945–1989 period:

- In the short term, united central control on a portion of Soviet nuclear weapons could break down. Resulting nuclear terrorism and, notably, nuclear blackmail directed at third parties could represent an unprecedented threat with which even the more imaginative novelists have not yet grappled with.[4]

- In the longer run, precedents such as the disintegration of the Hapsburg and Ottoman empires are not encouraging. The still unresolved consequences of the breakdown of these geographically conterminous, authoritarian, multinational empires demonstrate how important it is for the outside world not to mismanage, through precipitate action, the disintegration of the USSR. History appears to be on the side of those who exercise caution in establishing new links with emerging republics in the USSR.

In summary, four points are clear. First, under its current leadership or under new management, Moscow will remain capable of influencing events in Europe to some degree. Second, in the near future, this influence will diminish rather than grow. Third, hard-line policy changes in Moscow would turn the world against the initiators, whereas Moscow has at least avoided making enemies of its newly enfranchised ex-satellites. Fourth, the fate of the Soviet Union, including its current implosion, will have awesome consequences for the peoples of that state and for the world as a whole; nevertheless, the elements for a future European system have, to a large extent, their own dynamic, which will determine outcomes rather more crucially than will events in the USSR. In the long run, however, no stable European system will evolve if the eastern flank remains in a state of turmoil or, a fortiori, if it feels alienated vis-à-vis developments in Europe. Therefore, Europe has a stake in achieving a degree of nonadversarial stability in the USSR or its successor states.

TOWARD A EUROPEAN SECURITY SYSTEM

Architectural metaphors are less appropriate in discussing Europe's future security regimes than in analyzing the past, for a simple reason: In the past, Europe had an order—a clear-cut, comprehensive, and static structure, divided by very real walls. In the future, it is likely to have a system—a complex set of interacting and mobile elements. A system is not necessarily tidy, nor is even a successful one indefinitely adaptable: the Holy Alliance and the Concert of Nations, not to mention the interwar scene with its shifting eastern European alliances and inherently unstable *cordon sanitaire*, bear witness to this.

In predicting what sort of system will take hold in Europe, one must make a number of assumptions to reduce the field to manageable proportions. This section spells out three assumptions regarding a new European system, describes what will result if they are *not* valid, and then sketches the more desirable scenario that emerges if they are.

Assumptions Underlying the System

The first assumption relates to Germany and consists of three notions: (1) With a united Germany in NATO, western stationed forces may decline considerably, but they will not pull out entirely in the wake of Soviet withdrawals. (2) All ground-launched short-range nuclear forces will be removed before the mid-1990s. (3) The people of united Germany have learned the harsh lessons of history and are comfortable with the idea that peace is not simply a pause between two wars.

This assumption hinges on a successful ratification of the CFE treaty and its timely implementation, as well as on the two-plus-four agreement. There is no reason to doubt the keenness of German Chancellor Helmut Kohl's wish to achieve a common security—and eventually defense—policy within the framework of European political union, along the lines he and French President François Mitterrand spelled out in a letter to the President of the European Council in December 1990.[5] Such a policy will be achievable only if Germany eschews the temptation of functional neutrality and avoids amending its constitution to severely restrict defense outside of its territory or western Europe.

If this assumption proves wrong, Germany will eventually have to secure its own, purely national security guarantees (conventional or nuclear) with all of the associated uncertainties; this would have direct, negative effects on the following assumptions.

Under the second assumption, the European Community will pursue economic unification and integration and take the first steps toward political union. Furthermore, the achievement of German unity will continue to accelerate the integration process, and different members—including Germany—will, for diverse reasons, aim for a tighter community. This certainly was the case in 1990, when the EC members decided to convene the intergovernmental conference (IGC) on European political union from December 1990 onward, alongside the already planned IGC on the Economic and Monetary Union (EMU).

If this assumption proves wrong, a "concert of nations cum balance of power" system of the pre-1914 variety will become a strong possibility. Most important, Germany would go its own way politically. This would naturally affect the nature and content of the Euro-American relationship.

The final assumption is that the United States will not succumb to the temptation of neoisolationism and will pursue a dual-track policy of maintaining a close security relationship with western Europe and stationing forces in Europe for the defense of its military interests and those of its allies. The U.S. military involvement in Europe would no longer be geared to confrontation with a threatening Soviet Union, but would help maintain stability in Eurasia, an objective that is ultimately in the U.S. interest and would underpin U.S. influence in western Europe. Although in theory a permanent force presence would not be necessary under all circumstances, it would remain an asset for attaining both of these aims at much lower costs than apply today. Specific force levels should be a function of military requirement, which may lead to the kind of manpower level—between 75,000 and 100,000 soldiers—Senator Sam Nunn has cited.[6] This level would allow for the timely regeneration of forces in the event of a reconstituted threat. It would only partially accommodate the kind of U.S. force transfers made from Europe to Saudi Arabia during the Gulf crisis, but European bases would remain invaluable for such operations, and some ready U.S. forces would be available for out-of-area contingencies.

If isolationism does prevail in the United States, the western European nations will be left to their own devices in the face of a still powerful Russia—indeed, a Russia that will be, in military respects, the most powerful country in Europe. How the Europeans would cope with an eventually resurgent and revanchist Russia would be very much a function of their capability to pursue their integration within a political community. The same consideration would apply to emerging threats in the arc of crisis from the Mediterranean to the Himalayas.

One Outcome: A Nonintegrated Europe

Before examining the security system that could emerge if these assumptions prove correct, it is useful to describe a scenario in which these assumptions prove wrong. The backdrop of this scenario would be a deteriorating international environment. Germany—as Paris frequently assumes—would discontinue the presence of western stationed forces in the wake of reunification;[7] ultimately, it would reconstitute a general staff. Furthermore, in the face of instability in eastern Europe and turmoil in the USSR, Germany would increasingly consider a national nuclear deterrent. In reaction to this "loose cannon," France and the United Kingdom would act as security partners. Meanwhile, increasingly estranged in security terms from its neighbors, Germany would also balk at further economic and monetary integration of the European Community, not to mention refusing moves toward political union. With the overhasty accession of new member-states, the Community would eventually deteriorate into a more or less flimsy free trade area.

In eastern Europe, the absence of a strong and coherent western policy of economic assistance would accelerate the breakdown of inexperienced democracies unable to cope with the hardships associated with moves toward competitive market economies. Along with this "Peronization" of eastern Europe would come the violent breakup of the Soviet Union and Yugoslavia; the combination would lead to the reopening of innumerable border issues (Poland's eastern and Lithuania's southern borders, Romania's eastern and Bulgaria's western borders, and so forth). Massive population movements gener-ated by conflict and despair would create added challenges. In addition, out-of-area threats, notably from the Maghreb and the Middle East, would create opportunities for conflict, which an upsurge of xenophobia against Islamic communities in the increasingly inward-looking nation-states of a weakening European Community would accentuate.

All in all, this outcome would throw Europe back to the era before the creation of the EC, and the use of force to resolve interstate disputes would once again become current. As a whole, this scenario is unlikely, although some of its components are quite plausible (for example, Middle Eastern threats). Its likelihood is sufficiently high, however, to encourage those Europeans with a sense of history to ensure that these trends are avoided—and that the assumptions outlined above do indeed materialize. The checkered European action during the Gulf crisis, in which the United Kingdom and France conducted largely divergent national policies, demonstrates how easily Europe can slip back into traditional practices.

A More Desirable Outcome: An Integrated System

Provided the above assumptions prove true, how could the elements of an integrated European security system fall into place, in the short run (two to three years) and the longer term (a decade or so)? In attempting to grapple with this question, it makes sense to look at the role of the institutions that would drive such a system. The following have at least some relevance to security in a broader sense:

- The CSCE, the membership of which extends from San Francisco to Vladivostok

- The institutions of democratic Europe—the EC, the WEU, and the Council of Europe

- The Euro-American alliance, currently in the form of the Washington Treaty and NATO

The enumeration of these bodies in itself illustrates that Europe's limits do not lend themselves to a simple description.

For example, the eastern limit is located on the Elbe, the Oder, the Bug, the Urals, or the Pacific, depending on the issues or institutions one is referring to. In other words, there is no definable European home.

The CSCE

Of all these institutions, the CSCE comes closest to being pan-European: it now includes every European nation, plus the United States and Canada. In the early days of the 1989 revolutions, it was frequently (if not necessarily convincingly) put forward as the basic structure for collective security in Europe. A CSCE strengthened through the creation of a permanent secretariat (located in Prague), and extending its discussions into the broader political and security realms, could certainly accomplish a lot in the field of security; the crisis prevention center (in Vienna) and the election observation office (in Warsaw) are encouraging developments in these respects. Given its track record on issues such as human rights and confidence-building measures, and the legitimacy its decisions acquire through their unanimous adoption, the CSCE should be able to branch out to protect the collective rights of national minorities (a major concern in eastern Europe and the USSR); provide a forum for the political resolution of disputes; elaborate confidence-building measures aimed at defusing regional crisis in Europe; secure the broadest political agreement on issues of common concern, as was the case for the two-plus-four discussions; set agreed standards for free elections, and so on.[8] To this must be added the role the CSCE plays in arms control, both as the sponsor of the 23-nation CFE talks, and as the possible framework for a follow-up to those talks.

The CSCE could be extremely useful in these and other areas, not least because it ensures Soviet participation in the European system. In the long run, nothing would be more destabilizing than an excluded and frustrated Soviet Union, which marginalization under humiliating circumstances could drive to revenge. The CSCE can help avoid such an outcome, and this in itself explains the importance all players attributed to it in the 34-nation Paris summit of November 1990.

That being said, it is necessary to describe the limits of the CSCE's abilities:

- The CSCE's rule of consensus prevents it from imposing a course of action against any members; furthermore, unless all of its members perceive a common external threat, the CSCE is not likely to be capable of using force outside of its limits.

- It is difficult to imagine the CSCE changing its decision-making rules, in the field of security, either toward majority voting (the EC took 25 years to adopt limited majority voting, and that still excludes security affairs, inter alia) or toward a restricted European Security Council, a group of nations "more equal than others." Such a privileged group has no generally acceptable legitimacy, in contrast to the UN Security Council, which emerged as an expression of the results of World War II. Which nations would belong to such a group in Europe today, and what powers would the group have? Those who attempt to answer this question will recognize its inherent difficulty.

- The CSCE will face the growing challenge of how to accommodate the emergence of increasingly assertive sovereign republics moving away from the center in the USSR and Yugoslavia. At its Paris summit in November 1990, the CSCE prevented the Baltic states from participating as official observers. The CSCE faces no mean task in striking an acceptable balance between admitting bona fide new democracies into its ranks (such as Lithuania and Slovenia) and evading the appearance of fostering the breakup of the Soviet Union or Yugoslavia into ever-smaller ethnically bared states. In effect, the CSCE will be torn between its objective of full representation of Europe lato sensu, its rule of consensus decision making needed to protect minority rights, and the requirements of stable territorial arrangements.

In other words, the CSCE is in a position to greatly contribute to strategic stability in Europe. However, it cannot provide its members the kinds of security guarantees that NATO and the WEU do;[9] and expecting it to ensure collective security in the full sense of the expression is wishful thinking.

The Institutions of Democratic Europe

In terms of their mandate and geographic ambit, the Council of Europe (with its 24 democracies),[10] the EC (with its twelve members), and the WEU (with its nine members, all of which belong to both the EC and NATO) vary considerably. However, these institutions need to be mentioned collectively, not only because they are in a geographic sense strictly European.

The Council of Europe and the EC have a sui generis justification that insulates them to a considerable extent from the consequences of the ending of the Cold War: whereas the attenuation of the East-West polarization calls NATO's identity into question, the same is not true for these two bodies. European economic integration and political cooperation will continue to have a powerful raison d'être if the Russians go home. The Council of Europe finds new grist for its mill as new democracies emerge, and its European Court of Human Rights exercises mandatory jurisdiction; the Council is thus a unique body not only in terms of setting human rights standards but also in implementing them. These European organizations are in a dynamic phase; this is particularly true of the more powerful one, the EC, whose sphere of competence is expanding, in contrast with NATO's. These bodies can open perspectives to the eastern European countries, and provide institutional bridges to the West. The Council of Europe is the first, and most natural, bridge for new democracies to cross from East to West in a nonprovocative manner.

The EC serves as an economic and political magnet for the new democracies and should devise special forms of associate membership, above and beyond economic assistance. Such association agreements should open the door leading to eventual accession to the Community; even when membership is a distant prospect, such a light at the end of the tunnel could be of incalculable importance for the governments of the new democracies.

Providing the nascent democracies with the political and economic capability to weather the harsh transition ahead is not simply in the long-term political or economic interest of the parties involved. It is also essential from a broad security viewpoint: long-term security for Europe will not be possible if the continent's eastern portion becomes the seat of major instability and antagonisms. To avoid pitfalls of the pre–World War II variety, these countries not only have to succeed in their internal reform processes, but also should clearly belong to the group of countries whose values they are now adopting. That means membership in the Council of Europe first, associateship with the Community second, and eventually, full membership in the EC, once they are in a state to accept its disciplines.

Increasingly, the question will arise of greater involvement of the western European bodies—the EC and the WEU—in security affairs as a result of converging processes: the diminished military presence of the United States in a Europe less threatened by the Soviet Union; the new security requirements resulting from the strategic limbo in eastern Europe and challenges in the Middle East; and the growing confidence and ability of a western Europe that is moving toward greater economic and political union, and that will act as a centripetal confederation vis-à-vis eastern Europe.

For the short term, a somewhat paradoxical situation will probably limit the scope of western Europe's involvement in security affairs. In effect, the most broadly based and dynamic institution, the EC, is simply not ready, legally and politically, to actively and directly enter into the security arena. Meanwhile, the WEU, which has been doing good work and no doubt can do more, has too narrow a focus and too modest a track record to become, on its own, the pivot of the European security system.

Additionally, a natural inclination to avoid haste will slow the shift from the current NATO-centered system to a more European-focused one, for fear of losing the existing, concrete U.S. guarantee in exchange for the uncertainties of a still-abstract European system. This traditional consideration takes on greater salience as very large U.S. force withdrawals have become a near certainty, rather than a hypothesis.

Circumstances, however, may well change. Given the WEU's membership, one can increasingly make a case for its convergence (possibly even merger in the long run) with the EC, if the latter moves toward anything like the political union that the relevant Intergovernmental Conference (IGC) is currently addressing. This would be in line with the perspective the WEU's Ministerial Council adopted in the Platform on European Security Interests in October 1987.[11] In other words, in the field of security, the EC would initially have two speeds: the WEU core and those who would prefer staying out. While this type of arrangement is not, in itself, desirable, experience does demonstrate that it can be a condition for success; refusal to accept it, on the other hand, could mean a zero-speed Community. The European Monetary System (notably its exchange rate mechanism) illustrates how a two-speed approach can work.

Notwithstanding the great differences that exist within the Community regarding political union and EMU, the correction of the "democratic deficit" that currently characterizes the Community's institutions will fuel moves toward tighter integration and an expansion of the Community's ambit into security issues. Greater political accountability (be it of the Council, the Commission, or the European Parliament) translates into greater legitimacy, and legitimacy breeds assertiveness.

If this security union materializes, we should also expect that the budding U.S.–EC dialogue, put into place in the wake of Secretary of State James Baker's Berlin speech of December 1989,[12] will shift toward political issues.

Ultimately, the EC *could* become—and the emphasis on the conditional is crucial since the outcome supposes the successful jumping of numerous hurdles—the oft-invoked European pillar of a much changed Euro-American compact. Once the EC extends into the political realm, security and defense dimensions will inevitably come into its purview. A European Community with a security and defense dimension, and with Eastern European associate members, would be one possible way of answering, in a gradual and nondestabilizing fashion, the question the strategic limbo in eastern Europe poses. Similarly, such an entity could give the Europeans the clout they lacked during the Gulf risis. In a sense, the Gulf crisis demonstrated the difference between what the individual nation-states of Europe (notably the United Kingdom and France) can achieve on their own and what the United States can achieve. This is one clear case where the EC's basic principle of subsidiarity[13] would normally have entailed the posting of political and military assets at the European level, rather than the penny-packet approach the absence of a European security and defense organization made inevitable. Such a European organization will, however, be achievable only if the member-states are ready to proceed with a convergence of their security and defense policies akin to the convergence that the setting up of the European Monetary System and its exchange rate mechanism posited. Inter alia, this means that France will have to agree to subordinate its forces to a European organization and to coordinate its defense policy more generally this does *not* mean, however, that the French should simply return to the existing integrated structure of NATO); and Germany will have to accept that the defense of Europe beyond its borders is not the responsibility only of its partners' soldiers but also of its own.

The Atlantic Alliance

Whither, therefore, the alliance and its organizational expression, NATO? Indeed, one must now ask, *Whether* NATO?[14] The latter question is not a flippant one, nor is it born of a misguided sense of false symmetry whereby the disintegration of the Warsaw Treaty Organization demands that of NATO. Simply, if the general perceptions of a disappearing Soviet threat prevail, then the future of the Alliance is in the balance.

NATO may survive and the Alliance remain relevant, given a number of conditions. First of all, one must not forget that NATO is a child of the Cold War, with the clear purpose of providing, within a given geographic area, a common framework for the security of its members vis-à-vis the Soviet Union: its business is security, with defense at its core. Therefore, proclaiming that NATO must become "more political" to survive is not sufficient; one must look into what "more political" means. More consultations? But the mechanisms for consultation exist

and are readily available for use.—Excursions into new politic
or societal arenas? But in competition with what other organiza
tions? Or are we to witness a Mark II of NATO's Committee o
the Challenges of Modern Society?—Broadening the organiza
tion's limits? But analysts can be worried only when "out of area
is invoked as an institutional Alliance task, since that is usually
sign that NATO has trouble with its core business; out-of-are
threats can be very real indeed, but experience indicates tha
different challenges originating from a changing set of chal
lengers are best met by ad hoc responses (which can naturall
include NATO's consultative machinery). Would the interna
tional community have been better off if the coalition in the Gul
had been a NATO force rather than a much broader assembly o
29 countries?—More political content? NATO can hardly b
more political than it was when it drafted the Harmel Report i
1967; but perhaps a new Harmel Report is in order, not leas
because the objectives of that remarkable document are nov
being fulfilled. Indeed, one way to go is to set the post-Harme
goals and roles of NATO and, in so doing, address the har
questions that the emergence of a noncommunist eastern Eu
rope poses.

The communiqué of NATO's July 1990 London summit[1]
went some distance in this direction by establishing a number o
the political terms of the Alliance's future, building on the orga
nization's proven capability to act politically. In particular, coop
eration in lieu of confrontation, as exemplified (inter alia) by the
communiqué's proposals on the CSCE, belongs to the "Harme
revisited" category.

If the threat is receding, will NATO's security dimension be
sufficient to sustain it? The answer could be a cautious yes
provided NATO, particularly in its military aspects, accepts a
role as something akin to an "insurance policy," or risk manager
of the sort mentioned earlier—namely, by remaining an indis
pensable organization, but not always at the center of things.

In these circumstances, NATO may need to review the na
ture of integration. A reform of the concept of integration i
desirable not only to accommodate greater French participation
but to create a European defense identity as a pillar of the

lliance. In military terms, such a review could become possible. Vith the threat from the Soviet Union now waning, the Supreme llied Commander in Europe (SACEUR) may no longer have to laim the exclusive earmarking for assignment to himself of the ulk of standing military forces in central Europe; nor would he ecessarily need in peacetime an elaborate and permanently ctivated integrated command structure. Therefore, "double atting" European military units to both SACEUR (and in the rench case, to a national commander) and a European command would be worth considering. Such European forces would rovide the western Europeans with a tool capable of out-of-area ctivities that NATO could handle, or of participating in European contingencies in which NATO would not need, or want, to perate as such. "Dual basing" defense planning under the ntegrated Defense Planning Committee and the North Atlantic Council is another measure that could help to establish greater arity between the North American and western European legs f NATO. This does not, however, mean that SACEUR should ease to be an American: as long as the U.S. nuclear security uarantee remains important, an American SACEUR will be one f the most effective agents of transatlantic coupling.

Thus, NATO will remain a prudent hedge, and as long as he Washington treaty remains untouched, NATO should continue to focus on what it is good—and best—at: security policy. n so doing the organization will have to deeply revise its force osture and the doctrine these forces will operate under, as the entral front evaporates and the Soviets disengage from eastern Europe.

From NATO to EATO?

f a less-pivotal role of NATO as an organization is in the offing, n the long run the Atlantic Alliance itself will have to change in ature and possibly move from a treaty between sixteen legally qual nations, with the United States as primus inter pares, to a ompact between a smaller number of entities reflecting the new ole of the European Community: such a Euro-American alliance—involving the United States, the EC-cum-WEU collec-

tively, possibly Canada, and the non-EC European states—coul
also have an organizational dimension, EATO (European-Ame
ican Treaty Organization): a European security and, eventuall
defense arm of the alliance would then be in order.

EATO, with its substantial European content, rests on
heavy set of conditions, but these are not unrealistic, and th
relevant parties should take every measure to ensure their fulfil
ment—for the alternatives are hardly encouraging. If no pro:
pect of a Euro-American alliance appears, even as a recedin
horizon (or what the French would call a *mythe mobilisateur*), the
a coherent, workable security system may not emerge in Europ
Instead, the best that could be expected would be a "fair-weathe
architecture": an upgraded but limited CSCE, an incomplete E
that stops short of security issues, a NATO with a rapidly dimir
ishing relevance. This could be adequate if current benign ci
cumstances prevail ad libitum in Europe: a rambling, disjointe
structure with holes in the roof does not pose insurmountabl
problems if the weather is warm, the sun shining, and natur
generally at peace.

The difficulty is that in security, as in meteorology, th
weather inevitably does change, as the Gulf crisis demonstratec
When circumstances alter, we will need the benefits of a reasona
bly resilient and coherent system. Ultimately, achieving this wi
depend to an essential extent on the capacity of the West to offe
a political perspective to the new democracies of eastern Europe
on the capacity of the western Europeans to organize themselve
in conjunction with their North American allies to cope with th
new challenges flowing from the West's extraordinary success
and on the capacity of the North Americans and Europeans t
forge a new transatlantic compact, as Europe is at last becomin
whole and free.

NOTES

1. Soviet television, as quoted in BBC Monitoring Report: USSR, January 1
   1983.
2. The earthquake analogy was common at the time of the breaching of th
   Berlin Wall. See David White, *Financial Times*, November 11, 1989.

3. The Report on Future Tasks of the Alliance (Harmel Report) Brussels, 13–14 December 1967 is more than clear on this score, notably on the German question. See paragraph 8: "But no final and stable settlement in Europe is possible without a solution of the German question. . . . Any such settlement must end the unnatural barriers between Eastern and Western Europe which are most clearly and cruelly manifested in the division of Germany."

4. On the thriller treatment of nuclear terrorism, see Larry Collins and Dominique Lapierre, *The Fifth Horseman* (New York: Simon & Schuster, 1980) and Frederick Forsyth, *The Fourth Protocol* (London: Hutchinson, 1984).

5. Helmut Kohl and François Mitterrand, letter to Mr. Giulio Andreotti, president of the Council of Ministers of Italy, acting president of the European Council, December 6, 1990.

6. See Michael R. Gordon, "Nunn Sets the Terms for Military Debate," *New York Times* (published in *International Herald Tribune*, April 24, 1990).

7. At a press conference at the July NATO Summit in London, President Mitterrand remarked that "it will be logical for the French Army to go home when the role of the four has ceased first at the political and diplomatic level and then at the military one." See "Press Conference Held by M. François Mitterrand, President of the Republic, Following the NATO Summit, London, 6 July 1990 (Speeches and Statements—Ambassade de France à Londres)."

8. Prime Minister Margaret Thatcher's speech of March 29,1990, at the Königswinter Conference provides a source of discussion on what the CSCE can, or cannot, do.

9. Article 5 of the North Atlantic Treaty: "The Parties agree that an armed attack against one or more of them in Europe or North America shall be considered an attack against them all . . . each of them . . . will assist the Party or Parties so attacked by taking . . . such action as it deems necessary, including the use of armed force." Article 4 of the Treaty of Brussels: "If any of the . . . Parties should be the object of an armed attack in Europe, the other . . . Parties will . . . afford the Party so attacked all the military and other assistance in their power."

10. This number is bound to rise very soon. Hungary was the first of the "new democracies" to apply for membership and joined in November 1990; Czechoslovakia joined shortly thereafter and Poland has also applied.

11. The platform states: "We recall our commitment to build a European union in accordance with the Single European Act, which we all signed as members of the European Community. We are convinced that the construction of an integrated Europe will remain incomplete as long as it does not include security and defense."

12. The secretary stated: "we propose that the United States and the European Community work together to achieve . . . a significantly strengthened set of institutional and consultative links." Address by Secretary Baker to Berlin Press Club, 12 December 1989. See U.S. Department of State, Bureau of Public Affairs, "A New Europe, A New Atlanticism: Architecture for a New Era," *Current Policy Document* no. 1233.

13. Subsidiarity is the principle holding that decisions ought to be taken as near as possible to the level they affect, unless compelling reasons dictate otherwise.
14. The expression is from International Institute for Strategic Studies, *The Strategic Survey 1989–1990* (London 1990): "In early 1989, with the 40th Anniversary of the Alliance looming, the key question had been 'Whither NATO?' A year later that question remains valid and is no easier to answer, but a second question, 'Whether NATO?' lies not far below the surface."
15. "London Declaration on a Transformed North Atlantic Alliance," issued by the heads of state and government participating in the meeting of the North Atlantic Council in London on July 5–6, 1990, (NATO press communiqué S-1 (90) 36).

3

EUROPE'S INSTITUTIONS:
EUROPE'S POLITICS

Peter Ludlow

The European Community (EC) is in the throes of a major
constitutional negotiation involving basic questions about its nature and the proper balance between its institutions. This essay
attempts to explain the scope of the two intergovernmental conferences (IGCs)—on economic and monetary union, and on
political union—and to assess their significance in relation to
both the EC's internal development and the future of Europe as
a whole; it is important to note that this essay was completed
before the negotiations ended.

The collapse of communism and, more particularly, of the
German Democratic Republic, greatly influenced the timing of the
IGCs: their achievements can therefore only be properly assessed
within a pan-European perspective. The negotiators, whether they
like it or not, are laying the foundations of a new European order
that seems bound over the next ten years to involve the incorpora-
tion of most European states—indeed, perhaps all except the Soviet
Union—in the Community itself. In EC parlance, "deepening" and
"widening" are no longer mutually exclusive alternatives: they are
inextricably interlinked. The results of the IGCs will determine the
context in which the inevitable enlargement of the Community
takes place; the latter will put the achievements of the conferences
to their most serious test.

EC POLITICS AND INSTITUTIONS ON THE EVE
OF THE IGCS

While the scope of the 1991 IGCs is ambitious, they are intended
to develop and improve the EC system, not to overturn it. It is
therefore crucial to have a firm grasp of where we are at the

moment of departure, before speculating about where we migh
be if and when the task is achieved.[1]

The Primacy of the Member-States

In the course of the past fifteen years, the member-states of the
European Community have, individually and collectively, coun
tenanced a transfer of powers to the Community institutions tha
goes far beyond any achieved in the first 30 years after the Treaty
of Paris. The fact that this transfer has involved concessions no
to a supranational authority distinct from the member-states
but to a set of institutions they themselves control (through the
Council, on which each of them is represented) has facilitated
and to some extent masked it. As subsequent pages will show, the
Commission and Parliament have also been important. The
Council, however, has provided the decisive leadership.

Detailed explanations of why EC governments have con-
nived at such a significant redistribution of power over the period 1975–1991 lie beyond the scope of this paper.[2] There are
many, ranging from the seemingly banal but very important fact
that a transfer of powers on this scale was always the ambition of
the EC founders, to the impact of the global crisis of the 1970s,
which altered beyond recognition the political and economic
perspectives of both public and private decision makers in Europe. The character and extent of the process are evident in the
increasingly central role of the European Monetary System
(EMS) in European integration, the emergence of a powerful
coalition between European big business and the Community
institutions in favor of the Single Market and related policies,
and the less dramatic but growing consensus that the EC needs to
develop a common foreign and security policy.

The adjustments that these changes in national perceptions
and priorities have entailed for the member-states have varied
from country to country and from issue to issue. Two episodes,
however, deserve a central place in any survey of the European
Community in the last ten years: the French political and economic crisis of 1982–83, and German unification in 1989–90.

The French crisis was at once the coming of age of the EMS and the moment of truth for the second most powerful member of the Community. As a determined bid by the first Mitterrand government to mobilize a countercyclical national and socialist policy foundered, the French Left faced a stark choice between fortress France and the effective dismantling of the EC, and the reorientation of national policy priorities toward the European norm. The result was in many ways a foregone conclusion. Its consequences were, however, far-reaching as over the coming years the French government came to terms with the paradoxical reality that the most effective way of maintaining power even in policy areas hitherto regarded as central to national sovereignty was by exercising it through the Community institutions rather than apart from them.

The German experience was on the surface totally the reverse. The 1980s saw the consolidation of German primacy in the EC, especially, but by no means exclusively, in the EMS. The collapse of communism and, more particularly, the self-destruction of East Germany further highlighted the qualitative differences between Germany and its partners. The practical effect for the EC of Germany's growing strength was, however, identical to that of France's perception of the limitations of national power. France sought to maintain power through the collective machinery of the Community: Germany pushed equally vigorously to dilute its embarrassing strength by the same means. With the short-term exception of the United Kingdom, all France's partners shared and indeed, in the case of the smaller states, had anticipated France's interpretation of the new global and European realities, and acknowledged the self-imposed constraints on German policymakers; the result was a revolution in Community politics from below that was more effective and sustainable than any that idealists, constituent assemblies, or inspired Commission presidents could have imposed from above.

The impact of these changes on the functioning of the Council machinery was profound; the IGCs are still coming to terms with them. Any list of important institutional developments in the 1980s would include the following:

- *Consolidation of the leadership role of the European Council.* The Single European Act incorporated for the first time a reference to the European Council; in this respect, as in so much else, it did no more than sanction a reality that was already apparent and that became even more marked as the decade progressed. As the Community grew increasingly political, it was inevitable that the role of those who exercised supreme power in the member-states should become more central in the Community process. By the second half of the 1980s, the European Council's Conclusions—which are published at the close of every meeting—had acquired a quasi-legal status in EC politics. If the Council decreed the line to be followed, the Commission and others had a far more realistic chance of implementing the requisite policies.

- *Extension of majority voting.* The articles in the Single European Act that sanctioned an extension of majority voting were both a symptom and a catalyst of change. They were symptomatic in that they would not have been agreed to in the first place had member-states not been unanimous about the need for a major advance toward the Single Market. They were effective because they undoubtedly facilitated the decisions that were necessary to achieve the 1992 program and because the behavioral changes that they induced in specific areas of Community business began to affect the conduct of Community business in general. EC business *does* proceed faster when majority voting is allowed than when it is not. Unquestionably, however, the system as a whole has become more flexible and fluid.

- *Proliferation of the Council machinery.* By the late 1980s, hardly any significant area of national politics was not in one way or another taken up in the Council machinery. In the last years of the decade, the Council, a term used to describe all meetings of ministers within a Community framework, met in various forms more or less 100 times a year. The General Affairs Council and the Economic and Finance Ministers held routine sessions, and groups of ministers as diverse as those responsible for tourism, justice, and education also had meetings.

This proliferation is significant for at least two reasons. First, it confirmed the inexorable extension of Community competencies as the interrelatedness of policy questions asserted itself. Second, and no less important, it demonstrated that the Community-Council procedure was taking precedent over ad hoc intergovernmental cooperation. In the early 1980s, one might have been tempted to believe that whether or not a state was a Community member was of little importance. By the second half of the decade, membership was clearly a matter of crucial significance, particularly to those on the outside.

• *Growing power of the permanent Council machinery.* At least three groups of officials have benefited from the increasing centralization of decision making in the Council machinery: the permanent representatives, the national coordinators of EC policy in member-state governments, and the Council Secretariat. Of the three, the last is particularly important. The Secretariat is still a poorly understood and largely ignored institution. Its power is very different from that of the Commission, of which it is not a rival. On the contrary, the Commission, like the member-state governments, draws on its help, particularly in the increasingly common situation in which outcomes are difficult to predict. The Council Secretariat is the powerbroker, an instrument of political management that no presidency can dispense with and most presidencies end up following.

These developments are indispensable for an understanding of what is and what is not at stake in the IGCs. All those principally engaged in the negotiations, including the Commission, have built their strategies not on the destruction of the member-state–based system, but on its continuance. A "victory for the Council" is neither surprising nor inimical to the further development of the Community system as a whole. The Council of the early 1990s is not the incarnation of the "intergovernmental" principle as opposed to the "supranationalism" of the other

EC institutions. On the contrary, it is itself part of the suprana
tional reality, both legislatively (as has always been the case) and
still more important, politically.

The Commission and Parliament

In the internal EC debate about institutional questions, it i
sometimes implied that an augmentation of the Council's powe:
must inevitably be at the expense of the Commission. The histor
of the 1980s suggests the opposite is the case. Far from being ;
brake on the Commission, an effective Council is the precondi
tion of its effectiveness. An ambitious Commission requires ;
strong Council; a strong Council requires an ambitious Com
mission.

The Commission's capacity to turn the new strength of the
Council to its own advantage stems partly from characteristic:
and rights that it has possessed from the beginning, and partly
from recent changes in leadership and internal organization. O:
the Commission's basic strengths, three have repeatedly prover
to be of major importance: its right of initiative, its permanence
and its multinational and pluralist character.

Commission President Jacques Delors himself has stressed
the crucial significance of the first of these three. The Commission's *right of initiative* is a mandate for leadership. It is not only a
right, but a necessity. The machine simply cannot work if the
Commission is not prepared to take the initiative. Governments
can and do have ideas: they cannot, however, act within the EC
framework to develop their policies unless the Commission takes
the lead.

The advantages of *permanence* are in a sense self-evident.
Every bureaucracy has this advantage over its political masters.
In the case of the Commission, the notion of permanence is more
complex, because it is more than simply a bureaucracy: it is a
political actor in its own right. The external relations of the EC
well illustrate the point. In an increasing number of contexts, the
Commission is the European Community to the outside world,
even though constitutionally its position is hedged by many constraints. European Political Cooperation (EPC) often, quite

'ightly, comes under criticism for its slow and cumbersome pro-
:edures, and for the fact that built as it is around six-month
Council presidencies, it projects an image of the EC that is
lifficult for outsiders to keep up with. An inevitable conse-
juence of this has been the increasing prominence in crucial
EPC initiatives of the Commission, which, unlike the Council
presidency is always there. An Irish or a Dutch or a Luxembourg
prime minister may go to Washington as part of the new dia-
ogue process with the United States, but that leader's moment of
glory will occur only once every six years. The Commission
president, by contrast, is there every time. This factor helps to
explain the finding of a 1991 Chicago Council on Foreign Relations poll that the U.S. public rates President Delors higher than
the Japanese Prime Minister Kaifu and only very slightly behind
Chancellor Kohl and President Mitterrand in the recognition
and warmth table.[3]

The *multinational and pluralist* character of the Commission
was illustrated in its handling of the German question in 1989
and 1990.[4] The Commission was throughout conspicuously in
advance of member-states. To some extent this must be linked
with the fact that as a multinational body including many Germans, it could not but regard developments in Berlin and elsewhere as a domestic affair.

Important though these structural points are, the changes
in leadership that took place in the 1980s have undoubtedly been
a significant, constructive factor. Delors and his colleagues have,
nevertheless, played the system; they have not of themselves
transformed it. The president's relations with and role in the
European Council provide a good illustration of how a strong
Commission president can acquire authority and leadership
through the intergovernmental machinery rather than in conflict
with it. Being the thirteenth member of the Council has been a
source not of weakness but of strength. Historical parallels
should not be pushed too far, but the contrast between the De
Gaulle–Hallstein episode in the 1960s and the tussle between
Prime Minister Thatcher and Delors in the 1980s is illuminating.
De Gaulle, like Thatcher, was clearly both fascinated and ap-
palled by a supranational upstart. Unencumbered by the Euro-

pean Council, he was nevertheless able to see his opponent off the field. Thatcher attempted to engage in single combat, by personalizing her attack on the EC as one on Delors. Her tactics misfired badly. The Commission president of the late 1980s was securely lodged in a mature institutional system. It was, therefore, not the Commission president himself so much as the European Council—on which Delors and Thatcher sat on a basis of practical, if not formal equality—that administered her increasingly frequent humiliations and eventual defeat.

The Commission's capacity to manage a complex machine such as the Council, which operates in so many policy areas and at such different levels, varies, of course, from situation to situation. Like the member-state governments, it must find its allies according to its specific needs on a particular day or in connection with a precise policy proposal. In matters of major significance in Community politics, however, the Brussels-Bonn axis has clearly played an essential role. It is much more than simply a personal matter between the German chancellor and the president of the Commission. As the negotiation of the European dimensions of German unification shows, the Commission as a whole was instinctively sound on the German question and, as a result, found the German government supportive in all manner of issues.

It was, however, the president who saw more clearly than anybody else the strategic significance of the relationship with Bonn from 1985 onward. Chancellor Kohl's support has been the sheet anchor of the Delors presidency. In the Delors-Thatcher conflict, Bonn's unwavering loyalty to the president was critically important. The same relationship has also enabled Delors to shrug off the disadvantages of being the French president's nominee. The latter's inevitable tendency to regard the president of the Commission as a former minister of finance and as a prospective prime minister if not president has been mitigated by the obvious success that Delors has had in building up strong personal ties with France's privileged partner. The relationship has been important in substantive questions, too. Bonn and Frankfurt were crucial to the five major themes other than the Single Market that have dominated Delors' agenda since

1985: the Community budget, the EMS and Economic and Monetary Union (EMU), the integration of the united Germany into a united Europe, the collapse of communism in eastern Europe, and the social dimension.

The changing relationship between the Commission and Parliament is also of considerable importance in any discussion of contemporary EC politics. Until 1989 at any rate, the common interests of the two institutions seemed so self-evident as to require little or no comment. Parliament reinforced the Commission and provided it with a platform for public leadership. Like any parliamentary institution, it also on occasion embarrassed or angered the Commission. Until 1989–1990, however, the relationship was by and large harmonious and in many senses highly advantageous to the Commission, since Parliament needed the Commission to impose its preferences on the Council.

Since then, the balance of interests has perceptibly moved. There are various explanations, some stemming from specific events, others from systemic changes. Among the specific developments that are worth mentioning, two stand out: the solution of the budget problem in 1988, which dedramatized an issue that had been central to the political relationship between the two institutions, and the shift to the left in the 1989 parliamentary elections. The new Parliament has been more self-confident and less reverent than the former one. A number of systemic developments have made these "accidents" all the more important. As this essay has repeatedly noted, the Commission had come by the late 1980s to realize how successfully it could operate within the existing Community institutional system and, more particularly, in the Council. For many in Parliament, however, the position of the Council was and is the root problem thwarting a proper development of parliamentary power. A consolidation of the Council's role in any constitutional negotiations could only therefore be seen as a negative development. On several occasions in both 1989 and 1990, before the IGCs began, President Delors and parliamentarians clashed over the president's obvious desire to combine a major extension of the Community's power with the maintenance, as far as possible, of the existing institutional balance.[5] The Commission's preparatory documents for the IGCs stated this objective quite openly.[6] Naturally, the Commission maintained that this aim was not incompatible with serious steps to reduce the democratic deficit. The argument was counter to parliamentary orthodoxy, and many parliamentarians suspected collusion between the Commission and the Council at their expense.

Ironically enough, the efforts of Parliament's friends in the Council (notably Germany and Italy) to strengthen Parliament's role has further complicated the triangular relationship. Some of the more obvious steps, including granting Parliament some right of initiative and a more prominent role in the legislative process, can be conceded only at the expense of the Commission. It would be misleading to suggest that by the end of 1990, the Commission-Parliament alliance had broken down. The two institutions still had important common interests. Yet, it is quite obvious that EC politics cannot any longer be described in terms of a Commission-Parliament coalition against an overpowerful Council.

THE IGCS

The IGCs on economic and monetary union and political union should by December 1991 have negotiated a comprehensive revision of the original treaties; ultimately, a single treaty will incorporate the results of both conferences. Nevertheless, the two processes had distinct political antecedents and their rate of progress has been quite different. It is therefore appropriate to discuss them separately.

EMU

The quest for EMU is over 20 years old, and many of the concepts currently under discussion have been in circulation from the beginning. The practical experience of many member-states in working together, first in the Monetary Snake and subsequently in the EMS, goes back almost as far. As a result, all the member-states except the United Kingdom displayed a substantial degree of consensus about what the negotiations ought to achieve. The Conclusions of the European Council of October 1990—which in effect terminated Margaret Thatcher's prime ministerial career—listed the main points of agreement.[7] They included a common understanding of the basic characteristics of the economic union ("an open market system that combines price stability with growth, employment and environmental protection and is dedicated to sound and sustainable financial and budgetary conditions and to economic and social cohesion") and on the principal features of the monetary union. The centerpiece of the latter was to be a new monetary institution comprising member-states' central banks and a central organ, exercising full responsibility for monetary policy. This institution's prime task would be to maintain price stability. It would also be "independent of instructions," and it could (and probably would) issue a single currency.

Members agree, too, about the main landmarks that would have to be passed on the way to the final achievement of EMU. By the second half of 1990, the Community had already initiated Stage One. The Council therefore agreed that Stage Two should begin on January 1, 1994. With this in view the revised treaty should provide for the new monetary institution, the prohibition of monetary financing of monetary deficits, and the exclusion of any responsibility on the part of the Community or its members for any member-state's debt.

In Stage Two, the new monetary institution and the other Community institutions involved were to be given an opportunity to strengthen the coordination of monetary policies, develop the instruments and procedures needed for the future conduct of a single monetary policy, and oversee the further development of the EMU. At the latest within three years from the beginning of Stage Two, the Council would be obliged to consider moving on to Stage Three, at which point the central bank would be fully operational and, it was assumed, a single currency would be introduced.

Underpinning this agreement on broad principles were a number of papers on the nuts and bolts of the new regime; these included a draft treaty, prepared by the Commission, and draft statutes of the future central bank, submitted by the Central Bank Governors Committee.[8] Despite continuing efforts by the British to suggest that the Community had "hardly begun" to think about what EMU involved, it was already obvious by the end of 1990 that the negotiations would have to focus on remarkably few major issues.

The negotiations themselves have confirmed this judgment. Three questions have assumed particular importance: the treatment of budgetary indiscipline, the timing of the progression toward full monetary union, and the stance to be taken toward the United Kingdom by its partners should it choose not to join the EMU. Differences of opinion on the first of these questions had already surfaced in the Delors committee, where the Germans and the Dutch in particular argued that the union would have to be armed with powers to deal with member-states whose fiscal policies were deviant or disruptive. Representatives of the other countries in the Delors committee and the Commission president himself were inclined to believe that a combination of rules prohibiting the new central bank from funding member-states' deficits, the exclusion of any "bailing out" of one member-state by its partners, market forces, and peer pressure would suffice. In the end, the German-Dutch position prevailed.[9] As the IGCs have progressed, it has become increasingly likely that the new treaty will contain specific provisions to enforce budgetary discipline, including, for example, Community-supervised and publicly reported detoxification programs for countries addicted to budgetary excess and, if necessary, the termination of all transfers from the Community budget.[10]

The question of budgetary discipline has inevitably been prominent in the discussion of the timing of progress toward EMU. Once again, the Germans have been in the forefront of the negotiation. Their views have been put forward in various quarters, and by nobody more trenchantly than the outgoing president of the Bundesbank, Karl-Otto Poehl. His object was not, it should be stressed, to torpedo the whole negotiation: the debate has been about means, not ends. Essentially three issues are at stake: the timing and duration of Stage Two, the conditionality that should be attached to the entry into force of Stage Three, and the political and economic implications of a "two-speed" EMU.

On the first of these points, nobody, including the authors of the Delors report, much liked Stage Two. Its purpose was and is essentially political: to provide a bridge between present reality and final destination. Economically, Stage Two as the Delors plan envisages it has many weaknesses. It would signal the EC's intentions to the market without providing those responsible for managing monetary policies with the legal and financial powers they really require. Several prominent figures have therefore urged that it be avoided altogether; even those, like the Commission, advocating its maintenance have agreed that it should at all costs be made as short as possible.

The debate about the other two issues, conditionality and two-speed Europe, has significantly influenced the nature of the compromise that has emerged in the negotiations on this point. In widely reported remarks to the European Parliament in March 1991, Karl-Otto Poehl suggested that five or six member-states could, if they so wished, proceed immediately to EMU, dispensing altogether with Stage Two.[11] The obstacle to such a development, however, was and is a general distaste for a two-speed Europe, particularly if, as would be inevitable, the slower group included such manifestly "pro-European" countries as Italy and Spain.

The most important features of the emerging compromise are: agreement that there should be a Stage Two, as planned, beginning on January 1, 1994; postponement of the establishment of the central banking institution to 1996 at the earliest; and immediate action to discipline the countries that appear least likely to fulfill the conditions required for participation in the monetary union.[12] *In other words, the effect has been to delay the institutional timetable, while advancing the economic discipline.*

In the middle of 1991, the Community significantly strengthened "mutual surveillance," by introducing a well-publicized grading system, under which member states' economic performance was assessed according to various criteria and each member state was given a grade: white for good, grey for somewhat worrying, and black for downright bad. Only Luxembourg emerged

TABLE 1   COMPARATIVE PERFORMANCE OF MEMBER STATES

Country	Inflation (percent) 1991	1992	GDP Growth (percent) 1991	1992	Lending (+) or Borrowing (−) As percentage of GDP 1991	1992
Belgium	3.25	3.5	2.25	2.5	−6.25	−6
Denmark	2.5	2.5	1.5	2.25	−1.25	−1
Germany, Federal Republic of	3.5	4.25	2.75	1.75	4.75	−4
Greece	18	13	0.75	1.5	−15.5	−10.75
Spain	6	5.25	3	3.5	−2.75	−2
France	3	3.25	1.5	2.5	−1.5	−1.5
Ireland	3	3	1.75	2.25	−3.75	−3.5
Italy	6.25	5.5	1.75	2.5	−10	−10
Luxembourg	3.5	3.5	3	3.25	+1.75	+1.5
Netherlands	2.75	3.0	2.75	1.75	−4.75	−5
Portugal	11.5	9.75	2.75	2.75	−5.5	−5
UK	6.5	5	−2.25	2.25	−2.25	−3.25
EC average	5	4.75	1.25	2.25	−4.5	−4.5

Source: EC Commission, European Economy, Supplement A, No. 5, May 1991.

with a totally clean sheet; only Greece with an almost totally bad one. The report did, however, confirm that Italy is bound to be at the center of discussion in the coming years. In terms of its budgetary deficit, it is now in a totally different league from every other member-state except Greece.

The problem is, of course, not new. It also contains a distinctively Italian complication that some politicians in Rome have been quick to exploit: the fact that although the budgetary situation has deteriorated, Italy's general economic performance has in most other respects, including inflation and the growth of gross national product, significantly improved both in terms of the country's own past and in relation to its Community partners. Given the capacity of the Italian political elite to procrastinate and the fundamental importance for their position of the political clientalism that is an essential corollary of the public-sector problem, a quick cure of the Italian sickness is unlikely.

From the political debate in the first half of 1991, however, it is clear that Italy's "fitness for Europe" is going to be a central theme of domestic political debate for months and years to come, and that far-reaching reforms of the whole political system, including possibly the establishment of a presidential system on French lines, will figure prominently on the political agenda.

The Italian story promises to be by far the most interesting political spin-off of EMU in the present decade. By comparison, the question of whether the UK will eventually enter the EMU is increasingly stale. Margaret Thatcher's resignation as prime minister has certainly improved the atmosphere between the UK and its partners, but it is improbable that Prime Minister Major can deliver on EMU before an election. As the latter may well not take place before 1992, he has signaled—and his partners have agreed—a let-out arrangement, whereby the other eleven will go forward and the UK will reserve its position.[13] By the time the political decision has to be taken on Stage Three, however, it is scarcely conceivable that the UK will attempt to maintain the fiction of national sovereignty in the face of the reality of EMU.

European Political Union

In contrast to the negotiations on EMU, the IGC on political union has in many respects been exploring unknown territory. The Community has, of course, always had a high political ambition. The Schuman Plan in 1950 spoke of the first step on the way to a European federation. Since then, the political dimension of the EC has frequently been reasserted, not least in the Single European Act, which defined the goal as European union. The mandate the foreign ministers of the Community and, more particularly, their personal representatives received in April 1990 to prepare the groundwork for the IGC on political union was, however, strong on rhetoric but short on detail. Statements by both the German chancellor and the French president made it clear that questions of political accountability and a common foreign policy would figure prominently. Important though both themes were, they scarcely added up to a concept of union.[14]

Against this background, it was only natural that the personal representatives proceeded tentatively in the first round of discussions in 1990, and that outside commentators deduced from their caution that the negotiations were unlikely to result in any radical departure for the Community. This impression was in some ways confirmed by the early agreement, fully endorsed by the Commission if not by the Parliament, that the second IGC should not attempt to alter fundamentally the existing institutional balance. This was obviously intended to indicate that the Council would remain at the center of Community politics and that brave new departures such as those signaled by the draft treaty of union the European Parliament adopted in 1984 under the leadership of Altiero Spinelli were therefore not in the cards.[15]

As the months have passed, this early note of caution appears to have been rather misleading. Certain individuals, particularly in Parliament and among federalist groups, are still convinced that the outcome will be disappointing. If the measure by which it is tested is a federation on the U.S. or German model, they are right. If, however, this unrealistic measure is abandoned, the second IGC can be seen as a major negotiation.

Whence this momentum? Three factors are crucially important: the continuing impact of German unification, which refocused the attention of both the Germans and their partners on the need to strengthen EC institutions as a safeguard against the reemergence of a "German problem"; the built-in momentum of an open-ended negotiation into which participants quickly began to throw all kinds of ideas, with the result that almost 100 "nonpapers" were submitted in the first five months of 1991; and the impact of the Gulf crisis, which highlighted both the weaknesses of the Community and the dangers that would result if they were not repaired.

The negotiations will not be completed until the European Council meeting in Maastricht in December 1991; it is therefore impossible to be certain about all the details of the final agreement. It is nevertheless possible to make some judgments on the general scope of the negotiations and to identify the major issues that have emerged.

The five headings under which the conference initially organized its work indicate *the scope of the negotiations:* Community Competence, Democratic Responsibility, Efficiency, European Citizenship, Foreign and Security Policy. The draft treaty incorporates two fundamental constraints on the centralization process. The first is a more explicit commitment than hitherto to the principle of subsidiarity, according to which the Community institutions should seek to do only what they can manifestly do better than the nation-states or other lesser authorities. The second is built in to the design of the treaty, which distinguishes between three modes of collective activity: the classic, Community method; a hybrid system, involving the Council and the Commission in the field of foreign policy and security; and intergovernmental cooperation. Obviously, items mentioned in the third section of the treaty, such as judicial and police matters, will be less subject to the process of centralization than will policies such as environment or consumer protection, which figure in the first part.

Even if allowances are made for these general limitations, the extent to which the powers of the Community institutions are redefined or enlarged is still striking. A later section of this essay will discuss the issue of a common foreign and security policy in more detail. It is enough at this point to list the other topics that have figured in the negotiations and seem likely to appear in the new treaty:

- *Responsibilities that are already acknowledged to be within the Community's sphere of action but are to be extended or better defined.* The subjects concerned include social policy, cohesion, the environment, research and technology, fiscal policy, and vocational training.

- *Fields in which a specific legal basis for Community action is to be provided.* These include health, animal welfare, civil protection, the arts, education, tourism, consumer protection, energy policy, telecommunications, and trans-European networks (e.g. transport infrastructures).

- *Fields now dealt with in the framework of intergovernmental cooper*
  ation that can be usefully codified in treaty form. These comprise
  frontier control, visa policy, political asylum, immigration
  policy, the fight against drugs, judicial cooperation, and
  joint efforts to combat crime.

All these topics have involved negotiation, and on some of
them important differences have emerged. Six major issue
have, however, dominated the conference: social policy, commu
nity finance, foreign and security policy, institutional balance
the unity of the treaty, and the actual and potential position of
the United Kingdom in the negotiations and vis-à-vis the fina
treaty.

The debate about *social policy* is, of course, not new. It is
primarily a question between the United Kingdom and its partners. The latter, under the rule of either Socialists or Christian
Democrats, have had relatively few reservations about proposals
to enhance the social dimension of Community policies and in
particular, to facilitate the appropriate legislation by extending
majority voting. The British, by contrast, have been consistently
negative on both substance and procedure. It is still difficult to
see how a bargain can be struck, but it is undoubtedly important
that British Prime Minister John Major has openly endorsed the
concept of a social market economy and encouraged Conservatives in the European Parliament to move toward a formal link
with the Christian Democrats.[16] Nevertheless, a gap remains.

One of the major surprises in the conference on political
union has been the emergence of the *financial issue.* The Spanish
are principally responsible. They gave warning of their intentions in the prenegotiations in 1990. As a result, the Council
Secretariat's report to the General Affairs Council in December
1990 was liberally punctuated with formal reservations of "one
member-state" (i.e., Spain), which made acceptance of the proposal in question contingent on the provision of adequate public
finance to compensate the poorer member-states for the adverse
effects of greater integration.[17] Once the formal negotiations
began, Spanish demands became more open and comprehensive, culminating in May 1991 in a proposal that the Community

levelop a financial mechanism along the lines of the German
"inanzausgleich.[18] Both the Commission and the majority of
Spain's partners have been fairly cool toward such a radical
nnovation. Spanish persistence has, however, had the effect of
ocusing negotiators' attention on Community finance a year
before all concerned must in any event renegotiate the five-year
compromise on the Community budget arrived at in 1988. Even
f the Spanish do not make major headway in the treaty itself,
they will undoubtedly use every opportunity in 1992 and beyond
to press for a significant extension and redirection of EC public
expenditure. The North-South theme in EC politics will be an
important ingredient of the 1990s.

The discussion about *foreign and security policy* acquired particular significance in light of the Gulf crisis. A minority—principally, but not entirely, in the United Kingdom—seized on the
opportunity the Community's incapacity to maintain a united
front created to preach the message that the EC, and more
specifically, the IGC should not become involved with matters so
clearly beyond the Community's present range of abilities. A
larger number of contributors to the discussion drew the reverse
conclusion: the weaknesses the Gulf crisis exposed, made a
strengthening of the EC's competence in this respect more,
rather than less, necessary. The French and German governments, the Italian government, and the Commission all tabled
significant papers with this as their central theme in February
1991.[19] Intensive diplomacy involving, among others, the secre-
taries-general of the North Atlantic Treaty Organization (NATO)
and the Western European Union (WEU) backed up their efforts.
The internal EC debate has been complicated by NATO's simul-
taneous review of strategy and structure. The recommendations
on force structures to which NATO defense ministers agreed at
the end of May 1991 were widely perceived as a victory for the
"Atlanticists" against the "Europeans."[20] France in particular
protested against an apparent attempt to foreclose Europe's
options. London's obvious satisfaction with the agreement, and
especially with the new rapid reaction force, only fueled French
suspicion. These anxieties are, however, almost certainly premature. It is probably better to view the NATO recommendations as

a partial and temporary success for a coalition involving the defense establishments in most NATO countries, backed up by certain governments, of which the UK is the most conspicuous EC member state. The NATO report is likely to prove relatively unimportant in the longer term for at least two reasons. First, its conclusions have emerged from a strategic vacuum. Second, the recommendations' scant relation to the positions of politicians rather than defense professionals within the context of the IGC suggests that they will be modified over time. As in EMU matters, so in political military questions, it is usually sensible to listen not to the professionals with their vested interests, but to the political leaders.

The best guide to EC thinking is the June 1991 presidency draft treaty. According to that text, the Community will commit itself to the development of a common foreign and security policy in the fullest sense of the term. Progress will, however, be evolutionary, under the general, strategic leadership of the European Council. Thus, the speed of the EC's advance toward a common foreign policy will be significantly faster than its progress toward a common security policy. Member-states are already committed through the Single European Act to systematic political cooperation. They will undertake in the new treaty to develop common actions in certain agreed areas. A preliminary list includes armaments production; the transfer of military technologies and armaments exports; nuclear proliferation; arms control, particularly within the context of the Conference on Security and Cooperation in Europe (CSCE); peacekeeping efforts in the UN; humanitarian actions; and, possibly, the CSCE process as a whole, relations with the Soviet Union, and relations with the Unites States.

The institutional structure will be different from the classic Community structure. Even so, it will mark a significant advance on procedures followed hitherto in European Political Cooperation (EPC). Its principal novelty lies in the centralization of decision making in the ordinary institutions of the Community: the European Council, the General Affairs Council, the Committee of Permanent Representatives (COREPER), and the Council Secretariat, which will absorb the EPC Secretariat.

These proposals have been interpreted in some quarters as a victory for 'intergovernmentalism' over the Commission. This view represents a dangerous oversimplification. If we must think in terms of winners and losers, the Political Directors in national capitals clearly head the list of the latter, while the Commission—which will, as always, be fully involved in the Council pro-cedure—is equally obviously among the winners. A straightfor-ward transfer of competence from national foreign offices to the Commission was never in the cards—and the Commission itself, whose own paper on external policy envisaged essentially the same hybrid system, did not seek it.[21]

In the security field, the emphasis on evolution is still stron-ger. Hence the importance of the discussion about the WEU. The UK's paper on foreign policy and security issues, submitted to the IGC at the end of February 1991, admitted the need for close coordination of foreign and defense policies, but located the latter firmly in the WEU and placed the WEU itself equally firmly in NATO.[22] To the extent that the Europeans were to act outside the NATO area, for example, their efforts were to be based on "the European elements of the Alliance's reformed collective structure." WEU ambassadors and NATO ambas-sadors would be one and the same; EC permanent representa-tives would be a breed apart. The French and Germans agreed on the utility of the WEU, but only as a transitional instrument.[23] Their fundamental objective was to establish a link between the EC and the WEU by way of the European Council, thereby opening up the possibility that the European union would ab-sorb the WEU when the latter's treaty expires in 1998. The WEU would act as a bridge to NATO, but would be organizationally separate at the ambassadorial level and in every other way.

Despite some concessions to the British, the essentials of the Franco-German position seem certain to be preserved. The treaty will thus include a declaration that the union is to be responsible for 'all aspects' of a common foreign and security policy, including eventually, the framing of a defense policy. It will also establish a clear link between the European Council and the WEU. Finally it will probably provide for a review of the EC-WEU relationship by 1996 at the latest, as part of the further definition of a common defense policy. The EC will therefore be equipped with the authority to move forward as far and as fast as it feels the need to. How far and how fast will depend partly on political leadership, but still more on international developments, particularly changes inside Europe and North America. At the moment, everything in the security field is provisional. In these circumstances, it is more important to identify where the seat of political authority lies than to move dwindling forces around in a political, economic, and strategic void.

The negotiations' impact on the *institutional balance* in the EC has provoked a great deal of reaction among both participants and commentators. On one point, all seem to be agreed: the Council will emerge with its place at the center of the Community system confirmed and its efficiency reinforced. This judgment holds true of the Council machinery in general and of the European Council in particular. The latter is set to become the keystone of the arch linking the various elements of the union. The Council machinery as a whole will also benefit, however, from the extension of majority voting to most areas of Community policy and the consolidation of its role in foreign and security policy.

This "victory for the Council" need not and indeed should not be seen as a defeat for the Commission. On the contrary, as the first part of this essay suggested, a strong Council is an essential precondition of the Commission's leadership role. As the discussion of foreign and security policy has already shown, the Commission stands to gain from the centralization of decision making in the Council machinery. It will also be associated as of right in the intergovernmental discussion of judicial and police questions, which was not the case hitherto. Finally, but by no means least, the affirmation of the integrity of the union which the earliest articles of the treaty seem bound to include, will further strengthen the tendency of Community business to converge into common patterns and procedures.

Why, then, one may ask, did the Commission itself appear to encourage the general atmosphere of discontent with the negotiations in the second quarter of 1991? The answer is complex and cannot be developed at length here, but one point is particlarly relevant. For a variety of reasons, the Commission did not manage to assert its leadership in these negotiations to anywhere near the extent that it had in 1985 when the Single European Act was drafted. Everybody wanted and had a say in a process that was extraordinarily open-ended. The Commission's frustration was heightened by one or two significant defeats, particularly in the discussion of external policy: as the Commission attempted to "tidy up" arrangements concerning external economic policy, in which it has long had a central role, it overplayed its hand and offended even allies such as the Dutch and the Belgians. Against this background, a certain amount of resentment on the Commission's part was inevitable. If, however, one looks at the negotiations as a whole, it is very difficult indeed to conclude that the Commission will emerge weaker. On the contrary, both the general thrust of the negotiation and the specific provisions regarding the Commission, which will almost certainly allow for a reduction of the number of full commissioners from seventeen to twelve, thereby allowing a streamlining of its internal organization, suggest that its role will continue to expand in the 1990s as it did in the 1980s.

Where will the treaty leave the Parliament? Without a radical restructuring of the Community system, and more particularly the transformation of the Council of Ministers into something like an upper legislative chamber, the European Parliament's position will always suffer from certain weaknesses. Representatives of the member-states cannot be accountable to a supranational Parliament. Even so, a number of improvements can be made within these limits, and thanks to the pressure exercised by the Germans and the Italians, it seems highly probable that many, if not all, the more obvious measures will in fact be adopted. For example, the cooperation procedure the Single European Act introduced will be significantly extended, and in certain areas of legislation, Parliament will be given the right of codecision and veto.

Changes in the legislative process have attracted the most attention. It is arguable, however, that the real test of Parliament in the future will be in its ability to exploit its political powers and opportunities in a Community that, as a result of EMU and the movement toward a common foreign and security policy, will engage in more and more actions of a political rather than legislative character. Here, too, the new treaty will help, by providing Parliament with stronger rights to demand testimony and to supervise the management of EC policies, particularly in the financial sphere. Parliament will also play a role in the appointment of the Commission. The Council will continue to nominate the president and other commissioners, but it will be obliged to consult Parliament, and once the choice is made, to submit the Commission as a whole to parliamentary approval. Only when Parliament has given approval will the Commission be able to enter into office.

The fifth major issue in the negotiations, the unity of the union, may at first sight appear arcane,[24] but the argument has considerable political and practical significance. Politically, the majority of member-states' rejection of the Luxembourg presidency's initial draft which underplayed the linkages between the union's three modes of activity, marked an important victory for those who believe the Community should openly admit that its final objective is a union on federal lines. As the amended text the presidency tabled in June 1991 was based very largely on a Commission draft, the episode was also important for the internal morale and external reputation of Commission negotiators. Finally, and by no means least, the evident isolation of the British reopened deep divisions on European policy inside the Conservative Party and in doing so weakened the government's electoral prospects and negotiating hopes.

Arguably, however, the practical implications of the strengthening of the definition of the union's purpose and character are likely to prove still more important than their immediate impact on the politics of the Community and its member-states. The Community's handling of issues such as human and financial resources and enlargement, both of which are discussed in the final section of this essay, will be much easier if the eventual objective of a union of federal character is firmly embodied in the treaty. The EC will undoubtedly have to be accommodating in both economic and political terms to the special interests and problems of candidate countries. The new treaty should, however, leave those who wish to join the Community in no doubt about its ultimate purposes. Given the continuing problems between the majority and the UK almost 20 years after the latter joined the Community, this can only be interpreted in a positive light. Lastly, a clear statement that the ultimate objective is a union along federal lines will both hasten and facilitate another IGC, which, unlike the present one, will presumably alter the institutional balance fundamentally.

This leaves one other matter: *the attitude of the British*. In such a complicated negotiation, it is inevitable that no member-state will be entirely happy with everything and that some will feel strongly about matters that are not settled in their favor. The Spanish, for example, will probably not achieve all their demands regarding financial transfers. Similarly, it is difficult to imagine that the pro-parliamentary governments, Italy and Germany, will be entirely satisfied with the provisions regarding Parliament. Finally, the articles covering the common foreign and security policy may cause quivers in Dublin and may even provoke a repeat of the referendum process which had to be resorted to after the Single European Act. On balance, however, it seems safe to predict that eleven member states will be able to arrive at a compromise.

The British attitude is far harder to predict. In the early stages of discussions about political union, the British let it be known that although they had problems with monetary union, (Margaret Thatcher was still in power), they expected to be able to live with the rather muddled conclusions of the second IGC negotiations. The latter have, however, become much more extensive in scope than the British who took this line could have envisaged. As a result, some in London maintain that whereas a compromise on EMU is conceivable, patching over differences on EPU will be much more difficult.

Uncertainty surrounding the date of the general election makes the outcome all the more difficult to foretell. If they were free agents, it is probable that John Major and Douglas F. Hurd would in the end go along with their Community partners. In the present British context, however, with Margaret Thatcher still much more than a distant memory, they may well have to take

part in a charade in which the British opt out yet again. If the
do, the consequences would be inconvenient for all concerned
The Eleven will not, however, wait. Nor will the growing numbe
of candidates to join the union. Faced with those realities, it i
difficult to imagine the British maintaining their separatenes
for long.

THE UNFINISHED AGENDA

As the previous section has indicated, the IGCs of 1991 seem
certain to mark an important milestone in the evolution of the
EC. They will not, however, constitute the end of the story. On
the contrary, a significant unfinished agenda remains, and it
more important elements will dominate EC politics for years to
come, leading—sooner rather than later—to a further IGC. A
brief discussion of two of the more obvious items on this agenda
is essential for a proper evaluation of the 1991 IGCs.

The first involves *human and financial* resources. The EC has
traveled a very long way with a minute "central" bureaucracy and
a budget that, even today, amounts to no more than 1 percent of
gross domestic product (GDP). Federal spending in the United
States, by contrast, accounts for approximately 25 percent of
GDP. Given the maturity and, in most cases, the proven efficiency of the member-states' own administrations, a highly de-
centralized system in which most of the management of common
policies and virtually all government expenditure remain the
responsibility of national bureaucracies is both desirable and
feasible. It seems highly doubtful, however, whether the present,
totally lopsided allocation of resources between the Community
institutions and national administrations can be maintained for
long.

In the case of human resources, the Brussels-based components of the "government of Europe"—comprising the
Commission, the Council Secretariat, and the permanent repre-
sentations—employ fewer personnel than a big ministry in any of
the larger member-states. Daily transfusions of national ministers and bureaucrats borne by planes and trains already take
place on a massive scale; they will presumably remain a part of

ommunity life in the future. Nonetheless, anybody who has
atched the Brussels bureaucracy at close quarters or, for a less-
npressionistic appraisal, has perused the Court of Auditors'
ncreasingly sharp reports on the quality of Community surveil-
ance of common policies, must conclude that if the institutions
re to keep up with the responsibilities that have been thrust
pon them, a major review of the allocation of personnel be-
ween the Community level (including the Permanent Represen-
ations) and national capitals is necessary.

The Community is still, however, far from being able to
ustain a "rational" discussion of these matters. On the contrary,
nyths of overpaid and overstaffed bureaucracies in Brussels die
ard. Although many officials even in Bonn now admit that the
problem is approaching crisis proportions, there is little indica-
ion that their political masters are ready to accept that a problem
xists, let alone to take the kind of decisions that are required to
esolve it. If the crisis is not dealt with, however, complaints by
nsiders and outsiders about the Community's capacity to deliver
on its high-sounding objectives will multiply, to the cost of all
oncerned.

The struggle on the budgetary front is likely to be fiercer
till. The previous section referred to the role of the Spanish in
he intergovernmental negotiations. They are unlikely to get all
hat they want in the IGCs, but this will not deter them. On the
ontrary, with a major budgetary negotiation already necessary
n 1992, as a result of the expiry of the 1988 agreement, Spain,
llied with Portugal (which holds the presidency in the first half
of the year) and other "southern" states, will return to the fray
with a vengeance. The increasing demands of central and eastern Europe, not to mention the Soviet Union, and the growing
ikelihood that enlargement negotiations will sooner rather than
ater encompass several of the states concerned can only
heighten their anxiety. In a remarkable interview that the *Financial Times* published in May 1991, Spanish Prime Minister Felipe
Gonzalez drew attention to the South-East divisions that seem
certain to become an increasingly prominent feature of EC
politics in the 1990s, complicating the already growing division
between South and North.[25] The prime minister's dogmatic

insistence that the West should not pay for 40 years of commu
nism may not have been particularly statesmanlike, or even poli
ically realistic: if the West does not pay, nobody else will, to th
general detriment of the West and everybody else. Decodec
however, the Gonzalez message is clear. If the West, especially th
EC, undertakes to provide major assistance to central and eas
ern Europe and the Soviet Union, this cannot be at the expens
of the South, both inside the EC and on the Mediterranea
littoral.

Gigantic increases in the Community budget are unlikel
and are probably unnecessary. It would not be surprising, how
ever, if over the next five years, the EC began to edge its wa
toward a budget that was comparable in scope to the "prefeder;
budget" of the 1977 MacDougall Report, involving 2.5 percen
or more of GDP.[26] The passage toward that goal will not, how
ever, be peacefully achieved.

The second major set of issues that will dominate the EC'
political agenda in the 1990s concerns the role of the Communit
in Europe—specifically, the problems associated with *enlarge
ment.* Until the autumn of 1990, it seemed safe to say that th
"deepeners" had fended off the challenge of the "wideners.
The decision to launch two IGCs was one indication. The deep
eners' victory was also apparent in the EC's strategy toward th
European Free Trade Association (EFTA) and the formerl
communist countries of central and eastern Europe. Jacque
Delors sketched the strategy in general terms in his Strasbour;
speech of January 1989.[27] In it, he looked forward to a "Euro
pean village" containing several houses, including the EC, th
Soviet Union, the EFTA and one or more central and easter
European groups. When in subsequent months the communis
regimes fell, the imagery changed, but the substance remainec
essentially the same. The EC was now seen as the cornerstone o
the new European system, on which other building blocks wer
to be aligned. One could always hear dissident voices, but th
Delors strategy prevailed and took practical shape in the negotia
tions with the EFTA and in the proposals for new-style associa
tion agreements with Hungary, Czechoslovakia and Poland.

In the winter of 1990–1991, however, opinion shifted visibly. n explanation of this shift is beyond the scope of this essay. Its nplications for the internal development of the EC are, however, rofoundly important, since it involves a vision of the EC not as the ornerstone of the future European system but as the system itself. : now seems inconceivable that the EC will deny admission to new pplicants from the EFTA and central and eastern Europe; as a esult, the EC may by 2010 contain 20 or even 30 member-states. Iost, if not all, the EFTA countries will probably lodge applications efore the end of 1992, and Hungary, Czechoslovakia, and Poland nay even beat some of them to it. Add to this number Malta and Cyprus, Bulgaria, Romania, Yugoslavia, and Albania, not to mention eventually the three Baltic states, and one arrives at a very large Community indeed.

The geopolitical implications of this change are worth many ssays in themselves. The impact on EC politics will be enormous. The issues involved concern both the viability of the EC nstitutional structure and the fundamental purposes of the nion. Can an EC of 20 or 30 members continue to be based on a Council structure in which the member-states have a final say? Will it be possible to avoid total paralysis without extending najority voting to the whole of EC business? Will the larger owers, particularly France and Germany, accept a system in which their influence will inevitably be diluted and their strategies will be constantly vulnerable to the contrary wishes of coalitions built essentially on small states whose elites have had little or no training in the realities of global politics? Will the substantial differences in quality between national administrations of such diverse backgrounds permit the maintenance of the present EC ystem in which the Council and the Commission delegate to national administrations so much of the actual government of Europe? Can the Commission maintain its collegial character without hopelessly compromising its efficiency?

Questions about the viability of a larger EC merge into more fundamental problems concerning its cohesion and purpose. The United States is constituted on the principle of the melting pot: the European Community has flourished hitherto on the basis of unity in diversity. Is this model sustainable when the diversity is as large as it will be in a Community of 20 or 30 an when the challenges the Community faces globally will continu to grow? Even if it is, how will diversity of this magnitude affec the global stance of the union? Will the union be able to develop common foreign and security policy, for example, or will it hav to allow for variable geometry in this respect and in others?

Enlargement poses a seemingly endless list of problems; systematic answer to all or even any of them lies beyond the scop of this essay. Inevitably, there are those who see the prospect as threat to more than 40 years of work: the corrosive effects o widening will quickly dissolve the achievements of the curren IGCs. These preoccupations are real. It would be facile to under estimate the difficulties that the EC will confront as it comes t terms with the full implications of the breakdown of East-Wes divisions inside Europe. It would be equally imprudent, how ever, to give way to premature pessimism. The EC will have t change. A further IGC is inevitable. Large-scale resort to specia regimes for individual countries will also be necessary. It i highly probable, for example, that Czechoslovakia, Hungary and Poland will be members before the end of the decade; yet, i economic terms, it is hard to see how they can be fully integratec with the rest of the Community until well into the next century

These unavoidable consequences of enlargement need no undermine the union. The Community has always counte nanced special regimes as long as they are in principle tempor ary. Nor have those involved been barred as a result from influence in EC politics. On the contrary, Spain and Portugal which still benefit from special arrangements, had a significan impact on Community politics from the moment they joined Variable geometry as a permanent feature of the EC systen would make union impossible: variable geometry as a temporary regime designed to facilitate the entry of new members of div erse backgrounds is not only acceptable, but well tried. Given a constructive attitude on both sides in the enlargement negotia tions, the EC can devise a number of transitional arrangement that do not threaten its basic cohesion or efficiency.

The EC can also derive confidence from a number of other considerations. It is enough simply to recall four:

- *The sheer complexity of what has already been established and the consequent difficulty of unraveling it.* The intra-German negotiations in 1990 provided a graphic illustration of how profoundly the reality of Community law penetrates all member-states.[28] Commission officials were obliged to take part in the internal German discussions themselves, since the Community as much as the Federal Republic was a "successor state." Unscrambling these *acquis* would be as difficult as it would be pointless.

- *The political unacceptability of variable geometry as a systemic solution, as distinct from a transitional device.* The relevance to the enlargement issue of the consolidation of the EC's institutional structure that has taken place since 1979 (principally because of the 1985 and 1991 intergovernmental conferences) is best seen in the internal debate in several EFTA countries. As a result of the European Economic Area negotiations, the EFTA countries will in economic terms be almost fully integrated with the Community, but politically "independent." Two decades ago, this solution would have seemed ideal to most, if not all, of them. By 1991, however, it is manifestly suboptimal. The Community institutions have become a major focus of political power. Outsiders, such as Sweden, have to be in the game to influence its outcome: nominal autonomy seems a poor substitute for the additional leverage that a country can obtain through full membership. By the same token, the new candidates do not want their entry to weaken the union, which they now regard as their inevitable destiny. Enlargement is, in other words, simultaneously a tribute to the magnetic power of the EC and a reinforcement of the latter. A transitional phase may be messy, but far from weakening the drive toward union, the newcomers seem likely to strengthen it

- *The reemergence of the "German problem."* This is an issue not only for Germany's partners, but also for a German political leadership that, like its counterpart in 1950, does not in any way relish a return to the responsibilities and dangers of a loosely integrated Europe of sovereign states on the nineteenth-century model.

* *The geopolitical factors that point to the need for a strong and united Europe in a multipolar system.* It was possible to predict even before the collapse of communism that the Community would need sooner rather than later to negotiate a deepening of its economic and monetary integration and an extension of its capacity to act externally. The Single European Act and the 1992 program were not lighthearted whims or idealistic gestures: they were hardheaded reactions to the more complex world order to which the changing role of the United States and the emergence of Japan testified. With the upheavals in central and eastern Europe thrown in as well, the need for a strong European union as a source of stability in Europe and in the wider international order became even more apparent.

All this does not mean that the problems enlargement pose can be easily overcome. On the contrary, like the dispute over resources, which the enlargement process will inevitably reinforce, enlargement will stretch political imagination and patience to their limits. Despite the major advances toward European Union in recent years, Europe's institutions and European politics still have a long way to go before they achieve a sustainable equilibrium. If the Community or the union did not exist, however, it would have to be invented.

NOTES

1. The following paragraphs develop and update themes already discussed at greater length in Peter Ludlow, ed., *The CEPS Annual Review of EC Affairs 1990* (London: Brasseys, 1990); and Stanley Hoffman and Robert Keohane, eds., *Decision-Making in the European Community* (Boulder, Colo.: Westview Press, 1991).
2. See Peter Ludlow, *Beyond 1992*, Centre for European Policy Studies Paper no. 38 (Brussels, 1989).
3. John E. Rielly, ed., *American Public Opinion and U.S. Foreign Policy, 1991* (Chicago: Chicago Council on Foreign Relations, 1991), p. 21.
4. Wolfgang Heisenberg, ed., *German Unification in European Perspective* (London: CEPS/Brasseys, 1991).
5. EC Official Journal, Debates of the European Parliament of October 23, 1990.
6. For example, *Europe*, Document Series 1687, European Commission explanatory memorandum concerning the draft treaty on EMU:

"Without it being possible or necessary to indicate at this stage the
final content and shape of European Union, care must be taken to
ensure that the conditions for transferring new powers to the Community—however important they may be—do not jeopardize the
existing institutional framework, which has a proven dynamism."

7. *Europe.* Document 1658. Conclusions of the European Council of October
27–28, 1990.
8. *Europe.* Document Series 1675/1676. Draft treaty amending the treaty
establishing the EEC with a view to achieving EMU. Document 1669/1670.
Draft statute of the European System of Central Banks and of the European Central Bank.
9. Report of EC Committee for the Study of Economic and Monetary Union
(Brussels, 1989), especially paras. 30, 33, and 59.
0. *Europe,* February 27, 1991, pp. 5/6
1. *Europe,* March 20, 1991, pp. 13/14
2. *Europe,* May 13–14, 1991, pp. 7/8
3. Major's speech in Bonn on March 11, 1991 gave the first public hint of a
compromise. The "Delors compromise," reported in *Europe,* May 13/14,
1991, and elsewhere was no more than an echo of the prime minister's
position: if you do not force us, we will not veto you.
4. *Europe,* April 20, 1990. Letter from President Mitterrand and Chancellor
Kohl to Prime Minister Haughey, April 19, 1990.
5. Fr. Capotortif etc. *Le traité d'Union européene.* (Brussels: Université Libre de
Bruxelles, 1985).
6. Speech by John Major at Konrad Adenauer Stiftung, Bonn, March 11,
1991. U.K. Government Information Service.
7. EC Council Secretariat. Paper on political union submitted to the General
Affairs Council, December 4, 1990.
8. *Europe.* May 9, 1991, p. 9.
9. *Europe.* Document 1690 bis Franco-German paper on Security Policy Cooperation.
0. Atlantic News, No. 2326, May 30, 1991. See also the communiqué following the meeting of NATO foreign ministers in Copenhagen, June 7, 1991.
1. *Europe.* Document 1697/98. Commission proposals regarding a common
external policy.
2. UK draft treaty provisions on common foreign and security policy (un-
published papers)
3. Ibid.
4. *Europe,* June 2–4, 1991, on the Dresden meeting of the General Affairs
Council, which included a discussion of political union in the IGC framework.
5. *Financial Times,* May 9, 1991.
6. Commission of the EC report of the study group on the role of public
finance in European integration. 2 Vols, Brussels, April 1977.
7. For a fuller discussion, see Ludlow, *CEPS Annual Review,* introduction and
ch. 2.
8. Heisenberg, *German Unification.*

4

THE EUROPEAN ECONOMIC AREA, THE NEUTRALS, AND AN EMERGING ARCHITECTURE

Wolfgang Danspeckgruber

Although the Cold War has ended, a substantially differen
European structure has yet to emerge from the post–Worlc
War II order. European states continue to function along tradi
tional postwar organizational lines: The European Communit)
(EC), the North Atlantic Treaty Organization (NATO), the West
ern European Union (WEU), the Council on Mutual Economi
Assistance (CMEA), and the European Free Trade Associatior
(EFTA). The EFTA consists of seven members—Austria, Fin
land, Iceland, Liechtenstein, Norway, Sweden, and Switzerland
All but Iceland and Norway are also linked with a phenomenor
some observers consider outmoded—the policy of classical per
manent neutrality. The changing European architecture i
bound to substantially influence the fate of these countries.

This chapter addresses the relationship between the EC anc
the neutral states, the effects of EFTA membership on the con
duct of neutrality, and the political consequences of the creatior
of the European Economic Area (EEA). The choices available tc
emerging eastern European democracies in regard to foreigr
policy and their relations with the EC and EEA are also exam
ined. Specifically, the issue is whether classical neutrality is still a
valid foreign and security policy option for the future, or
whether integration and regionalization will eventually "Euro
peanize" the continent.

NEUTRALITY AND THE NEW EUROPE

Classical neutrality is a geopolitical and perceptual status. I
focuses on sovereignty, autonomous decision making, and the

earch for security and prosperity. This implies that the neutral has great interest in maintaining the geopolitical status quo—a desire the political changes in Europe during 1989–90 rendered obsolete. Neutrality, though, existed before 1945 and the Cold War; Thucydides mentioned it with regard to the Peloponnesian War. Rather than the end of the East-West divide, the drive to intensified integration in all sectors of human life and concomitant regionalization and Europeanization alters the prospects for neutrality. Perception, the sometimes forgotten aspect of permanent neutrality, consists of an internal and an external dimension: even if a state believed in its own capability to remain neutral, other states could deny the feasibility of its doing so and, hence, the credibility of its neutral status.[1] Neutrality is successful only to the extent that it is appreciated abroad. Much depends, therefore, on the degree of national fulfillment of international expectations.

The events of 1989–1990 created five major, interrelated factors of particular importance to the neutral countries: a unified Germany; the dissolution of the Warsaw Treaty Organization (WTO); new eastern European democracies in search of adequate foreign and economic security orientation; an institutionalized Conference on Security and Cooperation in Europe (CSCE); and choices for the EC in the process of deeper integration. The unification of Germany commenced a "digestive process" that demands a two-way adaptation: Germany must search for a new identity and position in international affairs; and the international community must learn to live with the greatest accumulation ever of people, industry, and power in one country on the European continent (with the exception of a functioning Soviet Union). This, in turn, has implications for the EC, the CSCE, and the former WTO members. In the words of French President François Mitterrand, the EC desires to eventually develop into a "federal finality." The risk is that the new Europe may give rise to two kinds of Europeans—the wealthy ones (EC members) and the others. States outside the EC, therefore, aspire to membership, while recognizing the potential for the reemergence of tension between the Mediterranean states and the rich North. In addition, the specter of an old problem lingers

for eastern Europeans: The Iron Curtain may have disap
peared, but another obstacle—what Hungarian Prime Ministe
Joszef Antall calls a "Welfare Wall"[2]—is in the process of replac
ing it. Regarding security politics, it has become clear that th
CSCE cannot replace NATO, and that a future common Euro
pean defense policy may still rely on NATO and use the WEU a
a bridge to the EC.

What, then, will be the role and position of neutral EFT/
members, in light of their desire to join the EC and a certair
reluctance to give up neutrality?

The EEA will serve as an intermediary, perhaps long-last
ing, step to full integration. Many neutral states intend to join th
EC—most immediately Austria and Sweden—but final ratifica
tion and complete accession may take some time, and this dela
revalues the EEA. Czechoslovakia, Hungary, and Poland see
association agreements with the EFTA and will try to becom
eventually integrated into the EEA. Meanwhile, all of Europ
may adopt some of the essentials of the concept of neutrality—
nonaggression and peaceful solution of conflicts, even defensiv
strategies and force postures. Ultimately, as the new democracie
follow a path from dealignment to Europeanization, the inten
sified integration and cooperation of an increasingly region
alized Europe may reduce or even eliminate the reasons fo
adhering to classical neutrality.[3]

THE CURRENT SITUATION: THE EFTA
AND THE EEA

EFTA

With the exception of Ireland, none of Europe's declared per
manent neutral states holds EC membership. Instead, Austria
Finland, Sweden, and Switzerland form the EFTA with Iceland
Norway, and—since April 1991—Liechtenstein. EFTA repre
sents the largest trading partner of the EC nations, with which i
conducts more than 60 percent of its trade—far outstripping EC
trade with America and Japan.[4] But the current EC-EFTA free
trade accords cover only industrial goods, not agriculture or

ervices, and the EFTA nations face an array of technical bariers, including EC specifications on product size, origin, compoition, and safety.[5]

Since 1972, Austria, Finland, Sweden, and Switzerland have ʌad separate free trade agreements with the EC (the Swiss agreenent includes Liechtenstein). They also have concluded special greements for participation in EC scientific and technological ›rograms (such as BRITE and COST), and are members of the ̣uropean Research Coordination Agency (EUREKA) and the ̣uropean Space Agency (ESA). Total trade of Austria, Sweden, .nd Switzerland with EC members, especially Germany, has xceeded 50 percent. These neutrals, in turn, are among Gernany's ten largest markets, as well as being important markets or Italy and France. Germany traditionally has supported ⸲ttempts at a closer relationship between the neutral EFTA nembers and the EC.

The Single European Market (SEM) initiative has con'ronted the neutrals with a painful dilemma. Their economies 'equire maximum access to the SEM, but they harbor a very real 'ear of being closed out, or "satellized," once the SEM is com›leted by the end of 1992. The tariff-free access of EFTA indusrial goods has potentially become less valuable, and competition ⸲gainst Community firms has therefore decreased. A mutual ›pening between the SEM and the EFTA would increase compeition, force restructuring and internationalization of EFTA inlustries, positively influence price and wage levels, and generally ⸲nhance international competitiveness. Another powerful in ̣entive for neutrals to seek membership in the SEM is the desire o actively participate in the EC decision-making process and herefore be in a position to influence the EC bureaucracy. But wo sets of obstacles stand in the way: First, the envisaged Euro ›ean Political Cooperation (EPC) eventually will extend to secu ·ity and military issues, perhaps via the WEU, and thus would ̣onflict with the principle of neutrality. Second, because they are ⸲mall and lack economies of scale, the EFTA states fear excessive ·ransborder traffic (especially consisting of EC workers), foreign nvestment, and other problems.

EEA

In their 1984 joint Luxembourg declarations, the EC and the EFTA agreed upon the guidelines for a "dynamic and homoge neous" European Economic Space (EES). The EES was to resem ble the Organization for European Economic Cooperatior (OEEC) free trade area of the 1950s and create a free westerr European market for industrial goods. But soon the notion o "homogeneity" started to disappear. In 1988, the potential di mensions and framework of the EES seemed much more restric tive than the EC originally planned. In 1989 it was negotiatec into the European Economic Area (EEA).

EFTA and EC ministers meeting in January 1989 agreec upon far-reaching negotiations and to the so-called Delors Plar (named for European Commission President Jacques Delors) This plan for the EEA foresees many areas of cooperation be tween the EC and the EFTA, but not full access to the EC' internal decision-making process. Indeed, the EEA agreemen (like its SEM counterpart) covers the free movement of goods services, capital, and people; the preparation of similar condi tions for free location; the elimination of trade barriers by creat ing equal rules for competition; and "flanking" and horizonta areas. The entire *acquis communautaire*—with the exception of EC agricultural policy—will form the legal basis of the EEA. EFT/ members have agreed to adopt the entire body of EC legislatior without much alteration,[6] and will gain little if any voice in EC decision making. Nonetheless, the formation of the EEA make: them partner to the largest market in the industrialized world— comprising 330 million persons.[7]

Brussels characterizes the EEA as consisting of two pillar (the EC and the EFTA) linked by constant consultation anc equipped with one or more common organs, such as a join ministerial council and a special disputes tribunal (probabl composed of the EC Luxembourg Court and EFTA judges) Whether the EEA will take decisions by unanimous agreement as the EFTA does, or by majority voting remains to be clarified The EC also demands that EEA agreements take precedenc over national legislation. Brussels, however, does not like curren

EFTA lobbying of certain EC members—such as Denmark and Germany—to influence the outcome of the EEA negotiations.

EFTA CONCESSIONS

If EFTA's individual states were simply applying for full EC membership, they would have no choice but to accept the complete menu of existing Community rules and to participate in EC decision making. But, even with the EEA as the immediate goal, the burden of concessions falls more upon the EFTA. Its members have to accept the EC practices in mixing of technical standards; opening public procurement; cracking down on cartels and state subsidies; and allowing the free movement of labor, goods, services, and capital. As a concession on its part, the EC will not include a common agricultural policy—despite increasing EC demands for "cohesion requirements," or *Kohaesionsforderungen,* such as improved market access for fruits, a common fund for the poorer EC countries, or enforcement of the Schengen agreement (regarding the abolition of border controls) on EFTA territory.

The fundamental questions for EFTA-EC relations and the EEA remain as follows:

- How can the EFTA influence the decisions that will affect it in the proposed EEA?

- What kind of joint body will supervise the regulations covering the EEA?

- What joint legal institutions will be responsible for upholding the laws that cover both EFTA and EC areas in the EEA?

- What sorts of agreements can be reached regarding heavy trucking through Austria and Switzerland and on fishery rights and market access for Norway and Iceland?

EFTA AND EC: JOINT DECISION MAKING

Jacques Delors and others in the European Commission still hold that EC decision making should not be diluted by expanding the Community. The EC has offered the EFTA "a hearing" and a say at certain stages during the enactment of legislation, but no joint decision making; it also would permit the EFTA to participate in the work of various committees as either a permanent or a partial member. It is clear that as more states seek full participation, more states will apply at once. The chances for a "package" thus increase, whereby several states will be admitted at the same time. In that case the admission process might take longer than it does now, and membership will be delayed accordingly.

In the European Parliament, the widespread belief is that Austria and Sweden will try to obtain EC membership by 1995. For them the EEA accord is only a stepping-stone to EC membership; EC parliamentarians are therefore reluctant to accept too many limitations on the autonomy of the decision-making process—as would be placed on it by an EEA agreement—for, as the argument goes, much will be different in just a few years.

New demands on the EFTA by the poorer, southern EC states—Portugal, Spain, and Greece—as well as Ireland, present additional complications. These countries want the wealthier and more industrial EFTA to create separate financial funds to help them in the SEM.[8] The EFTA also fears that despite consultations, the EC Council of Ministers and the European Parliament could suddenly present it with unsatisfactory legislative surprises as *faits accomplis*. Brussels fears that extensive demands by EFTA countries could complicate the EC's internal decision making.

The real problems concern the supervisory bodies the EEA will require. The Community recently declared its willingness to approve the consensus principle for joint decisions in the EEA, thereby acceding to an EFTA demand. The two sides agreed to treat the rules they decide on jointly as international agreements that will come into force at the same time in all nineteen EEA countries. They also agreed to conduct ongoing consultations within a joint body set up for the EEA, but its precise composition and the extent of its powers (especially when the two sides fail to reach agreement) remain to be determined. It may be a mechanism similar to the EC Commission that can supervise and enforce laws within the EEA, in which case the multinational EFTA surveillance body would take over some of the national decision-making power. The EC also would grant EFTA countries the right to raise whatever questions they want, whenever, and at any level. Brussels would allow the national EFTA parliaments to make their views known in certain instances, but this implies that parliamentary approval may be necessary in some cases and in some EFTA countries, and a joint EC-EFTA parliamentary body may be created.[9]

COMPETITIVE ARRANGEMENTS

The EFTA is ready to drop its demands for certain permanent exceptions for various industries, and to ask instead for transition periods during which sensitive areas, such as finance, farming, and forestry, can adjust to EC or EEA open ownership rules with temporary safeguard clauses. It has indicated a willingness to establish its own body to monitor competition and control state aid to companies (important in Austria and Norway) and to cartels. This might introduce a significant supranational feature in the EFTA, but the real problems are the "mixed cases"—EC and EFTA companies. Progress has already been considerable in the "flanking areas" of the EEA: education, research and development, the environment, and consumer protection. It appears, indeed, that a successful EEA conclusion on these issues may carry certain advantages for the EC, as well. Then, at least, Brussels could play for more time with the new admissions, since the most urgent needs of the applicants would have been satisfied.

Despite the many problems still needing attention, bilateral means alone could hardly have achieved the intensity and high level that the EEA negotiations between the EFTA and EC have reached; hence, the negotiations themselves constitute a great leap forward. Indeed, they represent more than half of the negotiations that any country would have to conduct when applying for EC membership. Among the many intermediary results, national preparations for adaptation to the future administration of EC regulations and the experience of individually confronting the EC machinery figure prominently.

A unique advantage of the EEA is that once it is established, EFTA states will be able to participate to a maximum degree in the SEM while still negotiating complete admission to the EC. Whether the EEA is ratified in December of 1991 or later is less important than the great contributions its negotiations have already provided toward European integration.[10]

THE NEUTRALS AND THE EFTA–EEA–EC TRIANGLE

Small, neutral states appear to have two primary motivations for seeking admission to the EC and the SEM: economic objectives and national security policy—i.e., the absence of dangerous considerations for their neutrality. As in the case of neutral Ireland, geopolitical and psychological fears may also play important roles in Austria's efforts for full EC membership. Sweden decided under enormous economic pressure to seek admission and prepare its official application in light of the drastic alterations in European security since 1989–1990. Finland and Switzerland have remained more cautious; Iceland, Norway, and Liechtenstein show little enthusiasm for membership, still favoring the EEA.

The Pro-EC EFTA Members—Austria and Sweden

Austria applied for EC membership in July 1989. Sweden, one of the staunchest European defenders of an independent foreign policy, followed Austria's path and formally applied for EC membership in July of 1991. A Swedish EC membership, in turn, creates significant incentive for Norway and Finland to follow.

Austria

Economic and political considerations motivated Austria to seek EC membership; party politics and new interpretations of the legal basis of its permanent neutrality further encouraged it in this direction.[11] Since the end of the monarchy in 1919, Austria has had a latent fear of decoupling from western Europe; its sense of conflict between the western-liberal and eastern-conservative mentality adds a psychological dimension to the EC question. Nevertheless, Austrians widely view membership in the EC as a *sine qua non* for economic development, industrial competitiveness on the world market, and access to the SEM.[12] They have always perceived permanent neutrality as a product of superpower antagonism and the Cold War in Europe, a means for national identification, and a valid instrument in Austro-German relations. Democratization in eastern Europe and particularly the SEM project have, however, created an urgent desire to get closer to Brussels—though not necessarily at the expense of neutrality.

According to Federal Chancellor Franz Vranitzky, the achievement of full membership in the Community is a priority task of Austria's coalition government (composed of the conservative People's Party and the Social Democrats), even as it strongly supports the creation of the EEA.[13] Officially, Vienna denies possible constraints on its neutral foreign policy resulting from a European Political Union (EPU), although it is aware of differences between economic integration and the political-security aspects of EC membership.[14] Foreign Minister Alois Mock and Chancellor Vranitzky hint that their country will fully accept even certain security principles. Political union, in Vranitzky's words, would be "a positive contribution to the realization of the unity of Europe; Austria will on the basis of neutrality participate in solidarity in a future European security system within and beyond the EC."[15] Austrian participation in an EC army, however, is "out of the question."[16]

The Austrians hope that the Western European Union (WEU) will carry the brunt of European defense cooperation for the foreseeable future outside the European Political Cooperation (EPC) and that EC membership may therefore be possible with neutrality.[17] Much of Austria's internal debate and ambivalence about the future of neutrality is likely to reduce the general credibility of neutrality as an argument in negotiations with the EC. In the Gulf war, for example, Austria permitted Britain, Germany, and the United States to transport military materiel over its territory and through its airspace.

Formal negotiations on Austria's admission to the EC should begin in 1993. Sweden's application may prolong that time lag because the Commission may try to deal with both applicants at once. Traditionally, the principal opposition to Austrian EC membership has come from the Soviet Union; this has diminished, and with shifts in Soviet politics, further change remains possible. Recently, stronger opposition has come from some of the major EC members—specifically, France and the Netherlands. Paris fears that Austrian admission will create problems with an all-EC security policy; it also frowns upon an extension of a united German *Wirtschaftsraum* (economic area) toward the southeast. Austria's strongest supporters are Italy and Germany (Rome for the purpose of balancing German political and economic weight), and the rest of the Commission seems increasingly positive about Vienna's admission.[18] This was expressed in the *Avis* of the Commission in July 1991 which foresees the beginning of negotiations after 1992. Major tensions, however, may still arise over the transit issue between Austria and the EC: Vienna would like to reduce the steady stream of trucks through Tirol, but Brussels shows less flexibility.

Austria maintains intensive economic relations (including strong links between the Austrian schilling and the deutsche mark) with Germany, as its dominant neighbor.[19] In terms of geopolitics, the unification of Germany and the dissolution of the blocs have transformed Austria from a buffer state to a rim state, hovering at the southeast of a now huge Germany and becoming once again the entrance to the Balkans. From a national perspective, this suggests an important bilateral aspect in Austrian foreign affairs. The fall of the Iron Curtain has altered Austrian neutrality from abstention in bipolarity to active stabilization in a potentially unstable region. Neutrality seems on the verge of becoming a spiritual Austro-German border. An Austria outside the EC may further intensify its relationship with Germany, which could result in German hegemonic influence from the Baltic to Sicily.

As an EC member, however, Austria may augment its role in eastern Europe and the Balkans, since its industries meet the technological and managerial standards of the Community. In this regard, Austria's eastern neighbors see Vienna's EC efforts as a snowplow on their own icy road to Brussels. Austria may thus become the EC-Balkan revolving door that offers both regional expertise to Brussels and EC know-how to its neighbors.[20] In a sense, this would contribute to stability by limiting the overwhelming economic and industrial German influence in east central Europe.

Sweden

Sweden's economy has always been heavily dependent on international trade and unhindered communications, conditions that have enhanced the relevance of the country's neutral policy. Given its prominent role in Scandinavia (including implications for the political parameters of Finland) and the Nordic Council, major Swedish political decisions carry great regional weight.

In 1990, Sweden confronted its greatest economic challenges and problems in 50 years. Projections for 1991 are even worse: 10 percent inflation and 3–4 percent unemployment, the highest level since the early 1930s. In October 1990, the Swedish government announced a Kr 15 billion budget reduction, cutting health benefits and reducing the state bureaucracy. Many describe this as the end of Swedish socialism.[21]

Its problems notwithstanding, the country is still the greatest industrial, economic, and military power in the Nordic region. Many factors speak for Stockholm's strong bargaining position in any dealings with Brussels—among them the powerful Wallenberg Group of industries (Ericsson, Saab-Scania, SAS, ASEA); and Sweden's strong presence in overseas markets, especially the international mergers exemplified by Volvo-Renault, Saab-GM, and ASEA-BBC. Indeed, in many respects, Sweden's significant economic-industrial involvement in the EC market (particularly with Germany, Britain, the Benelux countries and France) already provides it with quasi-EC membership status.

Swedish Socialists have traditionally maintained a negative stance toward EC membership, but they now opt for full EC membership even in view of the disadvantages for neutrality and for certain domestic sectors (for example, farming). Sweden's economic crisis has persuaded even the Socialists to place a higher value on international competitiveness and a healthy economy than on neutrality. (International détente, of course, has reduced the potential jeopardy of relinquishing neutrality.)

In December 1990, the Swedish parliament approved the government's proposal for EC membership, which was welcomed by Jacques Delors.[22] On July 1, 1991, then Prime Minister Carlsson submitted the application for EC membership in Brussels.

Nonetheless, Sweden continues the EEA negotiations and hopes for a breakthrough. This would enable Stockholm to expedite its preparation for full EC membership.[23] Basically all political forces, including the country's two main employer organizations and Carl Bildt's Christian Democratic party, have come to support EC membership. Additional backing has come from the Conservatives , the Moderates and the Liberals. They all feel that the eventual EFTA-EC agreement will be too limited and believe that German unification and the end of the Cold War diminish the role of Swedish neutrality.

Economic considerations are certainly in the forefront in Sweden's application to the EC, but a substantial problem may arise if military cooperation also becomes a requirement for membership; Sweden would then either have to adjust its application or change its neutrality status. The official line is to say "no" to any limitation of Swedish neutrality, for the USSR (or the Russian Republic) is still a major power and NATO still exists.[24] Sweden will, however, only decide on eventual alterations in its neutral status once the EPU and related defense policy issues have found their solution in Brussels.

The Other Neutral EFTA Members—Switzerland, Liechtenstein, Finland

Switzerland
Switzerland has had little to worry about regarding changes in relations with other states—except with Liechtenstein, which in 1990 began to break away from "Swiss diplomatic hegemony." The issue of ever closer economic integration into the EC, however, may dramatically affect Switzerland's diplomacy, as well as its federal structure, business, agriculture, direct democracy, labor policy, immigration policy, and even neutrality. Until Jacques Delors suggested joint negotiations between the EFTA and the EC, Switzerland had preferred to maximize bilateral agree-

ments; it has fully exploited articles 224 and 238 of the Rome treaties, the development clauses of its association agreement. Its most notable success so far has been the 1988 agreement on reciprocal establishment rights for Swiss and EC insurance companies, ending several years of negotiations.[25]

Although Swiss officials consistently understate the case, they fear that the implementation of EC rules on Swiss territory will subvert federalism (and contradict the *Kantoenli-Geist*—or desire for maximum independence of the Cantons), as well as undermine direct democracy. Even the implementation of less-stringent EEA decisions is difficult for them to accept since it would entail adherence to EC rules over which the Swiss have little or no control. The EEA may become a costly agreement that offers them little input but significant consequences. The prevailing sense is that the Swiss will accept extensive restrictions only if their government is going to have a say in the future organization of Europe.[26]

Thus arises the issue of what degree of independence and autonomy Switzerland is prepared to give up. Now 700 years old, Switzerland has been among the most independent, autonomous, and, indeed, self-centered of European states. The Swiss, especially the Germanic Swiss, have never been submissive to any foreign power; they have fought for their autonomy and are accustomed to seeing their opinions imposed on other groups, not the reverse. (Consider the relatively one-sided internal relationship with the Italo- and Swiss Romands.[27]) The SEM and EEA developments demand Swiss rethinking that could result in a crisis of self-confidence.

Despite Switzerland's active conduct of the EEA negotiations in the second half of 1990 as chair of the EFTA, Swiss voices are increasingly labeling the EEA as only the "second-best solution" after their primary preference for full EC membership. Some Swiss remain opposed to any membership; others claim that the country should "develop further pragmatic cooperation with the EC as a sovereign state."[28] Only 20 percent of the Swiss population still remains undecided about EC membership; the rest are divided into supporters and opponents. Support is especially great in French- and Italian-speaking areas; the labor unions are also strongly in favor of membership because Swiss social rights (such as health and safety) and rights of labor unions lag behind European standards. For precisely these reasons, some Swiss businessmen oppose EC—and even EEA—membership.

Swiss Foreign Minister René Felber has called his country's fear of the EC "basically a fear of Switzerland's weakness."[29] Felber argues that the Swiss have no choice but to join the EEA. In reality, much of Swiss business enjoys quasi-EC member status, especially banks, insurance companies, and large corporations because of their branches on EC territory. Small and medium-size firms that are faced with rising inflation, economic problems, and the ever greater likelihood of the SEM are more and more inclined to lean toward EC membership, even in Swiss-German areas. Bern has already developed a degree of cooperation with the EC over the last decades, establishing more than 130 bilateral agreements with the Community. EEA adhesion will not resolve the sticking point of being unable to participate in the EC's decision making,[30] but membership would have an important impact on agriculture, interstate trade and labor, regional voting, potential financial support for the Mediterranean, and—as in the case of Austria—transit through Swiss territory. If the EEA negotiations remain completely unsatisfactory, the country may seek full EC membership instead.

The decision to apply for EC membership would, under Swiss law, require a referendum, and government circles are concerned that in the event of a negative popular vote, another decade will pass before the application can be raised again, as the case of Norway proves. For the time being, the EEA option seems the most generally appealing.

Interestingly, the Gulf crisis revealed a Swiss flexibility not seen before. By agreeing to participate in the western embargo against Iraq following its August 1990 annexation of Kuwait, Switzerland deviated for the first time from its traditional policy of strict neutrality. Switzerland also approved several hundred million francs worth of aid to help Gulf countries affected by the conflict. Yet the denial of Swiss airspace to U.S. military trans-

ports from Germany indicates that the way from EC membership to EPC participation would still be very rocky.

Liechtenstein

The principality of Liechtenstein, a micro state-cum-constitu-
tional monarchy,[31] views participation in the EEA as a way to
experience integration without getting too quickly absorbed in
the EC framework.[32] Liechtenstein's small size and population
dictate many of its demands, such as those regarding free personal traffic, regulation of foreign investments (for example,
foreign acquisition of land and capital in the principality), free
economic contact, and, especially for its youth, access to EC
education and training and the possibility of practicing their
profession in EC countries. EEA membership also would put
Vaduz on a relatively equal footing with other EC members;
allow it to learn about the EC's institutions and decision process
close-up, allow it to participate in direct negotiations with the
Community; and facilitate its eventual application to the EC.[33]

Switzerland's prospect for full EC membership would demand a reassessment of Liechtenstein's pro-EEA position. Indeed, the question then would be whether the fact that
Liechtenstein's major neighbors—Austria, Germany, Italy, and
Switzerland—are EC members would not require at least institutional adherence to the EC. However, with a foreign policy staff
of only fifteen, Liechtenstein's ability to participate in the EC is
limited. But this does not seem relevant before 1996.

Finland

Finland's market economy, with one of the highest growth rates
in the western world in the 1980s, has been an unsung success
story. The mainstay of the Finnish economy in the last decade
was the dependable and protected eastern trade. The country's
trade relationship with the Soviet Union was like a colonial one:
Finland supplied the capital and skills; the Soviet Union supplied
the raw materials and cheap, unskilled labor. Finland paid the
Soviet Union for oil and other raw materials with high-technol-
ogy products (such as icebreakers or textile machines), other

goods, and the construction of hotels and infrastructure in the Soviet republics; sometimes Finland even sold the Soviets outmoded coats or shoes in return. Even the defense industry offered adaptation kits to raise Soviet arms to western standards. In 1985, 22 percent of all Finnish exports went to the Soviet Union.[34] Today that figure is 12 percent and rapidly declining. *Glasnost* takes its toll, and future developments within the Soviet Union will have further major economic impacts on Finland.

Now that the old organizational arrangements no longer exist, many contacts have been swept away. Finnish delegations in Moscow discover that they may have been dealing with the wrong organizations, many of which cannot pay their bills. Soviet companies owe an estimated Mk 7 billion to their Finnish customers for orders received.[35] Consequently, as Soviet economic ties are being dissolved, the EC is gaining a widespread popular appeal.[36]

Official Finland, the coalition government of Conservatives and the Center Party under Prime Minister Esko Aho, suggested recently a national debate over EC membership in order to make a formal decision—presumably pro-EC—by 1992. It is widely perceived that participation in the EEA as an "optional alternative" will not be enough.[37] The Central Federation of Finnish Trade Unions and the Agricultural Producers Association favor full adhesion to the EEA, but with agricultural policy remaining outside it. They hope for special treatment of agriculture by the EC but still understand industry's need for integration. The regional aspect, though, is of primary importance. "Finland wants to, above all, develop its policy together with the Nordic countries."[38] Fewer and fewer circles see neutrality as an obstacle to ever more firmly established European integration. Even the Finno-Soviet Treaty of Friendship, Cooperation, and Mutual Assistance has become questioned by Prime Minister Aho.

Finland obtained full member status in the EFTA only in 1986; until then, it had a special, politically limited position in the EFTA that was acceptable to Finno-Soviet relations. Finnish anxieties about a negative response from an as yet unpredictable Soviet Union, or one of the major Soviet republics, have demanded caution in tampering with neutrality, although the out-

:ome of the events of August 1991 has lent support to pro-EC forces.

Many Finns believe that "Finland runs the risk of isolation. We will have to join the EC. It is really just a question of time."[39] A possible joint Swedish-Finnish-Norwegian EC application, as the Swedish foreign minister proposed in the summer of 1990, has :aused official anger in Helsinki, but the reason was more the :ondescending tone than the contents of the proposal. For now, Finns await the results of the EEA negotiations and the inter-governmental conference (IGC) on political union. An adapted version of neutrality, "taking into account the way the world has changed," for instance—merely refusing to join an optional EC security community, especially in the form of greater EPC/WEU relevance—could allow Finland continued neutrality status and EC membership.[40]

Another push for integration is Finland's already strong involvement in the development of a Baltic subregion, especially the Vibor area of Soviet Karelia and Estonia, the "East Germany of Finland." The discussed creation of a free economic zone in the old Hanseatic way between Sweden, Denmark, Finland and the Baltics and Karelia (part of the Russian Republic) would be advantageous for Helsinki.[41] The Baltics, Karelia, and St. Peters-burg could act as an ice-free gateway to the West for the remain-ing Soviet republics.

The attraction of EC membership may be even greater if Norway also joins. Helsinki's way to Brussels would significantly shape the overall policy situation around the Baltic Sea, and would increase the economic development in the area around St. Petersburg and the new Baltic states.

The Nonneutral EFTA Members—Norway, Iceland

Norway
Norway went through important economic changes in 1990 that led to a rethinking of its EC option. "EFTA, a Dead End" was the title of an *Aftenposten* article indicating the increasing urgency of Norway's moving into the EC through the EEA. The Labor minority government under Gro Harlem Brundtland, however,

does not intend to make a quick application for EC membership although it has announced its readiness to join EEA negotiations fully, and to repeal concessionary laws that safeguard the country's industries, fisheries, and financial institutions from foreign ownership. The Labor and Conservative parties have a mutual interest in a rapprochement with the EC through the EEA instead of via full EC membership. The previous three-party center-right coalition wanted too many exemptions for Norway, even in the EEA,[42] and no Norwegian government wants to repeat the EC dilemma of the 1970s when the country was granted admission but could not accept when a popular referendum voted it down.[43] In the latest county Council elections, the Center Party and the Left Socialists—both virulently opposed to EC membership—once again made significant gains.

Recent polls even show Norwegians split on the EEA issue. Some argue that abandoning the EEA in favor of renegotiating the free trade agreement with the EC would be Norway's best strategy. Prime Minister Brundtland has asserted that Norway would be forced to take a stand on EC membership if the Storting rejected the EEA, which means a vote in Parliament may be necessary before Norway joins the EEA.[44]

Norwegians apparently have a deep-seated suspicion that too close a relationship with Brussels will lead to "selling out" and excessive foreign influence. In a related development, the European Commission has proposed that Norway and Sweden start to apply EC law on air transport even before the EEA is established.[45] This and a number of other factors would shed a favorable light on an application by Oslo in Brussels: the needs of its offshore oil industry; the appeal of bringing NATO member Norway into the WEU; and possibly an all-EC Scandinavia.

Iceland

In the case of Iceland, an adamantly Nordic country, the notion of Nordic independence once more conflicts with the benefits of greater European integration and the importance of NATO membership. But with a per capita income of $22,000 in 1988, and the fish-processing industry accounting for 71 percent of exports, the preservation of Iceland's 200-mile fishing limit and the included rights are vital.

On the other hand, Iceland does not have an army and depends completely on the United States for its defense. In a way, it can play this political orientation and important geostrategic position against EPC membership. If the EC objects to duty-free access for processed Icelandic fish—negotiated now with the EC—the country may have to look elsewhere for markets. (The fishery problems are also a principal item in the EEA negotiations—particularly with Spain.) Despite this implicit threat, Iceland tries to obtain its objectives through bilateral negotiations with the EC while remaining an EFTA member. Iceland will be under enormous pressure to seek EC membership if Sweden and the other Nordic Council members apply; nevertheless, Reykjavik will likely be among the very last to take that step, for reasons pertinent to the country's small population and remote location.

POTENTIAL FOR EASTERN EUROPE: THE EEA, EFTA, AND EC

Nearly all former members of the Council for Mutual Economic Assistance (CMEA)—especially Poland, Czechoslovakia, and Hungary—would like to become members of the EC. Despite predictions that some of them may be close to this goal by the year 2000, both the EFTA and the EC currently oppose their inclusion. Instead, the EFTA and the EC are independently beginning a series of negotiations on free trade arrangements (for industrial goods, agricultural products, and other items) with Poland, Hungary, and Czechoslovakia. The Soviet Union has also contacted the EFTA seeking more intensified cooperation. Talks with the Yugoslav federal government have been suspended for the moment, and there are potential problems between Czechs and Slovaks looming ahead.

Eventually, these talks may result in an association agreement, although there are still strenuous questions to be resolved, as the recent French demands for restricting beef imports showed. An additional set of negotiations may take place with the new Baltic states and eventually lead to the inclusion of the entire region in the EC. What has become clear is that the CMEA structure has disintegrated, owing to German unification and to the switch from barter to currency trading between the Soviet Union and its eastern neighbors,[46] and that all of the former CMEA nations will need greater access to western markets.

Negotiations with the EFTA could lead to an assimilation of certain eastern European states—Hungary, Czechoslovakia, Poland, and the Baltic states—into the EEA, and the EEA might require their acceptance into the EFTA as a condition of membership. But that development could also lead to a complete free trade agreement between these states and the EFTA, which could eventually transform into full EFTA membership. Thus, central and northern Europe would enter the EEA and become part of a 25-nation zone in which goods, services, and capital would circulate freely. Like the EFTA states, the central Europeans could treat EEA membership as a step toward EC membership, although that prospect will not figure explicitly in the association agreements.

In aiming at free trade, the EC accepts that at least in the first phase, it will have to open its market more than Poland, Czechoslovakia, and Hungary. Even so, access to the EC markets is unlikely to occur fast enough to compensate for the loss of CMEA trade. Brussels has given all eastern European countries the same Generalized System of Preferences tariff favors that Third World exporters get, but it has not offered any increase in steel import quotas, and it remains as protectionist on agricultural imports from eastern Europe as from any other region of the world. The dilemma is that if the EC does not do more to help eastern Europeans stay at home and earn a living, it might face massive westward migration.[47]

Presently, the EFTA would for several reasons not be very receptive to eastern European demands for full membership: the EEA negotiations with the EC would face additional problems, and expectations would have to decline concerning the potential of the EEA. Even to begin bilateral negotiations with eastern applicants would divert EFTA resources away from the negotiations with the EC and could undermine the already limited cohesion within the EFTA itself. Eastern European membership would entail a host of problems with visa and immigration regulations, and almost certain opposition from countries such as Switzerland and the Nordic states. In addition, since the average EFTA country is richer, more industrialized, has a much higher gross domestic product per capita, and maintains a higher standard of living—including environmental protection—than all but the most developed EC members, eastern European applicants would lag far behind. They would find it difficult to adapt and assimilate, despite geographic proximity and ethnic and historical links. A different route toward integration may therefore be necessary for the former CMEA countries.

Former CMEA members will, at least for a while, continue to trade heavily with each other for three fundamental reasons: First, the CMEA's traditional trade flow was largely with the USSR, and intra-CMEA trade has accounted for more than 60 percent of all its trade. Second, technological standards have been based on CMEA and Soviet norms. Third, the transition to convertible currencies will dramatically influence the cost of imports and exports in eastern European countries.

Hungarian Foreign Minister Geza Jeszensky has suggested that a series of bilateral trade agreements could replace the CMEA. Hungary, for example, wants to maintain its economic relations with former communist countries; it especially cannot afford to lose the Soviet market.[48] Additionally, certain CMEA states are intensifying efforts to recover the pre–World War II trade share with the West. Czechoslovakia, for instance, has indicated its intention to recapture some former economic exchanges, especially with Germany, with which it conducted roughly one-third of its trade.[49] In a way, of course, this also would underscore the key role Germany is likely to play in eastern European recovery.

A new, subregional financial mechanism or organization for the former CMEA countries could emerge in the framework of the London-based European Bank for Reconstruction and Development (EBRD), which the twelve EC countries, fourteen other developed countries (including Japan and the United States), and eight eastern European states established. The

EBRD will originally concentrate its lending on the private sector and on productive investment. With the combined involvement of the United States, the EC, and Japan, the EBRD could offer a better solution than a program modeled on the Marshall Plan. So far support programs exist with Poland and the Baltic states.

The question of how to attain neutral status for former Warsaw Treaty Organization (WTO) states is difficult. Neutrality has historically been an instrument to enhance national security, permit continued diplomacy and foreign trade, and offer stability and peace to potentially unstable areas. There are very few examples of former alliance members transforming their doctrine to a classical neutral status; no socialist country so far has made this transition (Yugoslavia became a leader in the nonaligned movement without having been a member in the WTO).[50] But the most serious concern is that traditional neutrality may be unproductive and improbable for the eastern European countries because of a lack of adequate resources, lack of domestic stability, and a lack of national consensus. Indeed, neutrality seems increasingly remote as the striving for continued westernization and modernization in these countries amounts to the precondition for successful and persistent democratization. Any diminished intercourse between them and the West, even in the benign case of neutrality, would undermine the original idea of breaking away from the WTO and CMEA.

A more realistic option for the young eastern European democracies and the new Baltic states is to change their Third World, anticolonialist, nonaligned orientation to a militarily independent, nonaggressive, Europe-oriented stance. The newly nonaligned states would then form a strategic triangle with WEU/NATO countries and the Soviet Union, leading to a transformation of the former rim states to buffer countries. It is already clear that they will try to participate to the widest possible extent in a policy shaped according to western needs, either within or close to NATO (if NATO accepts them) or the WEU. They will enter into regional agreements based upon bilateral treaties (such as the one between Prague and Warsaw on nonaggression, cooperation in training, and defense industries),[51] or through some "lightened form" of neutrality—in effect a "Euro-

)eanized nonalignment." Any such "Euro-nonalignment" could
)e sanctified under the auspices of the CSCE in agreement with
VATO, the EPC, the WEU, and the Soviet Union. Thus, a new
luropean security system might serve as supranational guaran-
,or for the validity of their neutral status, and for the compliance
)f all powers. But as Hungary's demand to join NATO demon-
,trated, even that might lose its appeal soon. And as a NATO
nember, Hungary would bring substantial problems for a per-
nanently neutral Austria.[52]

A FUTURE EUROPEAN ARCHITECTURE
AND THE ROLE OF NEUTRALITY

The framework of current developments in Europe may be reminiscent of the 1860s when German and Italian unification was
made possible by the relative absence of English and Russian
attention to the continent following the Crimean War. In today's
terms, one can argue that European unification may now be possible because of the relative decline of the hegemonic power and
interest of the USSR and the United States—including a major
thaw between them. Some would argue that any absence of hegemonic determination, any reduction of power, creates inherent
instability and a power vacuum. In the case of eastern Europe, this
phenomenon is particularly apparent in economic terms where the
gap between the fledgling market economies and the skills, technology, and economic standards of their western neighbors is enormous. It needs to be filled for many reasons, not the least of which is
to satisfy the expectations of their own peoples.

Western influence may come to replace postwar Soviet predominance in central eastern Europe. The question remains
whether that would be real western Europeanization or merely
"Germanization." The situation may in a sense become a quarrel
among three Bs: Brussels, Bonn, and Berlin. The eventual move
of the epicenter of German power to Berlin will create substantial economic and financial convulsion in the adjacent areas.
Another option is for certain states—namely, England, France,
and Italy—to stand apart from Brussels and seek optimal deals
also on a bilateral level.

But in the long run, Germany's capabilities and financial support may create an enormous attraction (indeed, a centripetal dynamic gravitation around it) for all the small neutrals and central European states in need of its expertise, managerial skills, and technology.

How long such an eastward drive of western—or German—values and capital may continue without creating tensions between the USSR or its major republics and Germany is not clear. This concern is even more relevant as multipolarity in a regionalized Europe replaces the bipolarity of postwar continental Europe. The principal question therefore relates only secondarily to U.S.-Soviet relations and weight, and primarily to the role Britain, France, Germany, and the USSR play on the continent.

This is another aspect reminiscent of the 1850s: Britain may eventually favor stronger Atlantic links to avoid too much damage to its sovereignty in greater European integration, especially in the EPU. Hence, England may once again become the balancer in European affairs between French, German, and Soviet interests—with a strengthened transatlantic spine. On the one hand, this may influence the Franco-German relationship; on the other, given the historically friendly "neighborhood" between the USSR and Germany, these countries may engage in increasingly intensified interactions once the domestic Soviet situation has been clarified.

Finally, the personality dimension—or political culture of European politics as personified by its leaders—may determine much of Europe's architecture. The once dominant Kohl-Mitterrand-Thatcher troika no longer exists, and Margaret Thatcher's departure gives rise to questions about England's future position. The successors of François Mitterrand and Helmut Kohl, possibly in combination with Boris Yeltsin as a successor to Mikhail Gorbachev, may provide Europe with yet another framework still to be defined.

Economic and Political Cooperation

In the economic area, the EC will move toward some form of a Single European Market—not fully completed by the end of

1992 perhaps, but sufficiently strong to maintain its dynamic and attract all nonmembers. The EC will certainly also find a working agreement on the emplacement of the Economic and Monetary Union.

In terms of political cooperation, the focus will be on assimilation of WEU principles into the EPC structure. The EPC is an upshot of the intensification of economic integration and its extension into the political and even security dimension; the WEU was the beginning of European defense cooperation in the 1950s; it reemerges as the link between NATO and EC politics. As was apparent in the results of the November 1990 CSCE Paris summit, a slight rivalry has grown between proponents of a CSCE-based European security architecture and those who would like the European Commission and an EC security community to take over such responsibilities. The latter solution would, of course, reinvoke intense discussion about intra-European security cooperation as expressed in article 30 of the SEM agreement, but only if membership were obligatory.[53] Meeting in February 1991, WEU ministers agreed in principle that the WEU should become a bridge between NATO and EPC/EC members. The French are in favor of the WEU's serving as a defense arm of the EC; the British and Dutch prefer a more balanced role for the WEU. The Franco-German position suggests the WEU should be a channel of cooperation between the Community and NATO and move to Brussels. Both France and Germany emphasize the case for giving WEU observer status to Denmark, Greece, and Ireland. Eventually, all twelve EC states should become members of the WEU. Even Turkey and Norway, both non-EC and non-WEU members, attended WEU meetings during the Gulf crisis.[54] The EC Commission suggests that the EC write the WEU mutual defense clause into the Community treaties and take the rest of the WEU over once the latter's treaty expires in 1998. A collective European security system thus formed should be acceptable to the EFTA members and EC-neutral Ireland.

It seems likely that the 38-member CSCE will remain the major all-European, American, and Soviet negotiation forum, but it will not replace the WEU or NATO. Rather, the broad consensus is that the CSCE should not evolve into yet another engrossment of hundreds of government officials—like a suggested Organization for Security and Cooperation in Europe.[55] Furthermore, the CSCE's taking over NATO's mission would jeopardize the sustained U.S. interest in remaining in Europe since it is improbable that the United States would ever accept the majority voting of the CSCE. All of this is true despite the CSCE's commitment, spelled out in its Paris Charter of 1990, to enhance its program of consultation between foreign ministers and senior officials, and to form several new divisions: a permanent secretariat in Prague with some ten to fifteen officials; a conflict prevention center in Vienna; an election observation office in Warsaw; and a parliamentary wing—the Assembly of Europe—enabling members of Parliament from all member-states to meet at regular intervals.

Given the continuation of the current U.S.–Soviet thaw—apart from the Gulf crisis, and barring any disastrous internal events in Yugoslavia and the Soviet Union—much of Europe might act according to nonaggression principles eminent in classical neutrality. Such a European collective security system would enhance stability and peace.

Under that hypothesis, the less-powerful countries, such as the Benelux and the neutrals, will have diminishing roles in the formation of European politics in general and CSCE politics in particular. Yet in light of the reduced power of sovereignty and the strengthening of European institutions, particularly the EC and its Parliament, the distribution of influence among European countries might be more even.

Perhaps only the Soviet Union—or, if it dissolves, several of its republics—might remain outside of an EC-dominated security landscape in the long run. For them and other eastern European and Balkan countries—perhaps also former republics of Yugoslavia and Czechoslovakia—the CSCE will retain its value as a negotiating forum for specific pan-European "security interests." In the future, eastern European countries may be put in the position of the former group of the neutrals and the nonaligned (N&N). The possible adhesion of certain neutrals to the EC will weaken the N&N group; meanwhile, the non-EC memers of eastern Europe may over time take their place in a new, special role within the CSCE.

For many reasons, Japan is likely to participate extensively in the CSCE. Principally, the CSCE should undertake to attract Japanese affiliation, for without Tokyo's sustained industrial interest, no long-term modernization of central eastern Europe and the Soviet Union seems possible. Much of the technical, industrial, and managerial know-how for modern, consumer-oriented industries lies in Japanese hands; and much of the world's disposable capital is in Japanese banks and industries. For Europe to ask only for that, however, without seeking broader and serious Japanese involvement in its current evolution, would be unwise.

Regionalization

A major aspect of the current international system, especially in Europe, is the trend to regionalization. This leads to the emergence of subregions, divided according to ethnic, historical, geographic, and climatic similarities. For parts of central and northern Europe, these tendencies represent a continuation of a development interrupted since 1919. Natural affinities link specific areas with each other and form functioning communities that derive from strong interaction in transports, environment, social infrastructure, and certain ties in energy and industrial cooperation.[56]

These emerging subregions will challenge the traditional notion of national sovereignty, much as technological development and interaction shape the international system and geopolitics. Expanding infrastructural cooperation, communications, regional trade, environmental needs, and demands for economies of scale—all of these will require a sizable amount of area and population. Also, the existence of smaller areas with strong ethnic, religious, and cultural similarities will demand intensified cross-border cooperation and, eventually, intensified subregionalization. (More globally oriented fields—such as telecommunications, electronic data, and aerospace industries—are largely excluded.)

Some analysts argue that the best approach to the long-range goal of European unification may be via the intermediary stage of regional cooperation. One of the most attractive aspects of regionalization is that problems within a smaller area may be amenable to solutions that directly benefit the people concerned.[57] On the other hand, the transfer of problems between minorities, nationalities, and environmental issues may create a dramatic form of negative interaction. Ensuing migration and reliance on cheap "imported" labor may cause tensions; incompetence or unwillingness to change plans for major construction projects may lead to fundamental political frictions.

Subregionalization is evident in the Danubian area, the Nordic area around the Baltic Sea (including the Baltic states, Finland, and Sweden) and in the larger Mediterranean area. The Pentagonale—launched in 1989 by Italy, and consisting of Austria, Hungary, Czechoslovakia, Italy, and Yugoslavia—is perhaps the most prominent example.[58] It aims to carry out transnational projects in transportation, telecommunications, education, and cultural affairs, along with support for small and medium-size enterprises. Projects agreed upon include four highways, six railroad links between the member-countries, an environmental data bank, and cooperation between news agencies and universities. Also, the group has submitted to the CSCE a joint resolution on the treatment of minorities, which indicates the possibility of cooperative action in high politics.[59]

Neutrality

The concept and policy of classical permanent neutrality face a profound fourfold attack: On the global level, the end of bipolarity and ideological antagonism raises the question of the continued rationale, as well as feasibility, of neutrality. On the continental level, neutrality may impede the movement toward greater economic and political integration and the formation of a "confederative Europe." On the local level, the emergence of subregions touches upon national sovereignty, the very essence of statehood and neutrality, and *de facto* stretches traditional state interests to different geographic dimensions. On the per-

onal level, the sheer intensity of transborder interaction, the
nhancement of imminent and intense interstate and inter-
humanitarian contacts, and a profoundly changed threat per-
eption—regarding dangerous impacts from economic, social,
nd environmental challenges, and migration—reduce public
readiness to remain neutral. The future of neutrality in Europe
s inextricably linked to the geopolitical consequences of shifts in
he balance of power, to the continued relevance of national
overeignty and the tension between that and economic and
political integration, and to the overall degree of political-strate-
gic stability.

In the long run, the intense and increasing legalization of
he European environment, the various charters, and, indeed, a
European security system may absorb the status of permanent
neutrality based on international law. With the enhanced role of
legal regulations, their stabilizing influence will obviate the need
for a legally agreed upon right to abstain from conflicts. Such a
framework may erase the requirement for national precautions
against foreign intervention, aggression, and so forth, given the
availability of a European supranational institution and force. It
seems also that in a tightly regulated environment shaped by
ntense economic and industrial integration, states will not have
much room to declare and maintain an independent, autonomous, and nonparticipant status like permanent neutrality.

Debates about how much "neutrality" a neutral will relin-
quish in exchange for membership in the SEM, however, most
certainly will enhance neither the credibility of neutrality nor the
bargaining power of the applicant in Brussels. The declaration
that neutrality is passé in modern European integration eases
the task for the negotiators of the EC; but, the expectation that
neutrality can be continued as always, even if the European
nations establish a common currency, is hypothetical. It may be
possible to retain neutrality as a member of the EC at least in the
near future, as long as other states continue to put national
sovereignty over Brussels' striving for total integration. It thus
may take some time until a fully working European security
community exists; even then, membership ought not be obligatory for all EC members, for what about dissenting opinions

between the great European powers? Also, persistent neutral
may, for instance, keep an observer status or remain otherwise
uncommitted—though an EC with several neutrals may be dif
ferent from one without. The EC may therefore, just for politica
purposes, demand that new members renounce their neutra
status as an expression of their acceptance of the Community'
supranationality.

The possibility of a "Welfare Wall" between the former
eastern and western Europe emphasizes the increasing role of
the economic and social dimensions of security. It may transform
the role of some neutrals, especially Austria and Finland, from
military buffers to interaction states, with a great obligation to
smooth the adaptation and modernization process of their east
ern and southeastern neighbors. Thus, the socioeconomic task
of nonmilitary support, distribution, and stabilization—such as
the acceptance of immigrants—may supplement or even replace
solely military dimensions of neutrality. That "Europeanization
of neutrality" may result in a "Euro-nonalignment," which may
come to mean nonparticipation in military alliances and offensive operations, and declining the right to conduct war, while
accepting greater nonmilitary, technological, economic and political integration and regionalization.

On the other hand, if all European CSCE states—neutrals
and nonneutrals, eastern countries and EC members alike—
agreed to conduct an orchestrated security policy in Europe, that
is, to become relatively equal members of a functioning European collective security system, the status of permanent neutrality would lose much of its relevance. Such a development
would represent the "neutralization of Europe." It would also
strip the neutrals of their prominent role in the CSCE process,
particularly once they have joined the EC and are obliged to act
within the EPC—a fact that may even touch upon their national
identity. The degree of credibility under these circumstances—
as well as integration-cum-regionalization—remains to be seen.
For the time being, however, a classical neutral status may present the only option available for newly formed states in Europe,
especially those which may result from centrifugal events in
Yugoslavia, the USSR, or Czechoslovakia.

Nevertheless, in light of the current flux and transitory
phase in European politics, continuing the status of an adapted
neutrality appears wise for the traditional neutrals until a new,
all-European, collective security system has emerged and proven
its feasibility; in case of heightened instability, neutrality remains
welcome fall-back option.

Therefore, the question will be how Europe's neutrals satisfy the fundamental objectives of any foreign and security policy—to create peace, security, and national prosperity—and
what choices the rest of Europe will allow. That actual cost-
benefit analysis of autonomy versus stronger integration will
depend on national decisions. For most of the neutral EFTA
members, the immediate goal is the conclusion of the EEA treaty
with the EC. For Austria and Sweden, the search for greater
cooperation with the EC brought a direct application for EC
membership. If their path is successful other EFTA members—
Switzerland, Finland, and even Norway—may follow. Neutrality,
then, may be a minor issue in light of greater economic advantages. The question remains whether such a greater and wider
Europe is, indeed, what the European Community desires.

*The author would like to thank the following individuals for helpful comments: Ambas-
sador Bjoern Barth and Professors Robert Gilpin, A. James McAdams, Richard Ullman,
William Wohlforth, and John Zysman. This chapter was written under the auspices of the
Center of International Studies, Princeton University.*

NOTES

1. For further analysis of the future of neutrality, see Wolfgang
Danspeckgruber, *Classical Neutrality in Europe and Technological Challenges*
(Ph.D. dissertation, Graduate Institute of International Studies, Geneva,
and Princeton University, 1991), especially ch. 6; and Philip Windsor,
"Options for Neutral States," in Richard E. Bissell and Curt Gasteyger,
eds., *The Missing Link—West European Neutrals and Regional Security* (Dur-
ham, N.C., and London: Duke University Press, 1990). As an overview, see
Efriam Karsh, *Neutrality and Small States* (London and New York:
Routledge, 1988); and Joseph Kruzel and Michael Haltzel, eds., *Between the
Blocs—Problems and Prospects for Europe's Neutral and Nonaligned States* (Cambridge: Woodrow Wilson International Center for Scholars and Cambridge University Press, 1989).
2. "The Paris Conference: The Thrill of Europe's Rebirth," *Economist*, November 24, 1990, p. 50.

3. The term "neutrality" rooted in the Latin words *ne* and *utra* means "to be neither on one nor on the other side." Today's use is derived from the medieval word *neutralitas* meaning "to stand aside" or "not to participate in armed conflict or a military alliance." "Neutrality" hence had originally only a military-strategic meaning.

   Obligations for neutrals are fourfold: (1) The obligation of abstention prohibits a neutral from lending any active or passive support to warring parties. (2) The obligation of prevention requires a neutral to actively deny belligerents any use of its territory. In this obligation, the triangular relationship between a neutral and two opposing parties plays an important role. (3) According to the obligation of impartiality, a neutral has to treat belligerents on equal terms in all (nonmilitary) issues that are not subject to the obligation of abstention. The application of this clause is prohibited as a means for circumventing the obligation of abstention. (4) The obligation of tolerance requires a neutral to accept certain actions by belligerents (e.g. control of neutral ships on the high seas). Obligations for permanent neutrals comprise all actions and omissions that would challenge the capability to remain neutral in the case of conflict, such as the prohibition to join military alliances or start a war.

4. Trade flows between the EFTA and the EC are rather evenly spread. EFTA countries, on average, take almost as large a share from the EC as do EC members themselves (56 percent, as against 60 percent). Similarly, EFTA members export almost as large a share to the EC as do EC countries themselves (57 percent and 64 percent, respectively). See Per Magnus Wijkman, *Patterns of Production and Trade in Western Europe: Looking Forward after Thirty Years,* EFTA Occasional Paper, no. 32 (Geneva, 1990), p. 5.

5. See Paul Luif, *Neutrale in die EG? Die westeuropaeische Integration und die neutralen Staaten* [Neutral in the EC? West European Integration and the Neutral States] (Vienna: Wilhelm Braumueller Universitaets-Verlagsbuchhandlung, 1988).

6. Lecture by Georg Reisch, EFTA secretary-general, "Der Europeaische Wirtschaftsraum—Grundsaetzliche Fragen des EG/EFTA Verhaeltnisses" [The EEA—Principal Aspects of the EC/EFTA Relationship], Representation of the EC to the Federal Republic of Germany, Bonn, November 28, 1990.

7. Conversations with Georg Reisch, EFTA secretary-general, and Berndt Olov Johansson, EFTA deputy secretary-general, December 4, 1990, and February 22, 1991.

8. David Buchan and Robert Taylor, "EFTA Comes Closer to Setting Out Its European Stall," *Financial Times,* November 21, 1990, p. 3.

9. "EC Accepts Demands for Consensus in EEA," *Hufvudstadsbladet,* December 13, 1990, p. 5 (transcribed in Foreign Broadcast Information Service [FBIS], FBIS-WEU-90-243, p. 2).

10. Austrian Economics Minister Wolfgang Schuessel was chairman of the EFTA for the first six months of 1991. He had hoped for a ratification of the EEA treaty on June 24–25, 1991, in Salzburg, but a later ratification, perhaps Fall 1991 seems more likely. The treaty should come into force with the SEM treaty on January 1, 1993.

1. For the legal reinterpretation of neutrality, see Michael Schweitzer and Waldemar Hummer, *Oesterreich und die EWG. Neutralitaetsrechtliche Beurteilung der Moeglichkeit der Dynamisierung des Verhaeltnisses zur EWG* (Vienna, 1987); Wolfgang Danspeckgruber, "Implications of Current European Economic and Political Developments—A Comparison between Ireland, Austria, Sweden, and Switzerland," in Stefan Huber and Fried Esterbauer, eds., *The European Neutrals, the Council of Europe and the European Communities* (Vienna: CIFE Austria Publications, 1988), p. 75; Thomas Nowotny, "Neutralitaetspolitik—Mythos und Realitaet" [Politics of Neutrality—Myth and Reality], *Europa Archiv*, vol. 13 (1989), pp. 423–432, and Heinrich Schneider, *Austria and the EC*, Royal Institute of International Affairs Discussion Paper, no. 24 (London, 1989). It is relevant to mention that Austria emphasized its status as a permanent neutral state in its July 1989 letter of application to the EC.

2. More than 60 percent of the Austrian population favor EC membership, but more than 70 percent insist on continued neutrality. An analysis by the Vienna-based WiFo suggests that six years after an EC membership took effect, real gross domestic product would be 3.6 percent higher and prices would be 5.2 percent lower than would be the case if conditions remained status quo. With an EEA membership, the figures would be 3.2 percent and 4.9 percent, respectively. See Helmut Langsner and Helmut Weixler, "Waiting Room for EC?" *Profil*, November 26, 1990, pp. 34–35 (transcribed in FBIS-WEU-91-008, p. 1).

3. Statement to the Parliament by Federal Chancellor Vranitzky, Vienna, December 18, 1990 (transcribed in FBIS-WEU-90-244, December 19, 1990, p. 6). See also Per Nordrum, "Austria Sets Deadline for EEA," *Aftenposten*, November 28, 1990, p. 8 (transcribed in FBIS-WEU-90-233, p. 7). Nordrum reports on a press conference at which Austrian Foreign Minister Alois Mock stated, "Regardless of the EEA results, there can be no alternative to becoming an EC member as soon as possible."

4. Also, it seems much less difficult to solve the numeric and quantitative aspects of economic integration and standardization the SEM requires than to deal with the qualitative and perceptual—or even emotional—dimensions that the EPC creates. For instance, with German unification, the German-speaking population in the EC totals more than 70 million. If Austria were to join the EC, German-speaking people in the EC would number close to 80 million, and that bloc would substantially outnumber any other cultural and language group in the Community. Certain reservations from the francophone or Benelux countries have to be understood in this light. Also, the effects of political discussions about the past of Austrian President Kurt Waldheim have to be accounted for.

5. Statement by Federal Chancellor Vranitzky, December 18, 1990 (transcribed in FBIS-WEU-90-244, p. 6).

6. Austria also is not a WEU member, and whether or not EC membership would become inseparably linked with WEU membership is not yet clear. The possibility of observer status in the WEU remains and would please the neutrals as well as Denmark and Greece. See Christian Kotanko, "Participation in EC Army Out of the Question," *Kurier*, February 16, 1991, (transcribed in FBIS-WEU-91-035, p. 4).

17. How possible this will be in case of a common European defense polic
including a joint European army remains doubtful. See also Thoma
Klestil, "Austria: No Longer Caught in the Middle," *European Affairs*
Aug./Sept. 1991, Vol. 5, No. 4, p. 27.
18. "The Making of a New Constellation," *Economist*, August 4, 1990
pp. 41–42.
19. For instance, the German car industry is the major partner—and inves
tor—among Austrian subcontractors. The manifold ethnic and cultura
links between Austrians and especially the southern, Catholic German
may encourage this relationship. Meanwhile, German unification ha
caused a loss of the Austrian export economy and industry: East Germa
companies have been one of the most important trading partners an
suppliers of raw materials. Presumably, German firms will continue thi
relationship, though competition has been enhanced. In any case th
result will be even further Austro-German economic interdependence
The ultimate answer lies in Austrian EC membership.
20. The Austrian ambassador to the United States, Friedrich Hoess, likes t
refer to central and eastern Europe as an area forming an ellipse, with
Berlin and Vienna as the two focal points. Within that area lies the "golder
triangle" Berlin-Prague-Vienna. This author would like to argue that
geographic-economic analysis sees the line Hamburg-Berlin-Prague
Vienna-Budapest (ideally prolonged to Sofia) creating an axis aroun
which a prosperous, industrious, and stable central Europe may take
shape.
21. Robert Taylor, "Banks Say Sweden Is Heading for Recession," *Financia
Times*, November 30, 1990, p. 2.
22. The rumor goes that Swedish socialism and industrial capabilities make it
more welcome applicant to the EC Commission than Austria. Also, Sweder
does not mention its policy of neutrality in its application for EC member
ship.
23. Conversation with Staffan Carlsson of the Swedish embassy, Washington
D.C., November 16, 1990. See also Robert Taylor, "Sweden Consider
Timing of Application," *Financial Times*, February 9/10, 1991, p. 4.
24. "EC Chorus More Harmonious," *Dagens Nyheter*, June 28, 1990, p. 2
(transcribed in FBIS-WEU-90-177, p. 32); and "Andersson Says No to EC
if Military Role," *Dagens Nyheter*, November 4, 1990, p. 8 (transcribed in
FBIS-WEU-90-237, p. 36).
25. Christian Kind, "Die Schweiz in einem Veraenderten Europa" [Switzer-
land in a Changed Europe], *Europeaische Rundschau*, 1990.
26. Interview with Benedict von Tscharner, Swiss ambassador to the EC
David Buchan, "Gloom in EFTA after talks with EC Fail," *Financial Times*,
November 27, 1990, p. 2; and Mathias Mueller von Blumencron, "Europe's Old-Age Home," *Wirtschaftswoche*, November 11, 1990, p. 46 (transcribed in FBIS-WEU-90-240, p. 28).
27. Conversation with René Schwouk, Graduate Institute of International
Studies, Geneva, June 30, 1990.
28. Interview with Swiss President Alfred Koller, by Austrian Broadcasting
Corporation, Vienna, November 25, 1990 (transcribed in FBIS-
WEU-90-232, p. 22).

9. "Taking a Stand: René Felber for European Integration," *Journal de Genève*, November 26, 1990, p. 6 (transcribed in FBIS-WEU-91-005, p. 26).

0. Dusan Sidjanski, "La Suisse et son état a l'épreuve de l'Europe," [Switzerland and Its Situation at the Challenge of Europe], *Agence économique & financière, 77 journée des banquiers.*

1. Conversation with H.S.H. Prince Nikolaus von Liechtenstein, Liechtenstein's ambassador to Switzerland and chief negotiator to the EEA talks, November 26, 1990. Material gratefully received also from Ambassador Andrea Willi, Auswaertiges Amt, Vaduz.

2. Until 1990, the Swiss-Liechtenstein Customs Agreement of 1921 gave Switzerland the exclusive right of representing Liechtenstein in such negotiations. Liechtenstein could negotiate contracts, though primarily for agreements to which Switzerland is also party. On November 26, 1990, Switzerland and Liechtenstein signed a bilateral agreement permitting Liechtenstein to negotiate on its own and to accede unilaterally to international trade and customs agreements in the economic field (e.g. memberships in the EFTA, EEA, and EC).

33. See *Bericht über das Fürstentum Liechtenstein und die Europeaische Integration* [Report about the Principality of Liechtenstein and European Integration] (Vaduz: Government of the Principality of Liechtenstein, 1989 and 1990).

34. Five-year trade agreements fixed deliveries in advance, and competition from other countries hardly exists. Until 1988, Finnish industrialists at least knew with whom they were doing business in the Soviet Union, and the deals were honored to the letter.

35. Robert Taylor, "A View from the Edge," *Financial Times Survey: Finland,* November 15, 1990, p. 15.

36. Opinion poll findings show that in 1987, some 40 percent of Finns favored EC membership; in 1990, the figure was 60 percent, and only 13 percent opposed the idea. In an *Economist* straw poll of 24 Finnish middle managers, every respondent expected Finland to apply for EC membership by 1999. See "Finland: Out in the Cold," *Economist,* September 8, 1990, p. 43.

37. Taylor, "A View from the Edge," p. 15.

38. "Prime Minister Holkeri: Neutrality Is No Obstacle to Close Cooperation," *Helsingin Sanomat,* September 28, 1990, p. 9 (transcribed in FBIS-WEU-90-223, p. 41).

39. Paavo Lipponen, head of the Finnish Institute for International Affairs, quoted in Taylor, "A View from the Edge," p. 15.

40. "Finland: Out in the Cold," p. 43, and Statement by Prime Minister Aho, quoted in "Finland—Europe Aho," *Economist,* September 14, 1991, p. 56.

41. Personal communication with Mr. Heskinen of the Finnish embassy, Washington, D.C.

42. Buchan and Taylor, "EFTA Comes Closer to Setting Out Its European Stall," p. 3.

43. In 1972, the EC accepted Norway's application, but a national referendum rejected the Norwegian government's desire to follow the UK, Denmark and Ireland: some 54 percent of voters, representing a coalition of farmers, fisherman, leftists, and religious groups, opposed the government's policy, and the government had to step down.

44. Karen Fossli, "Brundtland Warning on EC Membership in Europe De bate," *Financial Times*, February 9/10, 1991, p. 4.
45. Under the proposal, the two countries would apply all EC rules in tha sector, including those introducing competition into the market and thos regarding state aid. A joint body would be set up in which the EC and th two EFTA countries would take decisions unanimously. The motivatio comes from Denmark, frustrated by the need to abide by EC rules while jointly owns its airline, SAS, with EFTA members Norway and Sweden. Se Lucy Kellaway, "EC-EFTA Talks Make Progress," *Financial Times*, Decem ber 13, 1990, p. 2.
46. In 1988, the German Democratic Republic, Czechoslovakia, and Bulgari depended on the CMEA for 72–81 percent of exports and for 64–7 percent of imports; the USSR conducted more than 50 percent of its trad with the CMEA. However, Hungary and Poland have maintained mor balanced trade: for Hungary, 42 percent of trade is with western countrie and 44 percent with the CMEA; for Poland, 44 percent is with the West an only 41 percent with CMEA states. The USSR has been particularly impor tant for Bulgaria, which has received some 42 percent of its imports from there. See Susan Sidjanski, "Le dialogue des deux Europes et le role de l Communaute Européene," [The Dialogue of the Two Europes and th Role of the EC], *Travaux et communications du Department de science politique* Université de Genève, June 1990, p. 10.
47. David Buchan, "World Leader of the 'Salvation Army,' " *Financial Times* February 4, 1991, p. 13.
48. Quoted in Josef Kirchengast, "Yugoslavia: Hungary Favors Consulta tions," *Der Standard*, February 28, 1991 (transcribed in FBIS-WEU-91-040 p. 6).
49. Leslie Colitt, "Czechoslovakia Poised to Go Back to Its Old Partner," *Finan cial Times*, November 27, 1991, p. 6.
50. For detailed differentiation between neutrality, nonalignment, equidis tance, and so forth, see Wolfgang Danspeckgruber, "Neutrality and Its Role in an Emerging Europe," in Wolfgang Danspeckgruber, ed., *Emerging Dimensions of European Security*, Liechtenstein Series, vol. 1 (Boulder, Colo. Westview Press, 1991).
51. An agreement on nonagression, mutual aid in the case of conflict, and good neighborhood, in the making between Romania and the USSR indicates the possibility of the re-creation of a series of bilateral neutrality and nonagression treaties concluded between the USSR and several east ern European states in the 1920s.
52. Conversation with Heinz Gaertner, Princeton University, March 1991.
53. Article 30 defines cooperation in foreign policy and in the economic and political dimensions of security without mentioning clear military compo nents.
54. Ian Davidson, "Differences Narrow over Role for WEU," *Financial Times*, February 22, 1991, p. 4. In this context, Martin Bangemann, vice president of the EC Commission, has argued that "the European neutrals would be obliged to participate in a future EC-Army, and a related action, partic ularly if it is suggested by the UN." He contends that "the EPC will lead to a

common defense policy and finally also to a European army." (Quoted in *Wiener Zeitung*, February 15, 1991.)

55. Stefan Lehne, "Vom Prozess zur Institution—Zur aktuellen Debatte ueber die Weiterentwicklung des KSZE-Prozesses [From Process to Institution—the Current Debate over the Development of the CSCE Process] *Europa Archiv*, vol. 16 (1990), p. 505. For a discussion of the institutionalization of European security, see Richard H. Ullman, *Securing Europe* (Princeton: Princeton University Press, 1991)

56. Conversation with Peter Gellman, Princeton University, December 1990.

57. See the interesting article on the Pentagonale by Hans-Peter Neuhold, "Renaissance of Regionalism," *Der Standard*, January 4, 1991, p. 4 (transcribed in FBIS-WEU-91-038, p. 2).

58. The Pentagonale is likely to soon become the Hexagonale when Poland becomes its sixth member. See "Regional Clubs: Hello Neighbors," *Economist*, July 13, 1991, p. 55.

59. See Neuhold. Other regional clubs include Alpen–Adria, Donaulaender, and Visegrad (between Czechoslovakia, Poland, and Hungary).

5

DEMOCRATIZATION AND CHANGE IN EASTERN EUROPE

F. Stephen Larrabee

The collapse of communism in eastern Europe in 1989 shattered the bipolar security order that characterized East-West politics for the previous 40 years. At the same time, it has made a rethinking of the foundations of European security necessary. If Europe is again to be "whole and free," any new security order will have to include eastern Europe. Otherwise, the new security structure is unlikely to be stable or durable.

Eastern Europe's integration into a new security order will pose major policy challenges for the West—especially for the European Community (EC). Prior to the revolutions in eastern Europe in 1989, the Community seemed well on its way to attaining a new stage of integration through the creation of a single internal market by 1992—in itself a major challenge. The anticommunist revolutions, however, have complicated this task and presented the Community with an additional dilemma: how to support democratization and reform in eastern Europe without disrupting the considerable progress toward integration that western Europe has already achieved.

Compounding the dilemma is the long list of prospective applicants whose claim to Community membership is as great as, if not greater than, that of many of the countries of eastern Europe. Austria, Sweden, Turkey, Malta, and Cyprus have already applied for membership; Norway, and Finland may soon do so. Furthermore, the EC has recently completed complex negotiations with the European Free Trade Association (EFTA) over the creation of an expanded European Economic Area (EEA), which will have an important impact on the Community's future.

Finally, the EC must deal with the consequences of German

unification. This will absorb a considerable portion of its time, energy, and resources. It is critical that the Community "get unification right." Together with France, the Federal Republic is the linchpin of the Community, and its weight within the EC is bound to increase as a result of unification. Germany's concern with unification therefore must not lead to a slackening of Bonn's commitment to the larger process of European economic and political integration.

UNCERTAIN TRANSITIONS

This is a rather full plate under any circumstances. And the significant transition problems of the eastern European countries, which are likely to prove more formidable than many observers in either eastern or western Europe initially anticipated, further complicate the challenges facing the EC. In the immediate aftermath of the 1989 revolutions, a certain euphoria about eastern Europe's "return to Europe" reigned. The joy over the collapse of communism tended to overshadow the immense problems confronting the eastern European countries as they attempt to create market economies and democratic political systems. Today the mood in both parts of Europe is subdued, and governments and multilateral institutions have a greater recognition of the problems and obstacles they must overcome before they can complete these transitions.[1]

In recent years analysts have devoted increasing attention to the problem of transitions from authoritarian to democratic rule.[2] In the case of eastern Europe many draw comparisons to the transitions in southern Europe, especially Spain. While some parallels exist, the differences are also important. The countries of eastern Europe face a number of problems that are likely to make their transitions more difficult and less certain.

First, the postcommunist states in eastern Europe will have to undergo a dual transition—that is, they will have to change their political and economic systems at the same time. In southern Europe and Latin America, by contrast, where authoritarian regimes have undergone transitions to democracy, market economies existed before those transitions began. These countries could thus devote their primary attention to political reform. Spain, for instance, underwent a significant period of economic liberalization and social change for two decades before Franco's death and the transition to democratic rule. By the mid-1970s, when Franco died, Spanish society was largely middle-class, capitalist, consumer-oriented and moderate. This transformation greatly facilitated the successful transition.[3]

Second, the countries in eastern Europe lack the advantage of strong democratic experience and traditions. All, except Czechoslovakia, were under some form of authoritarian rule in the interwar period. They must begin to build democratic institutions virtually from scratch. In this sense the transition problems in eastern Europe have more in common with the transition in Portugal than those in Spain and Greece, where democratic institutions had stronger roots.

Third, the enormous economic problems that the regimes in eastern Europe face impose an important constraint on the ability of the new elites to successfully complete the democratic transitions recently initiated. The transformation to market economies is likely to intensify these economic problems—at least in the short run. As market economies are introduced, unemployment will increase, prices will rise, and living standards in most eastern European countries will fall. A significant rise in social discontent will likely result, hindering the transition in many countries.

The high—and in many cases unrealistic—popular expectations in eastern Europe will make management of this discontent all the more difficult. A general expectation persists that with the collapse of communism life will radically improve almost overnight. After years of deprivation, eastern Europeans are tired of promises of a bright future that is just around the corner. They want prosperity *now*, not in ten years. Given the magnitude of the economic problems facing all of eastern Europe, however, the new democratically elected elites will have a hard time satisfying these demands. Indeed, in many cases, things will get worse before they get better.

For fragile democratic governments with little experience in dealing with the vagaries of the market, the gap between rising popular expectations and declining living standards will pose a severe test. Authoritarian governments can institute wage and price restraints or cut back on consumer demand relatively easily through repression (Nicolae Ceausescu's Romania provides a good example); democratically elected regimes must be sensitive to the demands of the population. Therein lies the central dilemma: while satisfying these demands for immediate gratification may reduce the prospects for long-term recovery, failure to do so may undercut support for the regimes and lead to growing social unrest and political instability that could inhibit the transition process.

Prime Minister Tadeusz Mazowiecki's poor showing in the first round of the November 1990 presidential elections in Poland highlights the dangers in this regard. He came in third behind Lech Walesa and Stanislaw Tyminski, an unknown Polish-Canadian entrepreneur, who promised a variety of "get rich quick" schemes and accused Mazowiecki of selling out Polish national assets to "foreign interests." Mazowiecki's low support suggests that the wrenching changes caused by the rapid transformation to a market economy have created a strong degree of dissatisfaction among certain parts of the Polish electorate.

Fourth, ethnic nationalism presents a threat to long-term stability in the region. Historically, nationalism has been a strong—and often "dark"—force in eastern Europe.[4] Communist rule did not eliminate this nationalism; it simply suppressed it. In contrast to western Europe, where genuine multilateral institutions—such as the EC and the North Atlantic Treaty Organization (NATO)—emerged in the postwar period, in eastern Europe no multilateral integrative mechanisms were developed which could dilute and moderate this nationalism. The Council for Mutual Economic Assistance (CMEA) and the Warsaw Pact were essentially instruments to assure Soviet control and hegemony. The collapse of communism threatens to create a political vacuum and lead to a resurgence of nationalism in some parts of eastern Europe.[5]

The existence of minorities with a strong sense of ethnic identity dispersed throughout the region compounds this problem. Democratization has provided new opportunities for these minorities to express their grievances and led to a resurgence of ethnic nationalism and tensions throughout the area. The anti-Turkish demonstrations in Bulgaria in January 1990 and the clashes between the Hungarian minority and Romanian population in Tirgu-Mures, Transylvania in March 1990 are a stark reminder that nationalism is far from dead in these countries. And as the rise of Slovak nationalism and separatism in Czechoslovakia underscores, this danger is not limited to the Balkans.

Fifth, is the problem of political institutionalization. Many of the forces that have been in the forefront of the revolutions in eastern Europe have been large, heterogeneous umbrella movements—Solidarity in Poland, the Civic Forum in Czechoslovakia, and the United Democratic Forces (UDF) in Bulgaria. As democratization and reform have proceeded, growing internal divisions have plagued these movements. (The division within Solidarity between Lech Walesa and Mazowiecki provides one example of this trend, the splits in the Civic Forum and Public Against Violence in Czechoslovakia another.) This internal bickering and fragmentation has inhibited the ability of these groups to rapidly implement important reforms. The key question therefore is whether these large movements can transform themselves into strong political parties able to carry out coherent reform programs or whether they will remain essentially philosophical discussion groups incapable of effective political action.

Together, these factors underscore the uncertain nature of the transitions in eastern Europe. Like transitions elsewhere, this process in eastern Europe is likely to be uneven and may be marked by considerable instability and, in some cases, even violence. Indeed, the danger exists, as Timothy Garton Ash has noted, that the recent efforts at democratization in eastern Europe could lead to the emergence of an intermediate zone of "weak states, national prejudice, inequality, poverty and Schlamassel," particularly in the Balkans.[6]

A final obstacle is posed by the danger of public apathy and disillusionment (*desencanto*). This disillusionment emerged in Spain in the late 1970s, inhibiting the transition process, and there are signs that it may be emerging in parts of eastern Europe as well. One sign has been the low voter turnout in some countries, especially Hungary.[7] This low voter turn out suggests a strong degree of apathy and disillusionment with the performance of the leading parties that could have long-term negative consequences for the development of a stable democracy in Hungary.

The strong support for Stanislaw Tyminski in the presidential elections in Poland in 1990 is another reflection of this danger. As noted earlier, Tyminski's success reflected dissatisfaction with Mazowiecki's economic policies. But it also represented strong disillusionment with the ability of the main established political forces, above all the communist party and Solidarity. Many Poles voted for Tyminski because he was an "outsider" and not associated with the political establishment. The calls for a restoration of the monarchy in Romania and Bulgaria should be seen in a similar light. They are less a reflection of strong support for the monarchy *per se* as a manifestation of disillusionment with the ability of the established political parties to manage the political and economic problems in both countries. This has led many Romanians and Bulgarians to look for salvation in outside forces and a mythical past.

A certain degree of disenchantment is, of course, to be expected, given the dramatic and wrenching changes underway throughout Eastern Europe. But if this disillusionment becomes too deep-seated or widespread, it could prove to undermine support for reform and provide fertile soil for the rise of extremist, anti-democratic forces that could inhibit the growth of stable democratic regimes in the region.

THE REEMERGENCE OF EAST CENTRAL EUROPE

Eastern Europe was always an artificial concept. It reflected the political division of Europe after World War II rather than the historical and cultural traditions of the countries that fell under Soviet occupation. Many of the countries in eastern Europe had more in common with countries in western Europe than they had with each other. Thus, two trends are likely to characterize the political evolution in eastern Europe in the coming decade: a reemergence of traditional political ties, institutions, and cultural patterns; and a growing differentiation within the region. Indeed, as reform proceeds, talking of "eastern Europe" as a specific geographic region is likely to make increasingly less sense.

Broadly speaking, since 1989, eastern Europe has undergone a two-tier, or two-speed evolution, which is likely to become even more pronounced in the 1990s. The first tier is composed of the countries of east central Europe—Hungary, Czechoslovakia, and Poland. These three have moved rapidly to develop market economies and multiparty political systems. The second tier is composed of the countries of the Balkans—Bulgaria, Romania, and Yugoslavia. In these countries, the transition process is far less advanced and the prospects for integration into Europe are more problematic.

Economically, Poland has embarked upon the most far-reaching reform. The government of former Prime Minister Mazowiecki, who assumed power in August 1989, adopted a program of "shock therapy"—that is, transition to a market economy in the shortest possible time. The program, introduced in January 1990, called for reduction of the budget deficit through sharp cuts in subsidies and investment spending; devaluation of the exchange rate; tight control on money and credit through a sharp increase in real interest rates; strict limits on wage growth; liberalization of prices; and an elimination of import controls to allow for a free import of most goods.

The reform has produced a number of positive results. Shortages have virtually disappeared, and shops are well stocked. Inflation, though still high, has dropped markedly. The reform, however, has plunged the Polish economy into a severe recession. Industrial output has declined significantly. At the same time, prices have risen sharply, putting many goods out of reach of the average Pole. Unemployment, which hardly existed before the introduction of the reforms, has also significantly increased: it reached nearly 1 million at the end of 1990 and could be as high as 2 million by the end of 1991.

The political risks associated with the continuation of the reform are highlighted by the poor performance of former Prime Minister Mazowiecki in the first round of the presidential elections in November 1990. The strong showing by Stanislaw Tyminski, who placed second, ahead of Mazowiecki, underscores this danger. Significantly, Tyminski did best among the most alienated parts of the electorate: unskilled and uneducated workers and farmers, especially from small towns and villages, and inhabitants of the poorer regions with a high rate of unemployment.

During the presidential campaign, Walesa sharply criticized Mazowiecki's economic program for being too cautious and called for an "acceleration" of the pace of reform. Walesa's economic policy in office, however, has differed little from that of his predecessor. Walesa retained Leszek Balcerowicz, the main architect of the Mazowiecki reform program, as finance minister, and to the dismay of many of his closest supporters has continued to follow the main outlines of Balcerowicz's policies.

The results, however, have been disappointing. During Walesa's first six months in office, there was no visible improvement in the economy.[8] Inflation and unemployment grew, while productivity declined. As a result, opposition to the reforms, both among Walesa's supporters and within the society at large, has grown. Opposition has been particularly strong among the workers—previously the backbone of Solidarity's support. The expansion of this discontent among the workers could pose a serious threat to Walesa's ability to carry out the tough measures associated with the reform over the long run.

Walesa's task has also been complicated by the fact that the Sejm (the lower house of the Parliament) remains dominated by adherents of the old regime. The elections in June 1989, which paved the way for Mazowiecki's assumption of power, were not truly democratic because Solidarity could compete for only 35 percent of the seats in the Sejm. The other 65 percent remained in the hands of the communists. New elections are currently scheduled to be held in October 1991. These elections should significantly change the composition of the Parliament and give

Walesa a majority truly committed to democratization and economic reform.

Regardless of the outcome of the elections, however, the Presidency is likely to be the main focus of decision making. Since Walesa's election, decision-making power has increasingly flowed from the Prime Minister's office to the Presidency.[9] At the same time, Walesa has maintained a certain independence from many of the groups that initially supported his candidacy, playing one group off against the other and refusing to become the captive of any one of them. Walesa's impetuous style and his emphasis on "personal diplomacy," however, could pose long-term problems for the consolidation of Polish democracy. If a stable democratic order is to emerge in Poland over the long run, it is essential that a strong party system, including a strong opposition, be developed.

How well Walesa meets these challenges will have a significant impact not only on Poland's political future, but on the whole process of reform and democratization in eastern Europe—and the USSR. Poland is a test case of whether shock therapy can succeed or not. If the Polish experiment is successful, it is likely to have an important demonstration effect, emboldening others in the region to take more radical steps. But if it fails or leads to some form of benevolent authoritarianism, it could set back the course of reform and democratization throughout the region.

Czechoslovakia's reform borrows heavily from the Polish experience, but is based on a more gradual approach. It includes removing price controls on 85 percent of goods sold; closing inefficient enterprises; restricting the growth of money; making the crown convertible; and reprivatizing some 70,000 small businesses, including shops and restaurants.[10] Czechoslovakia has certain advantages, however, that may help it weather the transition period. Along with the former GDR, it has the strongest industrial base and one of the most skilled work forces in eastern Europe. It also has a lower per capita debt than Poland and Hungary. Thus, it has somewhat more room to maneuver in modernizing industry or establishing a safety net for those disadvantaged by the reform.

However, whereas Poland took the most difficult decisions in 1990, Prague will have to implement its reforms at a time when Comecon is moving from a system of barter trade based on transferable rubles to one based on hard currency and when the capacity of the Soviet Union to pay for eastern European goods has diminished. This will significantly complicate the reform effort and make its implementation more difficult.

Economic conditions, moreover, have significantly deteriorated since the launching of the reform on January 1, 1991. Industrial production dropped six percent in the first two months of 1991 compared to the same period in 1990, while unemployment rose to two percent of the working force. The agricultural sector, once one of the most productive in Europe, is on the verge of collapse. As a result, criticism of the reform and calls for socially less divisive economic policies have increased. This mounting social unrest could undermine public support for reform and force its postponement and later resumption under significantly worse economic conditions.

Two other factors will likewise affect Czechoslovakia's reform. The first is the ability of the Civic Forum, an umbrella group composed of sixteen disparate opposition groups, and its counterpart in Slovakia, Public against Violence (PAV), to transform themselves into effective political parties. In the elections of June 1990, the Forum won 49 percent of the vote in the Czech National Assembly, while Public Against Violence came in first in Slovakia, winning 29 percent of the vote in the National Assembly. However, both organizations have had a hard time translating their initial electoral success into coherent legislative programs and transforming themselves into strong, effective parties.

In addition, both groups have shown signs of increasing fragmentation. In February 1991 the Civic Forum split into two factions, a conservative faction entitled the Civic Democratic Party, headed by Finance Minister Vaclav Klaus, and a liberal group, the Civic Movement, headed by Foreign Minister Jiri Dienstbier and Deputy Prime Minister Pavel Rychetsky. A similar process of fragmentation occurred within Public Against Violence in Slovakia. In March 1991, PAV split into two groups, a federalist faction led by Fedor Gal, and a more nationalist faction led by former Slovak Prime Minister Vladimir Meciar, entitled Public Against Violence—For a Democratic Slovakia (VPN-ZDS).

To some extent the fragmentation of both the Civic Forum and Public Against Violence can be seen as a natural process and a sign of the "maturing" of the Czechoslovak political system. The original umbrella groups were composed of diverse political views that were bound to collide at some point. However, the splits have severely weakened both groups in the Federal Assembly. There is a danger, moreover, that the fragmentation will become so great that it will be difficult to reach consensus on important issues within the Federal Assembly and the separate National Councils.

The growth of Slovak separatism also could seriously inhibit the reform process in Czechoslovakia. Slovakia, which Hungary ruled before 1918, has long bridled under what it regards as Czech economic and political domination. The centralization of major decision-making power in Prague, the capital of the Czech lands, during communist rule reinforced the resentment. Democratization has led to an increase in Slovak national feeling and separatism. Slovak sensitivities manifested themselves in the spring of 1990 in the "hyphen war" over the name of the new republic.[11] Since then, Slovak separatism and nationalist feelings have visibly increased. While the majority of Slovaks still prefer to remain part of a federative state with the Czechs, the percentage of those who prefer a separation has grown since 1990.

Slovak separatism also threatens the fate of the reform. Slovakia is the seat of Czechoslovakia's arms industry, much of which is uncompetitive. The reform has forced the closure of many of the largest arms factories and led to a significant rise in unemployment in Slovakia. (The unemployment rate in Slovakia is nearly twice as high as the unemployment rate in the Czech lands.) This has led many Slovak politicians, such as former Prime Minister Meciar, to oppose the rapid pace of the reform program and fueled separatist sentiments among Slovaks, who see the reform as an effort by Prague to weaken Slovakia economically.[12]

This growth of separatist sentiment poses a real threat not only to the reform, but to the preservation of the current federation. Constitutional amendments agreed upon at the end of 1989 involve a significant decentralization of power.[13] However, the real test will come in the negotiations over the new federal, Czech, and Slovak constitutions during 1991–1992. It thus remains to be seen how well the new federative system will work and whether the redistribution of power embodied in the new constitutions will assuage Slovak concerns over the long run.

Hungary has also moved rapidly to develop a market economy and a pluralistic democratic system. Because it had embarked upon a program of economic and limited political reform before the dramatic developments of 1989, it has had a firmer basis than other eastern European countries on which to construct a democratic system and market economy.

Prime Minister Joszef Antall, whose right-of-center Hungarian Democratic Forum stresses traditional "Hungarian" values, has rejected the idea of shock therapy, opting instead for a more gradual transition. The government's first concrete steps toward a national renewal program was the September 1990 passage of a law calling for the privatization of some 10,000 shops, restaurants, and small businesses.[14] The law applies only to the domestic sector, however, and does not affect foreign trade, which will undergo privatization in a second phase.

The Antall government, however, has failed to develop a clear-cut set of economic priorities. In addition, disagreements within the government about the pace of reform, and differences between the government and its coalition partners (especially the Independent Small-Holders Party) over the privatization of agricultural land, have impeded the implementation of legislation needed to get the reform off the ground.[15] Hungary's economic fortunes were also hurt by a severe drought in the summer of 1990, the rise in oil prices due to the Gulf war and the sudden collapse of Soviet trade. As a result, in 1990 Hungary experienced a 5 percent drop in GDP and a 10 percent drop in industrial output.[16]

The economic dislocation caused by the introduction of reforms has fueled rising popular discontent. A massive strike by taxi and transport workers at the end of October 1990 dramatized the depth of this dissatisfaction. The strike, called in reaction to the government's announcement of a 66 percent increase in the price of gasoline, paralyzed the country for three days, forcing the government to cut the projected increase by half. Public opinion polls, moreover, indicate that of all the eastern Europeans, Hungarians have the most pessimistic outlook about the economic prospects of their country.[17] This growing public discontent and pessimism could pose a major threat to the ruling party's support—and to reform itself.

Another sign of this discontent has been the low voter turn-out in elections noted earlier. In the local elections in September only 30 percent of the electorate turned out to vote. The majority, moreover, voted for independent candidates rather than the representatives of the national parties. The local elections in the spring of 1990 also showed a low voter turn-out. This suggests a high level of apathy and disappointment with the results of the transition to democracy so far.

Finally, differences with Romania and Czechoslovakia over the treatment of the Hungarian minority could aggravate domestic problems.[18] The Hungarian Democratic Forum has a strong populist wing, and the Antall government has made the treatment of the Hungarian minority a major issue. A repetition of incidents such as the clashes in Tirgu-Mures or an effort by Slovak nationalists to curtail the rights of the Hungarian minority in Slovakia could provoke nationalist and irredentist pressures in Hungary. A weak Hungarian government beset by growing economic problems might be tempted to play the nationalist card in order to bolster its popular support and divert attention from the deterioration of the economy.

THE BALKANS

The transition in southeastern Europe (Romania, Bulgaria, and Yugoslavia) is likely to be more difficult than that in the states of east central Europe, and is likely to involve considerable political instability. The countries of southeastern Europe have different patterns of political development, and their ties to western Europe are far more tenuous. With the exceptions of Slovenia and Croatia (which were part of the Hapsburg Empire prior to World War I), southeastern Europe was under Ottoman rule for long periods of time. For the Balkan states, the transition is therefore not as much a case of returning to Europe as of joining Europe.

The transitions in the Balkans have been less stable and far-reaching than those in east central Europe. Part of the reason is the lack of autonomous groups and the weakness of civil society in these countries.[19] In Poland, Hungary, and, to a lesser extent, Czechoslovakia, autonomous groups and organized political forces existed to pick up the reigns of power when the old order collapsed or was voted out of office. Such groups did not exist in Romania and Bulgaria. The opposition in those countries was weak, fragmented, and unable to fill the power vacuum that the collapse of communist rule created; hence, the former communists were able to cling to power by changing their names and by making cosmetic changes.

Romania is likely to have the most difficult transition. Ceausescu's government atomized Romanian society and brutally suppressed all manifestations of dissent. Ceausescu's power, moreover, was more personal than institutional. It rested primarily on his control of the organs of coercion, especially the secret police (Securitate), who were better paid and better equipped than the army and were loyal to Ceausescu personally. When he fell from power, the National Salvation Front (NSF)—a coalition of former communists, technocrats, and military officers—sought to fill the resulting void. The Front succeeded in doing so largely because no other organized institution was capable of providing effective authority and because it maintained strong control over the media and other mass organizations.

In the May 1990 elections, the Front won 67 percent of the vote. Several factors help explain this overwhelming victory. First, because of the personalistic nature of Ceausescu's rule, Romanians directed their enormous discontent against Ceausescu personally and his immediate entourage. In addition, the leaders of the two main opposition parties, the National Peasant Party and the National Liberal Party, were exiles who had spent much of the postwar period abroad and had little contact with contemporary Romanian realities. Finally, the NSF controlled the old administrative-bureaucratic system, particularly the media, which it openly exploited, at times resorting to intimidation and smear tactics against the opposition.

The Front's popularity has declined significantly since the elections in May 1990.[20] The opposition remains fragmented, however, and has been unable to capitalize on the decline in public support for the NSF. At the same time, the popularity of nationalist groups like Vatra Romaneasca (Romanian Cradle) and the army has grown.[21] Given the relative weakness of democratic institutions in Romania, the emergence of "civilian-military twilight"—to use Dankwart Rustow's phrase[22]—in which a weak civilian government rules with the support of the military, cannot be excluded.

Bulgaria's transition also seems likely to be bumpy. What occurred in Bulgaria in November 1989 was, in effect, a "palace coup."[23] Todor Zhivkov, who had been Communist Party secretary since 1954, was deposed by a coalition of his top lieutenants headed by Petar Mladenov, the foreign minister. The party renamed itself the Bulgarian Socialist Party (BSP) and embarked upon a course of moderate reform. The lack of a cohesive opposition, together with the party's strong support in the countryside, gave the BSP a surprisingly large margin of victory in the June 1990 elections. (The BSP received 48 percent of the vote, giving it 211 out of 400 seats in the National Assembly. The United Democratic Front (UDF) was runner-up, winning 36 percent of the vote and 144 seats.)

Since the elections, however, the domestic balance of power has steadily shifted in favor of the UDF. In July 1990, President Mladenov was forced to resign after video clips showed that he had urged the use of military force to crush the opposition months earlier; his successor was UDF leader Zhelyu Zhelev. At the end of November, after months of intermittent unrest, Prime Minister Andrei Lukanov, a member of the reformist wing of the BSP, and his government were forced to resign. A caretaker government headed by Dimitar Popov, an independent jurist, was formed to serve until the convocation of new parliamentary elections.

The UDF is likely to do considerably better in the next parliamentary elections than it did in June 1990. A UDF victory, however, would by no means ensure a smooth transition to a stable democratic order. The UDF suffers from many of the same problems that have plagued other large umbrella movements in eastern Europe such as Solidarity or the Civic Forum. It is a highly heterogeneous body, many of whose members have little in common with one another. As time elapses, the UDF is likely to have difficulty maintaining ideological discipline and could split, weakening its ability to achieve a consensus on key issues related to reform.

Finally, the UDF will inherit one of the most shattered economies in eastern Europe. The cutback in Soviet oil deliveries and the Gulf crisis hit Bulgaria particularly hard. Industrial and agricultural production fell by 15 percent and Bulgaria suffered serious food and fuel shortages during 1990. And, Sofia has had difficulty obtaining credit for imports because it stopped payments on its $11 billion foreign debt in the spring of 1990. Given this combination of economic and political constraints, Bulgarian politics seem destined to be unstable for some time to come.

The most acute problems, however, are posed by the disintegration of Yugoslavia. Tito held this patchwork quilt of nationalities together by using the coercive apparatus of the Communist party, backed by the army, to suppress all serious forms of ethnic dissent. He did not, however, resolve the national problem, he merely repressed it. His death in 1980 removed the main guarantor of Yugoslav unity and arbitrator of ethnic differences. As a result, many of the old ethnic problems resurfaced.

The revival of ethnic tensions was given greater momentum by Yugoslavia's economic decline in the 1980s, which increased the desire of the richer, more Western republics like Slovenia and Croatia for greater autonomy, and by the end of the Cold War, which removed the threat that any crisis would be exploited by the Soviet Union. With Gorbachev's ascendency and the emergence of "New Thinking," it became increasingly difficult for Yugoslav leaders, especially the army, to use the threat of outside intervention, as Tito had, to contain the force of ethnic nationalism.

The process of internal democratization has also tended to fuel ethnic nationalism. Many republican politicians have seen nationalism as a convenient instrument to further their political ambitions. However, whereas in Croatia and Slovenia nationalism has had a strongly anti-communist tinge, in Serbia and Montenegro communist leaders like Serbia's President Slobodan Milosevic have used nationalism to solidify their power. This division between a democratizing anti-communist north and a neo-communist south has tended to exacerbate nationality tensions as well as inhibit the effective functioning of Tito's complex institutional mechanism after his death. The reform program of Prime Minister Ante Markovic has had strong Western backing but Markovic's ability to implement the reform steadily eroded as power inexorably flowed to the republican leadership.

The increasing weakness of the central government has accentuated the role of the army and has thrust it more deeply into the political vortex. The leadership of the army is the main supporter of a unified Yugoslavia. It has tried to remain above politics and allow the republican leaders to work out their differences. However, its leaders have repeatedly warned that they are prepared to use force, if necessary, to prevent a break-up of the Yugoslav federation. Their intervention in Slovenia at the end of June 1991 raises troubling questions about the degree of civilian control over the military and suggests that a more independent policy by the military in the future cannot be ruled out. Indeed, if current differences cannot be resolved, the army, whose officer corps is composed primarily of Serbs, could begin to back Milosevic's calls for the creation of a "greater Serbia."

The break-up of Yugoslavia no longer represents the same threat that it did at the height of the Cold War. Today there is little threat that the Soviet Union would intervene or that the crisis would lead to a superpower confrontation. Nevertheless, the overall impact could be highly destabilizing. Given Yugoslavia's strategic position in the heart of the Balkans, civil unrest might not remain localized. It could easily spill over into neighboring countries, intensifying other disputes. If Slovenia and Croatia become independent, Macedonia is likely to follow suit ather than remain part of a rump Yugoslavia dominated by Serbia. This could revive the Macedonian question. The Kosovo problem could also be inflamed, prompting calls by the Albanians, who make up 90 percent of the province's population, for independence and eventually even unification with Albania. Other separatist and ethnic movements throughout Europe—the Baltics, the Soviet Union, Czechoslovakia, and even Ireland—could also be exacerbated. Thus the West has a strong stake in the peaceful resolution of the Yugoslav crisis.

Western policy-makers, however, have been slow to recognize the depth and significance of the Yugoslav crisis. Absorbed with larger issues—German unification, reform in the Soviet Union, and the Gulf war—they tended to ignore Yugoslavia and put it on the back burner. By the time they began to pay serious attention to it, the pot had boiled over.

Western policy, moreover, has been characterized by two somewhat contradictory goals. On the one hand, Western governments and the EC have advocated an expansion of democracy and human rights. On the other, they have supported the unity of Yugoslavia. These goals have tended to work at cross purposes with one another. The expansion of democracy has fueled nationalism and separatism in several republics, particularly Slovenia, Croatia and to a lesser extent Macedonia, undercutting support for unity. By contrast, the strongest supporters of unity are the republics which are the least democratic and which have the worst human rights records: Serbia and Montenegro. Hence Western support for unity has indirectly strengthened the position of the most anti-democratic and intransigent forces in Yugoslavia.

These contradictions in Western policy have made it difficult for Western governments and the EC to play an effective role as mediators in the crisis. Most west European governments, the EC and the United States have strongly supported the unity of Yugoslavia, fearing the wider implications of a break-up of Yugoslavia on European stability. But no country can be maintained by force. Yugoslavia was, and remains, an artificial construct, forged out of the remnants of several empires. In the post-war period, it was held together by the force of Tito's

personality and the stringencies of the Cold War. Both are now
gone. Not surprisingly, therefore, Yugoslavia has begun to come
unhinged.

The Yugoslav crisis is likely to have far-reaching consequences for the establishment of a new security order in Europe
and the role of the EC in that order. A diplomatic success as a
mediator in the crisis would enhance the EC's prestige and help
purge criticisms of its weak and hesitant role in the Gulf war. But
a failure could significantly tarnish its image and inhibit the
development of a common foreign and security policy. Hence,
how well the EC performs in the Yugoslav crisis could have a
major impact on the Community's future as well as the effectiveness of any new security order that emerges in the post–Cold
War period.

THE SECURITY DIMENSION

For the past 40 years, the Soviet Union has been the major
hegemonic power in eastern Europe and the main guarantor of
eastern Europe's security. The collapse of communism in eastern Europe, however, has radically altered the security environment in Europe. The Warsaw Pact has collapsed, leaving NATO
as the only existing alliance in Europe. Soviet troops are also
being withdrawn from eastern Europe. The Soviet troop withdrawals in Hungary and Czechoslovakia were completed in
mid-1991; those in the GDR are scheduled to be completed by
1994. Negotiations are also underway for the withdrawal of
Soviet troops from Poland. Thus by the mid 1990s, at the latest,
there will be no Soviet troops stationed in Europe.

Meanwhile, eastern European countries have begun to reduce and restructure their military forces. As part of the process,
they have revised their military doctrines, putting primary emphasis on national forces' defense of national territory rather
than dedicating their forces to participate in an integrated alliance defense against an attack from the West.[24] Polish military
forces, for instance, are now charged with defending the home-
land against aggression *from any direction*.[25] In line with this,
Poland has shifted a portion of its forces from its western border

to its eastern border. Czechoslovakia and Hungary have made similar moves.

To be sure, few eastern European leaders regard the Soviet Union as an immediate military threat. However, the disintegration of the Soviet Union and its potential spillover into eastern Europe increasingly worries them. Moreover, regardless of the outcome of the current negotiations to establish a loose confederation, Russia will remain a major military—and nuclear—power on the continent. At the moment, the Soviet Union is preoccupied with internal problems, but once this "time of troubles" is past, many eastern European leaders fear that the USSR's traditional imperial ambitions could reassert themselves.

The crackdown in the Baltics and the more conservative internal policy adopted by Gorbachev in early 1991 intensified these concerns, particularly in Poland, which shares a border with Lithuania. Whereas Soviet troops have been withdrawn from Hungary and Czechoslovakia, they are still stationed on Polish soil. A more conservative Soviet policy or a reversal of perestroika could directly affect the timing and pace of Soviet troop withdrawals from Poland.[26]

Prior to the failed coup in August 1991, moreover, there were signs that Moscow was intent upon pursuing a tougher policy toward eastern Europe in the future. A document prepared by the International Department of the CPSU Central Committee in January 1991, for instance, was highly critical of past Soviet policy toward eastern Europe and called for a more active Soviet policy toward the region.[27] The document pointed in particular to signs of growing "anti-Sovietism" in the area. At the same time, a growing debate about "who lost eastern Europe" emerged, suggesting that discontent with Gorbachev's policy was growing among conservative forces. Soviet officials, particularly within the military, expressed strong concern about the impact of the revolutions in eastern Europe on Soviet security interests.[28]

One important manifestation of the more active Soviet policy toward eastern Europe was the effort by Moscow to negotiate bilateral security agreements with its former east European allies that contain "negative security guarantees." The treaty signed with Romania in April, for instance, contained clauses which forbid either party joining an alliance directed against the other or to station foreign troops on their territory.[29] Moscow pushed the Romanian treaty as a model for other east European countries. Hungary, Poland, and Czechoslovakia, however, strongly opposed the inclusion of such clauses in any bilateral treaty with Moscow. So did the UDF, the main opposition party in Bulgaria.

These developments contributed to an evolution in eastern European attitudes toward security since early 1990. Initially, many eastern European leaders favored the dissolution of both alliances and tended to see pan-European security structures such as the CSCE as the primary instrument for assuring their security. However, most eastern European leaders now favor the maintenance of NATO and the continued presence of U.S. troops in Europe, which they see as an important element of stability and safeguard against any reversal in the Soviet Union.[30]

Some, such as Czechoslovak President Vaclav Havel, have come full circle. In early 1990 Havel called for the dissolution of both alliances and the removal of all foreign troops from Europe. Since then Havel has become the strongest proponent of close ties between NATO and the countries of eastern Europe. In his speech at NATO headquarters in March 1991, for instance, he made a strong plea that the door to NATO "not be closed forever."[31]

Havel's appeal cast into sharp relief the basic security dilemma that has emerged with the collapse of the Warsaw Pact: how to assure east Europe's security. Many analysts fear that the collapse of the Pact could lead to the emergence of a security vacuum in eastern Europe, especially if there is a serious political reversal in the Soviet Union.

In principle, this problem could be addressed in several ways. One possibility would be for NATO to open its doors to eastern Europe or provide a security guarantee to the countries in the area. Many NATO officials fear, however, that this would destroy the organization's coherence and military effectiveness. Additionally, such a move would run up against strong Soviet objections and might undercut Soviet willingness to make eeper arms reductions, especially in the nuclear area. France, which has traditionally opposed any expansion of NATO's membership or competence, also would probably object.

A second possibility would be for the eastern European countries to form a regional defense alliance among themselves. The Romanians, for instance, have proposed that Moscow's former eastern European allies form an eastern European Union analogous to the West European Union (WEU).[32] There is little enthusiasm, however, for such an idea in eastern Europe. Most of the countries in the region are opposed to setting up any new blocs. Moreover, without a western security guarantee, such an alliance would not likely be very effective.

Yet another alternative would be for a pan-European security system to guarantee eastern Europe's security. The CSCE is too large and unwieldy an organization to offer meaningful security, and absent a generally perceived common threat, it is highly unlikely that all CSCE members would agree to take collective military action. Moreover, working out an effective pan-European security system would take some time; meanwhile, eastern Europe would be in military limbo.

A final option would be for the EC to develop a serious security component, as German Chancellor Helmut Kohl and French President François Mitterrand, among others, have advocated. Such an organization might eventually be open to the countries of eastern Europe, if and when they meet requirements for entry into the EC.

At present the EC does not seem ready to take on an active security role, as its vacillation and disarray during the Gulf crisis underscore; but this situation could change. If the EC does move toward genuine political union, as Kohl and Mitterrand propose, the Community seems bound to develop a security dimension. The WEU, which played an important role in the Gulf war,[33] could act as a bridge between NATO and a more dynamic and cohesive European Community with a security/defense component.

Such an evolution, as François Heisbourg suggests, might be a way of answering in a gradual and nondestabilizing way the problem that the emergence of a strategic vacuum in eastern

Europe poses.[34] This more robust EC could form the basis for a restructured and reinvigorated Euro-American alliance—the Euro-American Treaty Organization or EATO—composed o the EC, the United States and Canada, and associated member of the EC.[35]

A restructured European-American alliance, however, is a long-term vision. At the moment NATO remains the only rea trans-Atlantic institution capable of providing real security—a fact that the eastern Europeans well understand. Moreover, i ensures a strong American presence in Europe which they consider indispensable at the moment. Many fear that a premature effort to forge a security/defense component could lead to a sharp reduction of the U.S. military presence and influence in Europe, decreasing their own security as well as that of western Europe.

While membership in NATO may not be feasible at the moment, over the long run the countries of central Europe—Hungary, Poland and Czechoslovakia—should eventually become full members of a transformed trans-Atlantic security community. The actual form this takes will depend on the evolution of NATO, the EC, and the WEU as well as developments within these countries themselves. In the meantime, much can be done short of membership to strengthen security ties to these countries and provide them with greater psychological reassurance.

As a first step, western countries should open officer training courses to eastern European officers.[36] This would allow the eastern European countries to train a new generation of officers with close working ties to the West and help to imbue them with democratic values. Because the top officer corps in all the eastern European countries are products of the communist system and in most cases were party members, this is particularly important.

The West should also explore selling limited military equipment to the eastern European countries at favorable rates.[37] Doing so would help these countries gradually reduce their dependency on Soviet equipment, for which they must now pay hard currency. Such sales, however, should be made only after a thorough review of the countries' defense needs in the next decade. The equipment should be geared toward strengthening these countries' ability to *defend themselves against outside attack,* not toward enhancing their ability to conduct offensive military operations.

Third, the West should encourage the central Europeans to cooperate more closely among themselves. Some small steps have already been taken, but more could be done, especially in the area of air defense. The goal of such cooperation should not be to create a new regional security alliance, but to reduce procurement costs of expensive military equipment and to encourage closer cooperation in other areas.

Finally, the West should help to train *civilian specialists* on defense and security issues. Defense and security issues traditionally have been the prerogative of the military in eastern Europe. This has left the new elites without a cadre of knowledgeable civilians who can provide an alternative perspective to the military on critical defense and security questions. An intensified program of professional training courses and graduate exchanges in security studies—a "Fulbright Program in Security Studies for Eastern Europe"—could make an important contribution to alleviating this problem over the long run.

None of these measures would unduly alarm the Soviet Union—or whatever entity emerges from the present turmoil. However, they would reassure the countries of eastern Europe and help to reduce the sense of isolation some of them feel. At the same time, they would lay the basis for expanding more formal cooperation in the security area as these countries proceed down the path to democracy and as NATO, the WEU, and the EC evolve.

THE ECONOMIC DIMENSION

The disintegration of the CMEA has compounded eastern Europe's economic and security dilemmas. Its breakdown has produced serious dislocations in foreign trade. In 1990 trade among the CMEA countries dropped in volume by about 20 percent, while volume between eastern Europe and the Soviet Union fell by 13–15 percent. Two factors in particular exacerbated the decline in trade: (1) the rapid pace of German unification, which led to a large fall in imports to the former GDR, and (2) a cutback in delivery of Soviet energy supplies. Moreover, on January 1, 1991, trade within the CMEA began to take place on the basis of hard currency. This has led to a virtual collapse of Soviet trade with eastern Europe and pushed the region deeper into recession and aggravated the problems of moving toward a market economy.

The Persian Gulf crisis added to eastern Europe's woes by drastically increasing the price of oil. The embargo against Iraq, moreover, deprived eastern Europe of one of its main alternative sources of supply. At the same time, Iraq refused to pay its debts to eastern Europe—some $4 billion, all told—significantly accentuating the economic plight of some of these countries, especially Bulgaria and Romania.

Together, these developments have significantly intensified eastern Europe's already serious economic dilemmas. In the long run, some of these developments may actually have a positive impact, forcing the eastern European countries to close unproductive factories and reduce their dependency on the Soviet Union. But in the short term, they have accentuated the region's economic problems and made more difficult the transitions these countries have initiated since 1989.

The CMEA was expected to be formally disbanded sometime in the summer of 1991. There is no agreement, however, on what, if anything, should replace it. Vietnam, Cuba, and Mongolia favor a transformed successor organization. But the east European members are strongly opposed to such an idea. Several prefer a loose consultative body, limited to eastern Europe, the main function of which would be to exchange information and assist the member-states' switch from command to market economies.

The demise of the CMEA, however, is not likely to mean the end of all economic cooperation between former members. The eastern European countries cannot simply reorient their pattern of trade toward the West overnight—however much they might want to do so. The Soviet Union is a major market for eastern European goods, most of which are of poor quality and could not

e sold on western markets. As noted earlier, the recent collapse
of Soviet trade has had a devastating impact on the eastern
European economies. Thus, one of the top priorities for eastern
Europe in the short term will have to be to find a way to revive
trade with the Soviet Union.

In addition, eastern Europe is heavily dependent on Soviet
energy and raw materials. Poland and Hungary, for instance, get
nearly 90 percent of their oil and 80 percent of their gas from the
USSR. This pattern of dependence cannot change quickly.
Thus, some form of intraregional trade is necessary during the
interim period as the countries of eastern Europe seek to restructure their economies along market lines.

The collapse of the CMEA has sparked an interest in new
forms of regional cooperation. Hungary and Czechoslovakia, for
instance, have formed the Pentagonale group with Yugoslavia,
Austria, and Italy. The goal of the group, which was established
at Hungarian initiative, is to promote regional economic cooperation in specific areas. It has set up working groups to encourage
cooperation in environment, transportation, energy, telecommunications, culture, information, research, small and medium-
ized businesses, and migration and minorities.[38]

The Pentagonale represents a promising initiative, but how
successful it will be in resolving the pressing problems facing the
countries of central Europe remains to be seen. On the political
level, the motivations of the individual countries are quite diverse. For Italy, the group represents an attempt to outflank the
Germans and ensure that Rome is an active player in eastern
Europe, while Austria regards it as an opportunity to expand its
influence in an area where it has traditionally had strong interests and as a possible hedge against rejection by the EC. For
Hungary, Czechoslovakia, and the Yugoslav republics of Croatia
and Slovenia, the Pentagonale represents a means for achieving
closer economic and political integration with the West.

Many of the same problems that have inhibited cooperation
elsewhere in eastern Europe, however, have impeded cooperation within the Pentagonale: an inadequate economic infrastructure, an antiquated communications network, and a lack of
experienced managers familiar with western business tech-

niques. These conditions have discouraged western businesses from investing heavily in many projects. Until these problems are addressed, the prospects for a serious expansion of cooperation on a regionwide basis are likely to remain limited.

Poland joined the Pentagonale in July 1991. There is a danger, however, that if the group expands too much it will lose its regional focus and original sense of purpose. The group began as an effort between Hungary, Italy, Yugoslavia, and Austria to intensify cooperation in the Alpine-Adria region in 1977–78. Czechoslovakia was later added. With the addition of Poland, the group's geographic area will extend all the way from the Mediterranean to the Baltic Sea.

Poland, Hungary, and Czechoslovakia have begun to increase economic cooperation in a number of areas, particularly environment and transportation. The USSR's crackdown in the Baltics and Gorbachev's increasingly conservative policy in early 1991 gave this cooperation an additional political impetus. In January 1991, the foreign ministers of the three nations met in Budapest to discuss the Baltic situation and coordinate policy; in mid-February their heads of state met in Visegrad, Hungary to discuss ways to expand cooperation and coordinate views.

At this point cooperation remains largely ad hoc and does not envisage a serious security component.[39] Its main function is to coordinate the approach of the three countries toward the EC and avoid a mad scramble toward Brussels. Nevertheless, with time it could develop greater momentum and take on a more institutionalized form.[40]

The Balkan countries have also sought to increase cooperation, especially in the economic area. Meeting in Tirana in October 1990, the six Balkan foreign ministers discussed several modest steps to strengthen cooperation including the setting up of a permanent secretariat and Balkan Development Bank.[41] But a number of ethnic and minority disputes continue to plague the region, making any serious expansion of cooperation difficult.[42]

Bulgaria, Romania, Turkey, the Ukraine, and the Caucasian republics of the USSR have also initiated efforts to establish a Black Sea Zone of Economic Cooperation. The current economic difficulties these areas face are likely to hinder any signifi-

ant progress toward economic cooperation on a regionwide
asis in the short term. Over the longer run, however, Turkey
ould emerge as an important economic power in the region.

THE EC AND EASTERN EUROPE

The success of the reform efforts in eastern Europe will depend
o a large extent on the response of the West, particularly the EC.
While the eastern European countries have taken important first
teps toward creating market economies, they still face important
external barriers to integration into the world economy. Removal of
many of these barriers could facilitate the reform process and help
ameliorate the transition to market economies. In addition—as was
he case in Spain, Portugal, and Greece—strong ties to the West,
especially to the EC, may provide an important bulwark against a
lide toward authoritarianism.

The east central European countries' desire for membership in the EC, however, presents a number of problems. First, it
accentuates the debate about "widening" versus "deepening"
hat has been raging in the EC since the Turkish application for
membership in 1987.[43] None of the eastern European countries
are likely to be ready for full membership for some time. Admit-
ing them too early not only could weaken the Community, but
impose insuperable problems for the eastern European coun-
ries themselves. Moreover, a number of countries waiting in
ine, particularly Sweden and Austria, have far greater claim to
membership on purely economic grounds.

Second, the eastern European claims come at a time when
the EC already has a very full agenda: it must complete the
transition toward the creation of an internal market, restructure
its relations with the EFTA, deal with the impact of German
unification, and develop a coherent policy to assist reform in the
Soviet Union. The clamoring of the east central European countries for membership adds one more problem to this already
formidable list and risks slowing progress in other areas and even
splitting the Community.

At the same time, for the Community to simply turn its back
on eastern Europe and leave those countries to stew in their own

juices would endanger—indeed probably kill—their prospect
for significant reform and democratization. Furthermore, a
economically depressed eastern Europe, plagued by seething
nationality tensions and ethnic conflicts, would be a seriou
source of political instability. It is unlikely that western Europe
could hermetically seal itself off from the social and politica
consequences of such a boiling cauldron even if it tried. Eventu
ally the unrest would spill over into western Europe.

However, as Helen Wallace has argued, it is important to
make a clear distinction between "active partnership," on the one
hand, and "hasty enlargement," on the other.[44] At the moment
most EC members appear to favor giving priority to deepening
over widening. The processes, however, are not mutually exclu
sive. Indeed, deepening may well be a condition for widening
Only if Community institutions are first strengthened will the
Community be in a position to withstand the stresses the appli
cants for new membership pose. In essence, the EC will need to
pursue a dual policy: proceed with consolidating its interna
reforms and strengthening its institutional structure, while si
multaneously developing an active partnership with the EFTA
and eastern Europe.

The new association agreements under negotiation with
Hungary, Poland and Czechoslovakia represent an importan
step in this direction. Although these agreements do not explic
itly envisage membership in the EC, they go considerably beyond
previous trade agreements, establishing complete free trade be
tween the Community and these countries over a three-year
period, with the Community making the biggest concessions
first. They also include provisions for political cooperation
thereby providing an important political anchor to the Commu
nity and an element of psychological reassurance that may help
the nascent democracies through difficult times ahead.

These agreements, however, need to be complemented by
other measures. The dual impact of the Gulf crisis and the
cutback in Soviet oil deliveries has rendered obsolete the original
assistance plans worked out in 1989 and 1990. In conjunction
with the other western industrialized nations, particularly the
United States and Japan, the Community needs to work out a

comprehensive stabilization and assistance plan for eastern Europe that goes substantially beyond the modest efforts to date. Without such a comprehensive plan of increased assistance, growing economic chaos and instability may undermine many of the fledgling efforts at democratization and economic reform in Eastern Europe.

A new comprehensive stabilization package should include the following elements:

- *Opening of western markets to east European products as part of the General Agreement on Tariffs and Trade.* The EC's agricultural policy remains a major obstacle to the export of eastern European agricultural products. Additional steps to open the Community market to eastern European agricultural products are necessary. Tariffs on steel and textile products—two other areas of concern to the countries of central Europe—also need to be lowered or eliminated.

- *Relaxation of western export controls on the import of technologies necessary for the construction of a modern market economy.* In particular, the CoCom list of sensitive technologies requires review and streamlining.

- *Debt relief.* This facet is particularly important for Poland. The decision by the Paris club in March 1991 to reduce Poland's debt by 50 percent should facilitate the government's economic reform and help to increase western business confidence in investment in Poland.[45] The community should also consider similar ventures for other countries—such as Hungary, which has the highest per capita debt in eastern Europe.

- *Expansion of credit and investment guarantees.* These credits should be linked to the willingness of individual countries to proceed with a comprehensive program of economic reform. In many cases tying credits to specific projects may be useful.

Moreover, the *political* impact of EC membership over the long term should be clearly kept in mind. This is underscored by the experience of Greece, Spain and Portugal. A little more than a decade after their regime changes, all three countries are well established, secure and flourishing democratic regimes with relatively similar socio-economic content. Although internal factors were instrumental in ensuring these successful transitions, EC membership, as Lawrence Whitehead suggests, played an important role in shaping political values and expectations of key elite groups in certain directions.[46] In short, while membership in the Community does not force member states to create similar institutions, it does set broad parameters that influence the development of internal structures of member-states and move them in broadly similar directions, thus helping to promote "democracy by convergence." This has important implications for eastern Europe and highlights the political benefits of full EC membership for these countries over the long run.

GERMANY AND EASTERN EUROPE

Another key factor affecting eastern Europe's future will be the role played by Germany. The Federal Republic currently is the largest western trading partner for all eastern European countries. In 1989, for instance, 60 percent of Poland's imports from western Europe came from the Federal Republic. The figures for Czechoslovakia, Bulgaria and Hungary were 57 percent, 52 percent, and 50 percent, respectively.[47] As eastern markets open up, Bonn will be in the best position to take advantage of new business opportunities.[48] Over the next decade, it is highly probable that the Federal Republic will regain the dominant economic position that it occupied in the interwar period.

While suspicion of Germany remains strong in some quarters in eastern Europe, eastern European attitudes toward Germany have shifted perceptibly in the past several decades. Bonn's *Ostpolitik* has largely succeeded in defusing the "German bogey," which in the 1950s and 1960s was a potent instrument for maintaining cohesion within the Warsaw Pact. In addition, the Federal Republic, particularly Foreign Minister Hans-Dietrich Genscher, has been a leading western proponent of East-West détente. As a result, fear and mistrust of Germany have significantly declined in eastern Europe, particularly among the younger generation, who did not experience the horrors of World War II.

The degree to which attitudes toward Germany have changed is highlighted by the approach that the countries of eastern Europe, particularly east central Europe, adopted to German unification and the membership of a united Germany in NATO. Rather than opposing unification, as one might have expected, most eastern European governments saw it as a necessary step in overcoming the division of Europe. Hungary, Czechoslovakia, and Poland openly supported Germany's membership in NATO, while Bulgaria and Romania voiced no strong objection to it. Thus Moscow was left isolated within its own alliance on the German issue.

This is not to say that German unification has not prompted any anxieties in eastern Europe. But the nature of eastern European concerns has visibly changed. Today the fear is not of a revival of German militarism, but of German economic penetration and dominance. Many eastern Europeans fear that Germany will simply "buy up" much of the industrial and natural wealth in the region and that the countries of eastern Europe will become little more than "German colonies."

These fears, however, appear exaggerated. The Federal Republic in the next decade will be primarily concerned with rebuilding the GDR. Moreover, the costs of this task are likely to be considerably higher than initially expected—perhaps as much as 1 billion DM over the next decade.[49] The escalating costs of rebuilding the GDR are likely to put significant constraints on the financial resources available for investment elsewhere, especially eastern Europe. Thus the problem may not be that "the Germans are coming," but rather that the Germans are *not* coming.

Despite the problems of rebuilding the GDR, however, Bonn is not likely to neglect eastern Europe. Many German politicians feel Germany has a special responsibility for eastern Europe and that it should be a "spokesman" for these countries. They see a close association of the countries of eastern Europe— or at least central Europe—with the EC as a prerequisite for the creation of a broader federal Europe "from the Atlantic to the

Bug."[50] The leader of the Free Democrats, Graf Otto Lambs-
dorf, for instance, has argued that Germany must act as a
"broker" for eastern Europe and "take the lead" in facilitating
their entry into the EC.[51]

On the bilateral level, relations with Hungary have been
strengthened. Historically, Hungary has maintained strong ties
to Germany—it fought on the German side in both world wars—
and there are no outstanding bilateral issues between the two
countries. Thus relations are not burdened by the historical
baggage that has complicated Bonn's relations with other countries in eastern Europe. Moreover, Hungary enjoys a special
sympathy in Bonn because its decision to open its borders in
September 1990 paved the way for German unification.

With Czechoslovakia relations have improved visibly since
the "velvet revolution" of 1989. A new Agreement of Cooperation and Friendship is being negotiated and should be ready by
the end of 1991. The treaty updates the agreement signed in
1973 and is designed to put relations on a new basis. Some circles
in the FRG have raised demands for compensation for the prop-
erty of the more than three million Sudeten Germans expelled
from Czechoslovakia after World War II. However, both sides
have consciously sought to play down the Sudeten German issue
and it is not likely to be a serious obstacle to improved relations.

The most significant change, however, has come in Germany's relations with Poland. Polish mistrust of Germany has
deep historical roots and has been a major *leitmotiv* of Warsaw's
foreign policy in the postwar period. The *Ostpolitik* and the
signing of the Bonn-Warsaw treaty in 1971, which normalized
relations between the two countries, did much to reduce this
mistrust, but did not entirely remove it. Many circles in Poland
continued to harbor fears that Germany would at some point try
to claim the territories in eastern Prussia which it was forced to
cede to Poland at the end of World War II.

Chancellor Kohl's unwillingness in the spring of 1990 to
unequivocally recognize the Oder-Neisse as the final border
between the two countries reinforced these fears. However, Polish concerns have diminished significantly since late 1990, with
the signing of the Final Settlement on Germany, which provides

an international guarantee for Poland's border, and the conclusion of the Polish-German border treaty, which unequivocally recognizes the Oder-Neisse line as the border between the two countries.[52] In Poland, the conclusion of the border treaty was an important litmus test of Germany's desire for reconciliation and has contributed to a major reduction in popular fears about a threat from Germany.

The treaty thus has greater political significance, not just for Poland but for European security as a whole. First, it removes the main source of tension in Polish-German relations and lays the basis for a far-reaching rapprochement between the two countries over the long-term. Second, it provides Poland with a secure western border for the first time in the postwar period, thereby relieving Warsaw of the need to rely on the Soviet Union as a protector and counterweight to German power. In addition, a second treaty regulating overall bilateral relations was signed in June 1991.

Taken together, the two treaties provide the foundation for a significant improvement in Polish-German relations over the long term. One potential obstacle, however, could be the attitude of the population in the former GDR. In contrast to the Federal Republic, the GDR never went through a deep-seated process of *Vergangenheitsbewältigung* (overcoming the past). Despite the slogans about "socialist solidarity," East Germany made little effort to address the real sources of misunderstanding between the two countries. The relatively sparse contact between Polish intellectuals and the East German dissidents further inhibited the process of reconciliation. As a result, anti-Polish sentiment remains relatively strong among the population of the former GDR.[53]

Unification could accentuate this sentiment and give it a sharper edge. Many East Germans may resent giving large-scale assistance to Poland at a time of rising unemployment and economic decline in the länder of the former GDR. They may be tempted to look for scapegoats for their economic problems, especially if the easing of visa restrictions leads to a large influx of Poles into Germany. This could exacerbate social tensions and lead to outbreaks of violence and anti-Polish sentiment among certain segments of the East German population.[54]

The long-term ramifications of unification on German foreign policy may, in fact, be greater than has generally been thought.[55] There is an underlying assumption among many Western policymakers and analysts that a united Germany will simply be the Federal Republic writ large. This assumption, however, may not be justified. The East German population holds a more critical view of the United States and the Atlantic Alliance than its West German counterparts.[56] Over the long term these attitudes could have an impact on West German foreign policy, especially relations with the United States and NATO.

IMMIGRATION AND EAST-WEST SECURITY

The outbreak of violence and social tensions surrounding the easing of visa requirements for Poland noted above highlights the degree to which immigration is likely to become an increasingly important security issue in Europe. Migration began to emerge as a security problem in Europe before 1989, but the collapse of communism in eastern Europe has given the issue a new dimension. In the coming decade, western Europe could be confronted with an unprecedented flow of refugees and asylum seekers, many of them from eastern Europe.[57]

Germany has traditionally been the main haven for most of these refugees. In 1989, it absorbed some 370,000 ethnic Germans from the Soviet Union and eastern Europe, and another 121,000 foreigners asked for asylum. Figures show increases for both groups for 1990.[58] This large influx has posed significant economic and social problems for the Federal Republic, accentuating social tensions and antiforeign attitudes in a number of large cities, particularly Berlin.[59]

The problem is likely to become more acute if the disintegration of the Soviet Union continues. With the passage of the new, liberalized passport law in the USSR, millions of Soviet citizens could come pouring into eastern and western Europe over the next several years. The effects would be particularly severe in Germany, already burdened by a large refugee problem and the need to integrate the 16 million citizens from the

GDR, but would also be strong in other western countries, particularly Finland, which shares a border with the USSR. Many emigrants will also flock to eastern Europe, especially Poland and Hungary, compounding these countries' considerable economic problems.[60]

The migration problem will become even more critical as the EC moves toward 1992. As a result of the Schengen agreement—which France, Germany, Italy, and the Benelux countries signed in June 1990—all border controls will be removed and movement of residents between these countries will be unimpeded. Thus, once immigrants or refugees have entered one of these six countries, they will be free to travel and work in the others.

Intensified cooperation between eastern and western Europe is therefore crucial to prevent the flow of expected immigrants from becoming a major source of tension. The Community needs to work out a comprehensive policy toward immigration. This should include the following elements:

- *Strengthening economic and technical cooperation with eastern Europe.* The goal should be to promote domestic reforms leading to increases in standards of living, thereby reducing the pressure from migration.

- *Harmonization of rules and practices related to granting asylum within the Community.* Chiefly, the Community members must agree on what constitutes a refugee. In addition, the EC needs to streamline the process of asylum adjudication.

- *Cooperation between the Community and the countries of eastern Europe regarding visa policy, measures to prevent illegal immigration, and deportation agreements.* Eastern European visa and immigration policies in many cases are very liberal for Third World nationals. Consequently, a proportion of South-North immigrants are diverted to eastern Europe and subsequently reach western Europe illegally. Greater cooperation regarding visas could reduce this flow, as well as that of eastern European nationals to western Europe.

- *Harmonization of policy within the Community on immigration from eastern Europe.* The goal should be a migration convention that establishes quotas for eastern European immigration and provides for effective and orderly migration.

- *Harmonization of rules related to foreigners' access to the labor market throughout Europe.* Again, cooperation of the countries of eastern Europe will be necessary to make such procedures successful.

- *Increased financial assistance to the countries of eastern Europe.* Aid should go to help these countries address the consequences of large-scale immigration, as well as create incentives to keep their own populations from migrating.

In the final analysis, the migration problem is closely linked to the larger question of the success of reform in eastern Europe as a whole. If the reforms are successful, the pressure for sizable numbers of citizens from eastern Europe to move west will be less. But if the reforms fail, many eastern Europeans will "vote with their feet." This prospect gives the West an added incentive to support measures to help stabilize the reforms now underway in eastern Europe. Without such support, these reforms could falter, increasing the prospects for instability and disorder in *both* parts of Europe.

The views expressed here represent the author's personal views and do not necessarily reflect the views of RAND or any of its sponsors.

NOTES

1. See Charles Gati, "East-Central Europe: The Morning After," *Foreign Affairs* (Winter 1990/91), Vol. 69, no. 5, pp. 129–145.
2. See, in particular, Guillermo O'Donnell and Philippe C. Schmitter, *Tentative Conclusions about Uncertain Democracies* (Baltimore: Johns Hopkins University Press, 1986), and Guillermo O'Donnell, Philippe C. Schmitter, and Lawrence Whitehead, *Transitions from Authoritarian Rule: Comparative Perspectives* (Baltimore: Johns Hopkins University Press, 1986).
3. Kenneth Maxwell, "Spain's Transition to Democracy: A Model for Eastern Europe?" in Nils H. Wessel, ed., *The New Europe* (New York: Academy of Political Science, 1991), pp. 35–49.
4. Istvan Deak, "Uncovering Eastern Europe's Dark History," *Orbis* (Winter 1990), Vol. 34, no. 1, pp. 51–65.
5. See Zbigniew Brzezinski, "Postcommunist Nationalism," *Foreign Affairs*, (Winter 1989/90), Vol. 68, no. 5, pp. 1–25.

6. Timothy Garton Ash, *The Uses of Adversity* (New York: Vintage Books, 1990), p. 300. For similar concerns, see David Halberstam, "Beneath Eastern Europe's Euphoria," *New York Times,* July 22, 1990.
7. See Judith Pataki, "Elections Show Voter Apathy and a Shift to the Left," Radio Free Europe/Radio Liberty Research (RFE/RL), *Report on Eastern Europe,* August 26, 1991, pp. 16–18.
8. Jan B. De Weydenthal, "The First Hundred Days of Walesa's Presidency," RFE/RL, *Report on Eastern Europe,* April 5, 1991, p. 10.
9. The beginnings of this process were evident during the selection of the new cabinet after Walesa's election. Whereas Mazowiecki had largely picked his cabinet himself with little or no outside consultation, Bielecki's choices for cabinet had to be discussed and approved by Walesa before they were announced.
10. Peter Martin, "Scenario for Economic Reform Adopted," RFE/RL, *Report on Eastern Europe,* October 19, 1990, pp. 5–8.
11. During the debate in Parliament over the name of the Federation, deputies from the Czech Republic favored the name Czechoslovak Federative Republic, whereas Slovak deputies favored Czecho-Slovak Republic. They meant the hyphen to underscore the equal status of the two constituent republics. In the end both sides agreed to compromise, settling for the Czech and Slovak Federative Republic. For details see Peter Martin, "The Hyphen Controversy," RFE/RL, *Report on Eastern Europe,* April 20, 1990, pp. 14–18.
12. The problems in this regard were highlighted in May 1991, when Czechoslovakia announced its intention to sell 300 tanks to Syria. Despite strong objections by the Bush Administration, the Havel government decided to proceed with the sale, largely because a cancellation of the sale would have had serious economic and political consequences in Slovakia, further fueling Slovak separatism. See "Hard-Pressed Czechs Retain Arms Trade," *New York Times,* May 3, 1991.
13. For a detailed discussion, see Michael Z. Wise, "Czechs, Slovaks Reach Agreement on Federal Regional Power-Sharing Plan," *Washington Post,* November 14, 1990. Also see Jan Obrman and Jiri Pehe, "Difficult Power-Sharing Talks," RFE/RL, *Report on Eastern Europe,* December 7, 1990, pp. 5–9.
14. See Karoly Okolicsanyi, "Privatization: Two Cautious Steps," RFE/RL, *Report on Eastern Europe,* October 19, 1990, pp. 24–27.
15. Differences within the government over economic policy were particularly acute between Finance Minister Ferenc Rabar and Antall's economic advisor, Gyorgy Matolcsy. Both men were replaced in a cabinet shuffle at the end of 1990. For a good discussion, see David M. Kemme, *Economic Transition in Eastern Europe and the Soviet Union: Issues and Strategies,* Occasional Paper no. 20 (New York: Institute for East-West Security Studies, 1991). Also see Karoly Okolicsanyi, "The Debate on Economic 'Shock Therapy'," RFE/RL, *Report on Eastern Europe,* January 11, 1991, pp. 11–13 .
16. Peter Falush, "Hungary's Reform in Low Gear," *The World Today,* April 1990, p. 58.
17. In a regional poll taken at the end of 1990, 84 percent of the Hungarians interviewed said they thought their country's economic situation had wors-

ened over the last year, and 88 percent said they expected 1991 to be worse. See Celestine Bohlen, "For a Gloomy Outlook, Hungarians Top All," *New York Times,* January 2, 1991.

18. About 2 million Hungarians live in Romania, most of them in Transylvania, and about 600,000 Hungarians live in Slovakia.

19. On the relationship of civil society and the development of a stable democracy, see John Keane, *Democracy and Civil Society* (London: Verso, 1988); ———, ed., *Civil Society and the State* (London: Verso, 1988).

20. See Michael Shafir, "Sharp Drop in Leadership's Popularity," RFE/RL, *Report on Eastern Europe,* April 12, 1991, pp. 23–24.

21. In recent opinion polls the army has headed the list of institutions that enjoyed the greatest public confidence. See Michael Shafir, "Public Opinion One Year After the Elections," RFE/RL, *Report on Eastern Europe,* June 14, 1991, p. 27.

22. See his *A World of Nations* (Washington, DC: Brookings Institution, 1965), p. 194.

23. For a detailed discussion, see Wolfgang Höpken, "Das Ende der Ära Zhivkovs," *Südosteuropa,* Heft 1 (1990), pp. 2–35.

24. See Dale Herspring, "Reassessing the Warsaw Pact Threat: The East European Militaries," *Arms Control Today* (March 1990), pp. 8–12.

25. See Michael Sadykiewicz and Douglas L. Clarke, "The New Polish Defense Doctrine: A Further Step toward Sovereignty," RFE/RL, *Report on Eastern Europe,* May 4, 1980, pp. 20–23. For a comprehensive discussion of the changes in Polish doctrine, see Thomas S. Szayna, *The Military in Post-Communist Poland,* (Santa Monica: RAND, forthcoming).

26. Poland was particularly upset by remarks by Lieutenant General Victor Dubynin, commander of the Northern Group of the Soviet Armed Forces, made in early January 1990. Dubynin implied that Moscow intended to go ahead with its planned withdrawal of Soviet troops from Germany through Poland, with or without Poland's approval. Warsaw viewed these remarks as typical of the "Stalinist" thinking that still pervades the Soviet military. To emphasize its sovereignty, in January 1991 Poland held up a number of Soviet convoys carrying troops and supplies from eastern Germany at the Polish-German border, refusing them permission to transit Polish territory. See Douglas Clark, "Poland and Soviet Troops in Germany," RFE/RL, *Report on Eastern Europe,* January 25, 1991, pp. 40–44. Also see "Ich Nenne Das Stalinistisch," *Frankfurter Allgemeine Zeitung,* January 25, 1991; Stephen Engelberg, "No. 1 Question for the Poles: When Do Soviet Troops Go," *New York Times,* January 17, 1991; and———, Poland Is Pressing Russians to Leave," *New York Times,* February 15, 1991.

27. The document appears to be part of a growing political debate on Eastern Europe that has pitted the International Department of the CPSU against the Soviet Foreign Ministry. See Suzanne Crow, "International Department and Foreign Ministry Disagree on Eastern Europe," RFE/RL, *Report on the USSR,* June 21, 1991, pp. 4–8. Also "Moskau will sich in Osteuropa feste Positionen sichern," *Frankfurter Allgemeine Zeitung,* June 7, 1991.

28. For details see Suzanne Crow, "Who Lost Eastern Europe," RFE/RL, *Report on the USSR,* April 12, 1991, pp. 1–5.

29. See Vladimir Socor, "The Romanian-Soviet Friendship Treaty and its Regional Implications," RFE/RL, *Report on Eastern Europe*, May 3, 1991, pp. 25–33.

30. See in particular the "Ten Principles Regarding the Future of Europe," agreed to by Czechoslovak foreign minister Jiri Dienstbier and German foreign minister Hans-Dietrich Genscher in Prague, April 1991. Principle six stresses the importance of close cooperation with the United States and Canada for European security in the future. See "Aussenminister Genscher und Dienstbier formulieren 'Prager Thesen' zu Europa," *Frankfurter Allgemeine Zeitung*, April 13, 1991.

31. For the text of Havel's speech, see FBIS-WEU-91-056, March 22, 1991, pp 1–4. See also David Buchan, "Havel Secures Little but Fine Words from NATO," *Financial Times*, March 22, 1990.

32. See the speech by Romanian foreign ministerr Adrian Nastase to the Conference on "The Future of European Security," hosted by NATO Secretary General Manfred Wörner and Czechoslovak foreign minister Jiri Dienstbier, in Prague, April 25–26, 1991.

33. The WEU played a particularly constructive role during the Gulf crisis. See William van Ekelen, "The WEU and the Gulf," *Survival* (November–December 1990), Vol. xxxiii, no. 3, pp. 519–532.

34. See Heisbourg's chapter in this volume, "From a Common European Home to a European Security System," pp. 35–58.

35. For a similar suggestion, see Stanley Hoffmann, "The Case for Leadership," *Foreign Policy*, (Winter 1990–1991), no. 81, pp. 20–38.

36. Some countries have already taken steps in this area. For instance, Germay has opened staff courses to officers from Czechoslovakia, Poland, and Hungary. Britain has also agreed to receive two Hungarian officers for training. And the United States has changed the rules to allow eastern European officers to attend officer training courses through its International Military Educational Training program (IMET).

37. Poland, for instance, has expressed an interest in buying U.S. F-16s. See R. Jeffrey Smith, "Poles Say They Want U.S. Weapons," *Washington Post*, December 5, 1990.

38. For details, see Ernst Sucharipa, "Die Pentagonale," *Europäische Rundschau*, no. 3 (Summer 1990), pp. 25–34. For a Hungarian perspective, see Geza Jeszenszky, "Regional Cooperation in Europe," *Review of International Affairs*, December 20, 1990, pp. 3–4.

39. At the Visegrad meeting, the three leaders went out of their way to emphasize the loose, informal nature of the cooperation and that it was not directed at any one country. See Stephen Engelberg, "3 East Europeans Confer, Gingerly," *New York Times*, February 17, 1991.

40. Hungary, for instance, has proposed formal talks on the creation of a free-trade zone in central Europe. The proposal is designed to facilitate trade between the three countries and help overcome some of the problems caused by the collapse of the CMEA.

41. For details, see Louis Zanga, "The Balkan Foreign Ministers Conference in Tirana," RFE/RL, *Report on Eastern Europe*, December 7, 1990, pp. 1–4.

42. See F. Stephen Larrabee, "Long Memories and Short Fuses: Balkan Security in the 1990s," *International Security* (Winter 1990), Vol. 15, no. 3, pp. 29–53.

43. For an excellent discussion, see Helen Wallace, *Widening and Deepening: The European Community and the New European Agenda*, RIIA Discussion Paper, no. 23 (London: Royal Institute of International Affairs, 1989).

44. Ibid., p. viii.

45. The Federal Republic holds the largest share of the official debt; the United States, United Kingdom, France, and Japan follow.

46. See his chapter, "Democracy by Convergence and Southern Europe," in Geoffrey Pridham, ed., *Encouraging Democracy: The International Context of Domestic Transition in Southern Europe* (London: Frances Pinter, forthcoming).

47. See Ronald D. Asmus, *German Unification and its Ramifications*, (Santa Monica: RAND, 1991), p. 43.

48. The decision of the Czechoslovak car manufacturer Skoda to merge with Volkswagen well illustrates this point. Volkswagen won out over several western car makers, including Renault-Volvo. The merger involves the biggest cross-border investment in European history and will likely stimulate further western investment in the Czechoslovak economy. See Jan Obrman, "Skoda Becomes Part of the Volkswagen Empire," RFE/RL, *Report on Eastern Europe*, January 25, 1991, pp. 7–12; and, "Einsteig des VW-Konzerns bei Skoda," *Neue Zürcher Zeitung*, December 12, 1990.

49. Ferdinand Protzman, "Germans Lower Expectations on East's Economic Recovery," *New York Times*, February 13, 1991.

50. See in particular the article by Horst Teltschik in *Die Welt*, September 22, 1990. At the time the article was published, Teltschik was Kohl's adviser on national security affairs.

51. See Lambdorf's interview in *Der Morgen*, October 2, 1990.

52. See Anna Sabbat-Swedlicka, "The Signing of the Polish-German Border Treaty," RFE/RL, *Report on Eastern Europe*, December 7, 1990, pp. 16–19. For the text of the treaty, see the *Frankfurter Allgemeine Zeitung*, November 15, 1990.

53. Many Polish intellectuals believe that the real obstacle to a far-reaching accommodation between Germany and Poland lies not with the Federal Republic, but with the population of what was the GDR. See, in particular, Anna Wolff-Poweska, "Polen und Deutsche in einem sich vereinigenden Europa," *Europa Archiv*, Folge 22/1990, pp. 679–684.

54. The lifting of visas for Poles in April 1991, for instance, led to a number of outbursts of anti-Polish violence by Neo-Nazi groups in East Germany. See Leslie Colitt, "German Neo-Nazis Assault Poles at Border," *Financial Times*, April 9, 1991.

55. For an insightful discussion, see Asmus, *German Unification and its Ramifications*.

56. See Ronald D. Asmus, *German Perceptions of the United States on the Eve of Unification* (Santa Monica: RAND, 1991).

57. See François Heisbourg, "Population Movements in Post–Cold War Europe," *Survival* (January/February 1991), Vol. XXXIII, no. 1, pp. 31–43.

58. A record 397,000 ethnic Germans arrived from Eastern Europe and the USSR in 1990. The largest groups came from the Soviet Union (148,000), Poland (133,872), and Romania (110,000). See "1990 Mehr Aussiedler Nach Deutschland als je zuvor," *Frankfurter Allgemeine Zeitung*, January 4, 1991.

59. The rise of anti-Polish feeling in Berlin and other large cities has been particularly strong because of the large influx of Poles who come for short periods and engage in black-marketeering and other speculative activities.

60. Both Poland and Hungary have been inundated with refugees, many of them gypsies from Romania. This is beginning to cause major social problems for both countries. See Carlos J. Williams, "Hungary: Reluctant Refuge for the Homeless," *Los Angeles Times*, November 26, 1990; Robert Hunter, "Europe Braces for Hungary Hordes," *Los Angeles Times*, December 3, 1990; and "For East Europe's Hopeful, Warsaw Glitters," *New York Times*, December 26, 1990.

6

INDUSTRIAL STRENGTH AND REGIONAL RESPONSE: JAPAN'S IMPACT ON EUROPEAN INTEGRATION

Michael Borrus and John Zysman

This chapter examines Japan's influence on the terms of European integration and the resulting international implications. The emergence of Japanese economic power helped to trigger European moves toward greater integration, and will continue to powerfully shape their character. Of course, to understand the details of European integration and particular choices European governments have made, one must look at domestic and regional political maneuvering within Europe. But after decades of frozen position, European business elites and government leaders moved toward the original treaty objectives of a single market at least in part because of the economic and political implications of Japan's industrial success. A brief look back will help to situate Japan's current influence.

The wrenching structural changes brought about by World War II sparked the original European movement.[1] After the war Europe was no longer the center of the international system, but a buffer between two superpowers. Political entrepreneurship came initially from the group surrounding Robert Schuman and Jean Monnet, who mobilized a transnational coalition supportive of integration. That coalition's core eventually included Christian Democratic parties of the original six (France, Germany, Italy, Belgium, Luxembourg, and the Netherlands) plus many of the socialist parties. Its fundamental objectives were to bind Germany to the rest of Europe, making another war impossible, and to rebuild the region's economies.

A number of explicit and implicit implementing bargains with the United States in finance, trade, and technology facilitated the objectives. In general, the United States agreed to keep its own market open to European exports while tolerating protection in Europe on behalf of economic development there. The United States simultaneously assured that development through extraordinary transfers of finance and technology. In turn, the United States benefited by providing technically advanced goods and services, and by purchasing European assets with surpluses and an overvalued currency.[2] In the bargain, U.S. firms operating in Europe received national treatment.

Through the 1980s, the impression of relative American decline and the incontrovertible evidence of rapid Japanese ascent helped to spur change in Europe. The altering industrial positions were seen to represent real shifts in the international distribution of economic power resources. Because the fundamental distribution of resources crucial to the international economic structure had shifted, the basic choices confronting Europe shifted as well. The issues of international control and influence, settled for three to four decades, were suddenly reopened.

Previously, Europe's options had centered on the United States. If Europe could not lead in technology, it could still acquire it relatively easily from the United States. If Europe could not structure financial rules to its liking, at least it could accommodate to American positions. If Europe were not first, it was second, and individual bargains by and between European governments and companies could suffice for generating economic growth and significant geopolitical influence. Japan's sudden rise severely constrained and complicated Europe's existing options: The prospect of being third was quite another matter altogether. To be even modestly dependent on Japan in finance, trade, or technology—or even to be less influential geopolitically—would be unacceptable without the integrated defense and trade ties that linked the Atlantic partners.

Three broad responsive options confronted European governments. Each country could seek its own accommodation through purely national strategies. Europe as a whole could reconcile itself to increased Japanese power and decreased European influence. Or Europe could restructure its own position to act more coherently—and more powerfully—in the changing world. The third option became Europe's choice.

JAPANESE INFLUENCE ON THE EVOLUTION OF EUROPEAN INTEGRATION

A variety of developments, including the dramas in eastern Europe, have shaped the trajectory of the European project and influenced its pace. Central among these has been competitive pressure in the economic sphere. European governments' and companies' responses to the new and intense competition from Japan, especially in consumer durables, will largely determine whether Europe remains open or becomes an economic region turned in on itself—a fortress. To be sure, the European commitment to open trade is strong, although Americans, who are so focused on their competition with Japan, often underestimate it. Indeed, despite the agricultural policy disputes that troubled the Uruguay Round of the General Agreement on Tariffs and Trade, we believe that European-American trade can be managed within mutual commitments to open trade. Competitive pressure from U.S. industry, while significant in some domains (chemicals and aerospace for example), will not compel Europe to adjust the rules of its region toward greater protection. By and large, the American presence is an established part of Europe's economic landscape, and the bilateral trade account is balanced enough to avoid substantial dislocation or destructive policy debate.

By contrast, intense competitive pressure in Europe from Japan and Asia may well produce much more contentious trade outcomes that unexpectedly rebound to provoke heightened conflict between Europe and the United States, conflicts that Europeans themselves do not really want. A few examples will suffice to demonstrate the potential.

Consider finance. When Willy de Clerq was external relations commissioner of the European Community (EC), his call for reciprocity in financial relations set off a great furor. The policy was aimed at opening access to Japanese financial markets for European firms, or at least at limiting a flood of powerful Japanese banks into Europe, but it hit most directly the interests of American financial institutions.

Or consider electronics. Charges of dumping which the Community brought against Japanese firms producing copiers in the United States forced the questions both of what entry strategies Europe would accept from Japanese firms and of what constituted a Japanese product. Remedies that specified local European content also hit U.S. companies by forcing the Japanese copier companies to design out U.S.-manufactured components. Similarly, the use of industrial standards to maintain markets in the face of Japanese competition is evident in the discussion of high-definition television (HDTV): when asked how many HDTV standards the EC would adopt, one European senior executive remarked that there would be as many standards as were required to keep the Japanese out of Europe.[3]

Finally, consider autos. The current debate on Japanese auto quotas in Europe may determine the extensiveness of trade protectionism Europe adopts to limit Japanese market penetration. But what will constitute a Japanese auto for those purposes? Will U.S.-made Hondas exported to Europe be subject to sanctions aimed at Japanese producers? What about vehicles jointly produced by Ford and Mazda? The U.S. government could well end up prosecuting U.S.–European trade conflicts on behalf of Japanese companies.

Such disputes take place in the established trade categories of reciprocity, dumping, standards, and quotas, but they are all symptoms of the fundamental challenge Japanese competitive strengths represent. Japan's enormous industrial success is built on production breakthroughs and organizational innovations that present exceptional problems for established European firms. Initially Europeans felt the pressure through trade. Japan's exports of manufactured goods to Europe more than doubled between 1980 and 1987, with very rapid increases in electronics and automobiles.[4] In the next decade, they will feel the pressure as direct foreign investment. The enormous profitability of the Japanese firms and the considerable export surpluses that have resulted from industrial advantage give Japanese firms and financial institutions considerable financial muscle. That financial strength permits Japanese firms to implant themselves in European markets; the production innovations will help them succeed there.

While Japanese firms are strong in global markets in a considerable range of industries, it is in volume consumer durables—such as automobiles and consumer electronics (and related high-volume office electronics, like fax machines)—that they have established unique advantages. The effective introduction by many Japanese firms of "flexible automation" or "lean" production systems has given them absolute advantages in cost, quality, and new product development.[5] The point is not simply that the best Japanese auto companies produce cars less expensively than their European counterparts. It is not simply that the quality of their product is higher as measured by defects or fit and finish. It is rather that Japanese firms can produce higher-quality cars—or other consumer durables—less expensively and in far less time from design to showroom than European companies. This translates into a capacity to respond to market shifts and introduce technological innovation much faster. As a result, Japanese capabilities press both the volume European car makers (including Volkswagen, Fiat, and Renault) and the top-end specialists (for example, BMW and Mercedes-Benz). The same market pressure exists in consumer and personal electronics, from camcorders and compact disc players to faxes, copiers, and portable phones and computers. Without a doubt, European skills in software, design, and systems integration—applicable equally to computer architectures and antilock brakes—provide potential advantages for European firms. Some firms—Electrolux is an example—are expanding scale and reorganizing factories to respond. But as the U.S. experience attests, Japanese strengths will provide formidable competitive pressures on established European market positions. And when market share is lost to imports, jobs are lost as well, with obvious political complications.

Perhaps more significant, however, the high-volume industries Japan dominates are increasingly becoming the driving force behind component technologies that are broadly applied across the industrialized economies. High-volume high technology is a crucial new category:[6] high-volume electronics applications from camcorders to electronic braking systems are already beginning to drive the development, costs, quality, and manufacture of technological inputs critical to computing, communications, military, and industrial electronics. At stake is a breathtaking range of essential technologies, from semiconductors and storage devices to packaging, optics, displays, and power supplies.[7] Similarly, in automobiles, electronic engine management, antilock braking systems, and communications technology make auto component firms sources of profound and broadly applicable innovation. In our view, for example, one of the most sophisticated electronics firms in Europe produces automotive components as its core business: traditional lists of European electronics firms do not normally even count Robert Bosch. But, like Motorola in the United States, Bosch is a major European exception to increasing Japanese dominance of high-volume high technology. That dominance will constrain the competitive strategies of a broad range of European producers—an issue we examine in detail below.

EUROPE'S RESPONSES

How will Europe respond to these Japanese challenges? Three issues are central. First, how much room will Europe provide for Japanese firms? The specific debate in the news is about the length and extent of protection for European automobile producers, but the general principle is whether trade policy will contain the pace of Japanese entry. Second, what will be the form, and who will be the agent, of public support for the necessary competitive adjustment of European firms? Precisely because the European Commission is trying to uproot state subsidy to national firms, trade protection is all the more probable—despite protestations to the contrary. Third, what Japanese development policies and corporate entry strategies will Europe accept? Here we find the question of dumping restrictions; the insistence on local production; and the demands for reciprocity in market access, technology, and investment opportunities in the Japanese market.

No single European answer to these questions is likely. Certainly, no common position exists among the governments, nor, for that matter, within the several departments in the European Commission. In fact, the range of views among the countries is extreme. In autos and consumer electronics, the Italians and French have sought to severely restrict Japanese access to the European market. The precise instruments and policy disputes—from local quotas to registration restrictions—are adapted to that general purpose. The British, by sharp contrast, see Japanese implants as a mechanism to rebuild Britain's manufacturing base. As discussed before, this is a matter not simply of investment, but of reorganizing production and introducing new notions of how labor and management can operate.

Other national views fall between, tolerating open competition the more competitive the nation's industries. Thus, initial German opposition to the auto quotas reflected the small but highly profitable export position of Mercedes-Benz and BMW in Japan and their confidence in holding position in the European market. The German position then reportedly shifted shortly after a careful evaluation of the Lexus (Toyota) and Infiniti (Nissan) entries in the luxury market. Along with Honda's NSX in the high performance market, the Lexus and Infiniti pose a real challenge to Europe's leading high-end producers.[8]

Nor does unanimity prevail within the European Commission. General Directorate (DG) XIII is essentially operating a developmental strategy for European electronics. DG IV (Competition) is increasingly challenging the legitimacy of that effort. It is gaining substantial prestige, and will continue to assert its influence against the rest of the EC bureaucracy and the member-states.

Thus, while the industrial and political views cover a broad spectrum, a uniform outcome may be coalescing from the initial mix of policies. That outcome is forced direct investment in Europe by Japanese firms, with local production consisting of increasing local value-added. The Japanese are a target here, in part because local production represents only 16 percent of total sales for their firms as against 79 percent for U.S. firms.[9] In turn, Japanese firms have certainly been responding to perceived pressure to increase their contribution to European economic performance: Inward investment accelerated sharply in the second half of the 1980s. Average annual inflows of Japanese investment into the eight leading EC countries were nearly seven times as high in the second half of the 1980s as in the first half.[10] Equally important, industrial investment (as opposed to investment in services or real estate) more than doubled its share of the Japanese total, finally becoming a significant factor. The majority of industrial investment has been concentrated in electronics and transport machinery, where Japan's greatest advantages lie.

Supporting the strategy of forcing Japanese investment into Europe is the belief that local Japanese production will be less disruptive than import competition. The belief rests explicitly on four assumptions Europeans commonly make, all of which are plausible, but each of which may be seriously flawed. First is the premise that if Japanese firms are implanted in Europe, national governments and the European Commission can control, influence or instruct them to accomplish European ends. On matters of plant location or employment policy this may well be the case. But on matters of technology development and accessibility, it is much less certain. Indeed, since Japanese technology investment is skewed toward some countries—the United Kingdom and Germany, for example—at the expense of others—including Italy and France—differential effects on national competitiveness could provoke political conflicts among European governments, limiting their abilities to deal coherently with Japanese industry.

Second is the assumption that Japanese production in Europe will limit competitive employment losses, or even lead to increasing employment. For many purposes—wages and taxes among them—employment in a Japanese plant in Europe is likely to be as good as that in a European-owned plant. However, overall levels of high-paying employment may decline radically if Japanese firms introduce more efficient production organization and European industries are forced to restructure comparably.[11]

Third, European producers contend that if Japanese companies operated under European social rules and union arrangements, their vaunted production edge might be neutralized. Preliminary evidence on the Japanese experience in the United Kingdom, however, indicates that some Japanese firms are able to achieve productivity and quality rates well above those of local competitors, occasionally even matching performances achieved in Japan.[12]

The fourth, and perhaps most critical, assumption is that if local content rules and high tariffs on components and subsystems compel the sourcing of parts in Europe, then European producers will hold on to much of the value-added protection even if final assembly moves to Japanese hands. Unfortunately, the American experience suggests strongly that local suppliers will have considerable difficulty fitting into Japanese systems and, often, meeting Japanese standards. Indeed, according to Japan External Trade Organization (Jetro) surveys, almost 70 percent of Japanese firms operating in Europe are dissatisfied with local suppliers.[13] If the U.S. experience is indicative, Japanese assemblers will pull their preferred domestic suppliers into Europe after themselves, supplanting European ownership and control of the supply of critical production inputs.

This question of supply base control may well directly affect long-term economic development opportunities in Europe. The supply base issue is a question less of foreign dependence than of the consequences of a particular "architecture of supply"—that is, the structure of the markets through which component, materials, and equipment technologies reach European producers and users.[14] By the supply base of an economy, we mean the parts, component, subsystem, materials, and the production equipment available for new product and process development, as well as the structure of relations among the firms that supply and use these elements. One may think of the supply base as the infrastructure of any given firm: it is external to the firm but broadly supports its competitive position by helping to delimit the range of its possibilities in global markets, while providing collective gains (for example, technological spillovers) for the economy as a whole.[15] What Japanese dominance of high-volume high technology threatens is potential control over precisely this significant infrastructural supply base.

The supply base shapes the possibilities confronting users by enabling or deterring access to appropriate technologies in a timely fashion at a reasonable price. The architecture (or structure) of the supply base matters precisely to the extent it influences such technology access, timeliness and cost. Therein are contained European capacities to adjust to market shifts. Although many elements of necessary supply are available on global markets, the capacity of firms in a given region to adjust in a timely fashion appears to turn on the locally available knowledge and skills. Local customers are able to compel appropriate access, price, and quality far more directly than can remote customers. This is a particular problem wherever remote suppliers are serving local competitors of remote customers—just as Japanese suppliers are linked to the industrial families of the major Japanese auto and electronics firms that compete in Europe.

Thus, the open question is, will the entrance of Japanese suppliers add to the pool of local know-how by bringing new techniques and technologies that diffuse into the fabric of the European economy? Or will those suppliers control technology access, price, and quality to the advantage of their major Japanese customers? The answer is not deducible analytically. It turns partly on whether European policy forces Japanese firms to move leading-edge activities to Europe, partly on how tightly Japanese firms link their product and technology development in Japan to their European activities, and partly on whether competition forces Japanese firms to bring more value-added to Europe than their strategies would otherwise dictate. The stakes are highest in the advanced electronics segment of the European supply base, simultaneously Europe's weakness and Japan's perceived greatest strategic advantage. Creation of state-of-the-art electronics supply in Europe, even if under Japanese ownership, would benefit European users of electronics. Conversely, huge competitive leverage is also at stake. Consider Toshiba's announcement that one of its affiliated suppliers has developed new battery technology for portable applications: Toshiba's unwillingness to disclose the supplier or permit access to the technology is suggestive of the potential leverage at stake.

These future considerations aside, for the moment Europe's overall industrial position is strong, despite the years of supposed sclerosis. The strengths are in traditional and scale manufacturing, from textiles to chemicals, and in manufacturing equipment and materials. In these industries, European firms have been very effective, often at the forefront, in applying advanced technology. They have been less effective at maintaining a market position in the range of advanced electronic products from semiconductors to computers. The development of joint electronics research efforts—including Esprit, Race, and Prometheus—was a response to this perceived weakness. But will such programs be sufficient?

Fujitsu's takeover of ICL; the huge retrenchment at Philips; enormous problems at Thomson, Olivetti, and Bull—all these suggest that the European cooperative technology programs may fail to deliver on their promise. Among traditional suppliers, only Siemens and the telecommunications powers, notably Alcatel and Ericsson, appear to be in a truly defensible competitive position. The other European computer firms are dangerously close to imitating ICL—becoming so dependent on Japanese competitors for hardware technologies that they end up being little more than distributors of Japanese systems. The relative weakness of European producers calls into question whether European research and development programs can support a sustainable technological response to Japan. As Japanese producers become more deeply entrenched in Europe, it will be increasingly difficult to exclude them from the cooperative programs. The aims of those programs may well change as a consequence.

These challenges to and changes in the European technology programs are occurring just as an effort is getting under way to dismantle programs of state subsidy to domestic producers. The decision to compel the Istituto per la Ricostruzione Industriale (IRI) subsidiary Finmeccanica to reorder the books of the sale of Alfa Romeo to Fiat is one instance. National subsidy has often served as an alternative to formal trade restrictions. It is economically like a tariff, but it avoids redirecting trade relations

oward retaliatory protection. Will formal bilateral restrictions
n trade be more likely in the absence of domestic subsidy? We
uspect so.

Finally, there is the question of how to counter activist Japa-
ese policies, and sometimes predatory business practices, when
hey affect competition in Europe. As the United States has
lone, Europe is responding to Japanese entry with concerns
bout both Japanese government support to help create advan-
age in global markets and domestic Japanese restrictions on
narket access, technology access, and inward investment. Politi-
ians as divided on other matters as Michel Rocard and Margaret
Thatcher have argued powerfully that only one thing can hold
)ack pressures for European trade retaliation: Japan's restraint
n its use of policy and pricing to create advantage and an
icceleration in opening domestic Japanese market opportunities
n trade, technology, and investment. Strict reciprocity would
seem to be the only viable policy. European opportunities—and
lemonstrated successes—in Japanese markets will, in the end,
nfluence Europe's stance vis-à-vis Japanese entry into Europe.

EUROPE AS ONE REGION AMONG OTHERS

While increasing direct investment by Japanese companies into
Europe will heighten interdependence, Europe's responsive
choices examined above—and Japan's in turn—could have the
opposite effect of helping to fragment the developed economies
into a set of regional trading groups. In our view, a multipolar
economic system with three separable but interconnected regions is emerging and could eventually produce a multipolar
security system. Each region has the political capacity and techni-
cal-industrial foundations for independent action. The question
is how the regions will relate to each other.

This is not to deny that firms in the advanced industrial
countries are increasingly global. Products, companies, and investments from each of the major industrial regions are present
in almost every market on earth. Imports of raw materials,
resources, manufactured goods, and even services from developing countries, in turn, penetrate the advanced countries. At

the same time, despite globalization, national policies and national markets continue to exhibit substantial differences; national—and regional—variations continue to matter. Indeed, place may matter more than ever.

We need a clear definition of the new code word *global*, to distinguish it from the earlier code words *international* and *multinational*. International firms sold abroad; multinational corporations produce abroad.[16] The British era of industrial pre-eminence was one of trade and fostered international firms. The American era was one of the multinational corporation, with firms that produced abroad in a variety of locations.[17] In both cases, a single preeminent power projected its advantage. To-day's cynic might observe that the newest era of globalization may merely be a euphemism for Japanese industrial domination. At this point, however, globalization implies multiple *geographic* sources of distinct production approaches and skills (for exam-ple, flexible automation from Japan, flexible specialization from Italy and Germany). Globalization means not only greater mar-ket volatility but also no clear leader or target. As each locale, nation, or region builds its response, variety will be reinforced.[18]

Indeed, the emphasis of both policymaking and certain market dynamics appears to be shifting to the regional level. Three roughly coequal and distinct, though interconnected, regional economies are emerging: a European region, centered on the European Community; an Asian region, centered on Japan; and a North American region, centered on the United States. The United States/Canada and western Europe each represent about 25 percent of global gross domestic product (GDP). In 1987, Japan represented 12 percent and Japan plus the Asian NICs represented 16 percent.[19] Because growth rates are substantially faster in Japan and the Asian region than in the United States or Europe, the importance of this region will expand. In addition, interregional trade is a quite limited part of GDP. Moreover, intraregional trade is steadily growing—that is, trade within each region is increasing at a faster rate than extra-regional trade in both Europe and Asia.

Consider first the Asian region, where strong market forces for regional economic integration exist, centering on Japan.[20] By almost any significant measure, Japan, rather than the United States, is the dominant economic player in Asia. Japan is the region's technology leader, its primary supplier of capital goods, its dominant exporter, its largest annual foreign direct investor and foreign aid supplier, and an increasingly vital market for imports (though the United States remains the largest single import market for Asian manufactures). Japan's own economy is decreasingly dependent on other world markets for growth. Japan's export dependency dropped from a high point of 14 percent of GNP to 10 percent in 1990, thereby reverting to its historical form of domestic demand-led growth.[21] Nevertheless, Japan's trade with Asia in 1989 surpassed its trade with the United States, more than doubling since 1982 to over $126 billion.[22]

Trade within Asia has grown faster than trade between Asia and other regions since 1985.[23] By 1988, trade within the Pacific Basin had risen to 66 percent of the region's total trade, from 54 percent only eight years earlier.[24] The major source of imports for each Asian economy is usually another Asian economy, most often Japan. In the late 1980s, for example, Japan supplied, on average, 25 percent of the NICs' imports (as against the 16–17 percent the United States supplied). Japan, in fact, supplied well over 50 percent of Korea's and Taiwan's total imports of technology products in the late 1980s, more than double the U.S. share. In turn, Japan's imports of manufactured goods as a proportion of total imports grew from 26 percent to 48 percent between 1979 and 1988, with other Asian countries becoming the fastest growing source of that expansion. Indeed, the NICs alone increased their share of Japan's imports of technology products from 14 percent to 19 percent between 1985 and 1989. Over that time frame, increased intra-Asian trade permitted the NICs to reduce their dependence on the U.S. market, and U.S.-bound exports fell from one-half to one-third of their total exports. The move offshore to other Asian countries by Japanese multinationals and smaller suppliers faced with an appreciating yen and protectionist measures partly explains the growth in intra-Asian trade.[25] Whether these trends will continue, with Japan becom-

ing as vital a market as the United States for high-value manufactures from the East Asian NICs, remains to be seen.

Financial ties further reinforce intra-Asian trade trends. By
1990, Japanese industry was investing about twice as much in
Asia as was American industry. From 1984 to 1989, the level of
direct Japanese investment in Asia equaled that of the previous
33 years, thus doubling the cumulative total. Japanese investment grew by about 50 percent annually in the Asian NICs, and
by about 100 percent annually in the Association of Southeast
Asian Nations (ASEAN). Perhaps even more telling in several
emerging Asian economies, cumulative NIC direct investment in
the second half of the 1980s surpassed the cumulative U.S. total
(by as much as five times in Malaysia[26]). Moreover, the use in Asia
of the yen as a reserve currency is expanding sharply.[27] The
result of such trade and investment trends is a network of component and production companies that makes Asia an enor-
mously attractive production location.

That regional production network appears to be very hier-
archically structured and dominated by Japan: Japanese technology lies at the heart of an increasingly complementary
relationship between Japan and its major Asian trading partners. Japanese companies supply technology-intensive components, subsystems, parts, materials, and capital equipment to
their affiliates, subcontractors and independent producers in
other Asian countries; the products ultimately assembled are
sold via export in third-country markets (primarily in the United
States and Asia). Conversely, nonaffiliated labor-intensive manufactures, and affiliated low-techology parts and components,
flow back into Japan from other Asian producers. Summarizing
these trends, the Ministry of International Trade and Industry
noted in 1987 the "growing tendency for Japanese industry,
especially the electrical machinery industry, to view the Pacific
region as a single market from which to pursue a global corporate strategy."[28]

As noted above, Japanese companies seem to be pursuing
that strategy with a vengeance. In automaking and electronics,
the strategy appears to have two key elements. One is to spread
subsystems' assembly throughout Asia, while persuading local

governments to treat subsystems originating in other Asian countries as being of domestic origin. The second is to keep tight control over the underlying component, machinery, and materials technologies by regulating their availability to independent Asian producers and keeping advanced production at home. The two elements together deter independent producers' too rapid catch-up to the competitive level of leading Japanese producers, while simultaneously developing Asia as a production base for Japanese exports to the United States and Europe to avoid bilateral trade frictions.

Increased intraregionalism in Asia may, of course, have limits. For example, Japan may not be willing to absorb continuing increases in levels of manufactured imports from other Asian economies. Japanese analysts already claim that the domestic market for labor-intensive imports is saturated.[29] Despite a competitive edge in some areas, Taiwanese and South Korean producers have not been able to establish an enduring position in the Japanese market.[30] Nevertheless, intraregional trade and financial ties continue to grow in significance in the area of the world that is expanding the fastest.

The importance of intra-European trade has also been steadily increasing. Trade within the EC has grown faster than trade between the EC and other regions since the establishment of the European Community in 1958.[31] From 1967 to 1987, the ratio of EC-EC exports to EC–non-EC exports rose from 79:1 to 115:1.[32] The ratio for each major country rose, most dramatically for Britain, where the ratio went from 39:1 to 79:1. Add in trade between the European Free Trade Association (EFTA) and the EC, and the picture of regional integrity is even clearer. Since 1967, intra-European trade, including both EC and EFTA countries, has increased substantially, as measured by both imports and exports. Intra-European (EFTA and EC) trade typically outweighs extra-European trade by 3 to 2, up from 1 to 1 a decade ago.[33] Discounting intra-European trade, Europe's share of world exports and imports drops: exports declined from 45 percent to 14 percent and imports from 43 percent to 11 percent.[34] These trends are likely to continue with the creation of the Single Market and the adherence of the EFTA countries to it, whether they formally join or not. As in Asia, financial ties now reinforce regional trade ties. The European currencies are increasingly bound to each other through the formal mechanism of the European Monetary System (EMS) and the predominance of the deutsche mark. The EMS pushes toward regional integrity by increasing the stability of each national currency. Progress is also being made toward formal coordination of fiscal and monetary policy, which could eventually culminate in a European central bank.

One should not underestimate Europe's regional capacities and fundamental strengths. They rest in an educated and highly skilled workforce, a sound foundation in science, and the enormous wealth built up through a long and successful industrialization. European industry has been much more successful than its U.S. counterparts in remaining competitive in traditional industries, production equipment and materials. It has added new strengths to this older foundation, including the successful application of advanced technology to existing industries, a capacity for systems development and integration, and the use of political will to retain final product markets in the face of foreign production or product advantage.

Now, as argued above, Europe is confronting the most obvious weaknesses of the postwar years. The subsidies flowing into electronics and information technology from national governments and the EC itself are enormous—ECU 3–4 billion just for semiconductors. Some of the programs, such as those in telecommunications, are likely to succeed; others, as discussed earlier, may fail to provide a viable response to foreign competition. But through a variety of mechanisms, ranging from subsidy to management of direct investment, the Europeans are attempting to maintain existing capacities and to rebuild others where weak. If the Japanese (or American) role in that effort does not seem to be constructive and to be offering reciprocal opportunities in Asia (or the United States), Europe retains the wealth and political will to develop autonomously.

In essence, then, both Europe and Japan are seeking and increasingly establishing an independent technological and industrial base. They are attempting to assure through domestic action the basis of regional autonomy. The conviction is widespread in Japan that it will be the dominant technological power by the end of the century. Indeed, some Japanese believe that the transition has already happened.[35] In any case, purposive political strategies of economic and industrial development remain central to Japan's surge to economic power. In parallel, European national governments, the European Community, and individual companies are increasingly investing resources required to overcome European weaknesses and play to its strengths. For them, 1992 is as much a vision as a program, a vision of Europe's place in the world. As a senior executive of Fiat declared, "The final goal of the European dream is to transform Europe into an integrated economic continent with its specific role, weight, and responsibility in the international scenario vis-à-vis the U.S. and Japan."[36] That dream is already producing a new awareness of European strengths and a seemingly sudden assertion of the will to exploit those strengths in competition with the United States and Japan.

Japan, with political capacity, has created economic resources. Europe, with extensive underlying economic resources, is creating the political capacity to exploit them. Each region is acting in the economic and industrial arena as powers traditionally act in the security arena. Each is maintaining capacity for independent action, minimizing dependence and perceived vulnerability in terms of economic development and security. At the moment, Europe and Japan are regional economic powers that have the technological and industrial capacity to put a strategic military machine in place. While the machine does not now exist, conflict—or simply diverging long-term geopolitical interests—between the United States and Europe or Japan could provoke its creation. So could European-Japanese collaboration on commercial technology development that was perceived to provide powerful new weapons potential when applied to defense needs.

Thus, we move from the economy to security. One should not discount changes in the security realm as a result of economic regionalism, if only because, in the post–Cold War world, confusion and complexity will prevail, and the nature of threat will be ambiguous and shifting. The circumstances that would spark a reformulation of Japanese or European security policy are diverse and could become compelling. In essence, Japanese economic success and Asian regionalism force Europe's hand in the security realm, as well as economically. Will Europe opt for greater international integration or greater regional autonomy?

Europe's commitment to international integration, like its concern with open markets, should not be underestimated even as European integration proceeds. Neither, however, should it be overstated. In a world of autonomous regions, Europe would have significant advantages—not least collective wealth, size, education, and political will. Mustering those assets to produce greater autonomy is, in the end, the very heart of the European project. Europe's responses to Japanese competition, especially the moves to compel Japanese investment in Europe, are simultaneously internationalist and regionalist moves—international because outsiders are invited in, regionalist because the significant economic activities must occur locally among foreign producers who act, and eventually become, European. Precariously balanced for now, Europe could be tipped in either direction, toward greater international integration or greater autonomy, depending upon how the Eurofication of Japanese business proceeds and how the resulting conflicts are managed. Europe's choices will thus profoundly influence Japan even as Japanese economic success continues to shape the path of European integration.

NOTES

1. Wayne Sandholtz and John Zysman, "Recasting the European Bargain," *World Politics*, Vol. XLII, No. 1, October 1989, pp. 95–128.
2. See, for example, Charles Maier, "The Politics of Productivity: Foundations of American International Economic Policy after World War II," in *Between Power and Plenty*, Peter Katzenstein, ed. (Madison, Wisc.: Madison University Press, 1977).
3. Private communications.
4. These data are from an excellent account of Japan's European investment: Stefano Micossi and Gianfranco Viesti, "Japanese Direct Manufacturing Investment in Europe," in L. A. Winters and A. Venables, eds., *The Effects of 1992 on Trade and Industry* (forthcoming, 1991).
5. James Womack et al., *The Machine that Changed the World* (New York: Rawson Associates, 1990), is a seminal work on the notion of lean produc-

tion. The authors attribute the phrase to one of their colleagues, John Krafcik. See also Benjamin Coriat, *L'atelier et le robot* (Paris: Christian Bourgeois Editeur, 1990); and Stephen Cohen and John Zysman, *Manufacturing Matters* (New York: Basic Books, 1987).

6. See Michael Borrus, *Competing for Control: America's Stake in Microelectronics* (Cambridge, Mass.: Ballinger, 1988).

7. Such products contain, for example, a wealth of silicon chip technology, ranging from memory and microprocessors to charge-coupled devices, and have been a principal factor behind the drive for Japanese semiconductor dominance. During the 80s, emerging high-volume digital products have grown from 5 percent to over 45 percent of Japanese electronics production, accounting for virtually all of the growth in domestic Japanese consumption of Integrated Circuits. With this segment continuing to expand at 22–24 percent annually, more than twice the approximate 10 percent annual average growth rate of the electronics industry as a whole, high-volume electronics will constitute an ever larger part of the electronics industry of the next century. See Dataquest Incorporated and Quick, Finan and Associates, *The Drive for Dominance: Strategic Options for Japan's Semiconductor Industry* (San Jose, Calif.: Dataquest, 1988), pp.4–7, citing Electronics Industry Association of Japan data.

8. For those who doubt this, note the October 1990 issue of *Car and Driver*, which rates the four leading sedans at any price. The Lexus 400 at roughly half the price of its German competition was third on the list, ahead of the Bentley, which was four times the price.

9. Unless otherwise specified, these and the following data are from Micossi and Viesti, "Japanese Direct Manufacturing Investment."

10. See Stephen Thomsen and Phedon Nicolaides, "The Evolution of Japanese Direct Investment in Europe: Death of a Transistor Salesman" (Draft, Royal Institute of International Affairs, 1990).

11. We note that Edward Graham and Paul Krugman predict negligible total employment effects from Japanese investments in the United States because the supply of labor determines employment levels. However, their argument does not speak to the compositional changes in employment (e.g., more in services, less in manufacturing) resulting from adjustment, as well as the costs of adjustment, which may be significant and could have the effects we suggest. See Edward Graham and Paul Krugman, *Foreign Direct Investment in the United States* (Washington,D.C.: Institute for International Economics, 1989).

12. See, for example, Nick Oliver and Barry Wilkinson, *The Japanization of British Industry* (London: Basil Blackwell, 1988).

13. Cited in Micossi and Viesti, "Japanese Direct Manufacturing Investment," p. 21.

14. We have drawn this notion of the supply base from a forthcoming work of Michael Borrus, from which we derive the definition and concerns set out here. For a very brief preliminary statement, see Michael Borrus, "Chips of State," *Issues in Science and Technology,* Fall 1990, pp. 40–48.

15. The economics of infrastructure is quite underdeveloped. In general, infrastructure is defined as being outside any individual firm, ubiquitously available, and indivisible, and as generating broad externalities (social

gains that are not fully capturable by private firms). On this definition, our supply base notion (especially given technological spillovers in advanced sectors, like electronics) qualifies as an infrastructure, with the caveat that the question remains of precisely how nationally "indivisible" it is. This is, of course, precisely the issue we examine in the text.

16. This is the basic definition that emerged from Raymond Vernon's project on the multinational corporation. See Raymond Vernon, *Sovereignty at Bay: The Multinational Spread of U.S. Enterprises* (New York: Basic Books, 1971).

17. Robert Gilpin, *U.S. Power and the Multinational Corporation: the Political Economy of Foreign Direct Investment* (New York: Basic Books, 1975).

18. Stephen Cohen and Benjamin Coriat developed this distinction, which they elaborated in "Globalization and Production" (paper prepared for Berkeley Roundtable on the International Economy (BRIE) Conference on Manufacturing and Production, held April 14–16, 1991).

19. Bureau d'Information et Prévision Economique, *Europe in 1992* (Paris, 1987).

20. The following data and arguments are from Michael Borrus and John Zysman, "The Highest Stakes," in Sandholtz et al., ed., *The Highest Stakes: Technology, Economy and Security* (New York: Oxford University Press, forthcoming 1991.) Particularly useful among those sources is Yung Chul Park and Won Am Park, "Changing Japanese Trade Patterns and the East Asian NICs" (paper prepared for the National Bureau of Economic Research (NBER), Conference on U.S. and Japan Trade and Investment held in Cambridge, Mass., October 19–20, 1989.

21. These figures are from a presentation by Kazuo Nukazawa, managing director of the Keidanren, at Chatham House, Royal Institute of International Affairs, London, July 27, 1990.

22. "The Rising Tide: Japan in Asia," *Japan Economic Journal*, Special Supplement, p. 4.

23. See also Takashi Inoguchi, "Shaping and Sharing Pacific Dynamism," in *Annals of the American Academy of Political and Social Science*, Vol. 505, September 1989, pp. 46–55.

24. Data calculated from various sources by Lawrence Krause, in "Pacific Economic Regionalism and the United States" (paper prepared for the symposium on *Impact of Recent Economic Developments on U.S.–Korea Relations and the Pacific Basin*, University of California at San Diego, November 9–10, 1990).

25. Park and Park, "Changing Japanese Trade Patterns."

26. Malaysian Industrial Development Authority.

27. These figures are from a presentation by Nicholas Colcester, financial editor of *The Economist*, at Chatham House, the Royal Institute of International Affairs, London, July 27, 1990.

28. Ministry for International Trade and Investment (MITI), *1987 White Paper on International Trade and Investment* (Tokyo, 1987), as cited in Japan Economic Institute, "Economic Regionalism: An Emerging Challenge to the International System," *JEI Report*, June 29, 1990.

29. Daiwa Securities, cited in Park and Park, "Changing Japanese Trade Patterns."

30. Yung Chul Park and Won am Park in *Far Eastern Economic Review*, Vol. 8 June 1989.
31. These figures seem to be quite different from those in Michael C. Webb and Stephen D. Krasner, "Hegemonic Stability Theory: An Empirical Assessment," *Review of International Studies*, vol. 15, no. 2 (1989). It is unclear to us how the authors calculated their figures, which appear to be significantly mistaken and which therefore support a conventional interpretation of regional economy.
32. Economie Prospetive, International Revue du CEPII, Numero Special Europe la Documentation Francaise, 43m3 trimestre 1989, "Les Trois Europe."
33. Calculations done at BRIE.
34. CEPII, op cit.
35. Shintaro Ishihara, *The Japan That Can Say "No": The New U.S.–Japan Relations Card* (New York: Simon & Schuster, 1991). Originally released as Shintaro Ishihara and Akio Morita, "The Japan that Can Say 'No': The New U.S.–Japan Relations Card," translation by the U.S. Department of Defense. With less controversy and greater technical accuracy, journalists, industrialists, and government officials have expressed similar views.
36. Personal communications to the author.

7

BALANCE, CONCERT, ANARCHY, OR NONE OF THE ABOVE

Stanley Hoffmann

The evolution of a reunified but highly heterogeneous Europe, and of its relations with the two great powers that had divided and dominated it, continues to baffle commentators. The year of euphoria is over. The era of confusion and complexity is not. This essay attempts to examine, first, some general issues in the theoretical debate that has been raging for over a year; second, recent events and puzzles; third, the future of the European Community (EC) and of its relations with the countries of east central Europe—especially Czechoslovakia, Poland, and Hungary; finally, European-American relations, that hardy perennial. My main point is that Europe, thanks to a combination of democratic regimes, diffuse threats, and extensive institutionalization, may be on the threshold of a new kind of politics that goes beyond such traditional categories as balancing alliances or alignments, loose cooperative concerts, or junglelike anarchy. Whether Europe will cross this threshold, by extending and deepening its institutionalization, depends on the chief actors inside and outside the continent, but ultimately on the United States and Germany above all.

ISSUES IN THE DEBATE

The theoretical debate that has pitted John Mearsheimer's stark neorealist analysis[1] against his multiple critics has had one merit: it has exposed, in a concrete case, the sterility of neorealism. Mearsheimer's gloomy view of a Europe of states returning to its troublesome past results not from any empirical evaluation of present-day Europe, but from a theory—that of Kenneth

194

Waltz—combining two sets of dogmas. One (the "structural" approach) views international politics as a condition of anarchy in which the distribution of military power in an endless contest for survival and security to a large extent dictates the moves of states. The other contrasts the notion of bipolar stability with the instability of multipolar systems (and describes the new Europe as part of an emerging multipolar system).

This second idea is debatable for several quite different reasons. It is not clear at all that the ideal types of multipolarity and bipolarity fit the current international system, with its different hierarchies of states, depending on the functional domain and the kind of power required in each. Nor is it clear that the end of the Cold War—that is, of highly conflictual bipolarity in the strategic realm—and the acute crisis of one of the superpowers mean the end of the military preponderance of the United States and the USSR. Moreover, even if one characterized the present condition of Europe and of the world as strictly multipolar, one would have to point out, with Stephen van Evera,[2] that multipolarity, in history, has ranged from very unstable to moderate; furthermore, as Raymond Aron showed many years ago,[3] the bipolar system that led to the Peloponnesian War was hardly stable. It is, indeed, impossible to understand the nature of an international system without looking at the character of the leading states. By refusing to do so in order to produce a more economical theory, Waltz and his disciples have not only failed to achieve greater rigor, but produced exactly what they charge their critics with: reductionism. Structure matters, of course. It limits, restrains, and creates both risks and opportunities for the policies of rational actors. But the key questions are: How much does structure matter, and what *is* structure?

Critics of Mearsheimer have, at times exhaustingly, shown how today's Europe and, particularly, Germany differ from the Europe and Germany of 1913 or 1938.[4] I will not do so once more here, but three points, important for both theory and empirical research, deserve emphasis. They all concern the conceptual poverty of neorealism.

First, neorealism's core concepts are misleading. It starts with the notion of anarchy as the key feature of the international political system. But if anarchy means only the absence of central power above the states, it tells us nothing of interest about the countless forms the game of international politics may take (depending, for instance, on who the actors are). If anarchy is supposed to mean a permanent struggle for power, a zero-sum game, the "state of war," then it accurately describes *some* international systems, but not others. (I once referred to two great theoretical and historical types: "state of war" and "troubled peace"; we may, in Europe, witness the birth of a third type altogether.)

The international system of neorealism is a system of states: self-propelled billiard balls endlessly attempting to knock one another out of the field of battle. The world system of today is—if I may refer to myself once more[5]—a complex game played at three levels: a world economy that creates its own rewards and punishments, and provides both opportunities and constraints for the players (not all of whom are states); the states themselves; and, increasingly, the peoples, who intervene insofar as they are unhappy with the effects, inequities, and inefficiencies of the world market, or with the inadequacy of established borders, or with the nature of their governments.

A concept of structure that focuses on the distribution of military power is doubly at fault. On the one hand, it obscures the fact that states, today, do not play only the traditional strategic-diplomatic game—in which such power is indeed either essential for survival and security or important as the gold reserve behind the paper currency of "soft power" used for influencing others, to borrow Joseph Nye's excellent concept.[6] States also play the modern games of economic interdependence. These require very different *kinds* of power, and place sharp limits on the *uses* to which such power can be put. On the other hand, in the traditional arena, the salience of military power depends on the nature of the threats to survival and security. Neorealism (like the cruder versions of realism) posits a kind of existential threat, built into the condition of statehood-in-anarchy. To be sure, theoretically, any independent actor can at any moment be threatened by a neighbor, rival, or partner. In real life, it makes a difference whether one is in, say, the Europe of rival alliances of

1914 and 1939, or the Europe of today, where threats are diffuse, often hard to identify, and not all manageable through
armed might.

In the parched landscape of neorealism, states cope with
their security dilemma by balancing power (rather than "bandwagoning"), so as to thwart the designs for domination great
powers recurrently concoct. Three things are wrong here.
One—which Stephen Walt discovered[7]—is that states often balance against perceived threats, rather than against objectively
greater power. Also, the repertory of anti-imperial or anti-
hegemonic moves, especially in multipolar systems, has often
included bandwagoning coalitions around the status quo power,
aimed at isolating the would-be hegemon, and at confronting
him with overwhelming power should he attack. Finally, the
present-day repertory in Europe contains original creations un-
heard of in neorealist circles. The EC could be seen as a shrewd
attempt—an invention of the wily French in 1950 (after the
failure of a "traditional" hostile approach to the solution of the
"German problem")—to "balance" German power not by building a coalition *against* Germany but by bandwagoning *with* Germany. With respect to Soviet power, the Conference on Security
and Cooperation in Europe (CSCE) is only one of the many ways
in which, since 1970, western powers have tried to tame the
threat from Moscow, not merely by military balancing, but by
tying up the Soviet Union in a tangle of agreements that it would
not be in Moscow's interest to break. This is, obviously, not classic
balancing, and it goes way beyond the ill-defined European
Concert of the nineteenth century.

Secondly, the refusal to consider what goes on within states
is perhaps the most serious flaw of neorealism. Because independent states are all in the same situation of anarchy, Waltz has
dismissed as secondary the differences which the nature of the
political regime, the character of the domestic economy, and the
specific features of the relations between state and society may
make for foreign policy. Yet, international politics is the interplay
between the constraints and temptations "structure" provides
and the ambitions or needs of the actors. Often, purely domestic
factors— interests, ideologies, coalitions, and so on—shape these

ambitions and needs, and they can, if the actor is powerful enough, reshape the system itself. This is why the critics of Mearsheimer have underlined the differences between the second and third German Reichs, on the one hand, and the Federal Republic, on the other. Just because Germany remains in the middle of Europe, and is again more powerful (but *not* in all dimensions) than its neighbors, is there really no difference between the revisionist imperial Germany in clumsy search of a world role, the rabid revolutionary Germany of Hitler, and the satisfied, cooperative and world-shy new united republic?

My third point also refers to a glaring gap in neorealism. Just as neorealism downplays the effects of economic interdependence, especially among industrial societies and welfare states, it tends to dismiss the significance of institutional links among them. To be sure, actors continue to be deeply concerned with *national* security and the satisfaction of *national* economic and social goals. Especially in the realm of security, they may remain less concerned with joint gains than with ways of limiting the gains of rivals.[8] But the important fact in present-day Europe is the role of a bewildering array of overlapping institutions, within and through which states seek altogether joint benefits, the balancing of partners who are also potential adversaries, national advantage (by forming institutions in which they have the greatest freedom of maneuver or influence over those which others are better able to manipulate),[9] and a variety of insurance and reassurance policies. One can distinguish at least three important roles these institutions play.

First, within the EC, the density of institutionalized links and the structure of governance have blurred the distinction between domestic and foreign policy and between national sovereignty and federal (or community) powers. At the national level, while elected governments must continue to think first about internal priorities and the satisfaction of domestic interests, the gigantic mesh of the Community limits the extent to which the members can act autonomously and get away with it. Such attempts boomerang, as François Mitterrand's France discovered in 1982–1983, and Great Britain found repeatedly in the 1970s and 1980s. In other words, at that level, the existence of

"Brussels" cannot help affecting the way in which governments (if not the Bundesbank) define the national interest and select the instruments and procedures for achieving their goals. At the level of "Brussels," there occurs what lawyers would call a *dédoublement fonctionnel:* the representatives and agents of states, in pooling state sovereignties for joint rules and directives, also behave as (incipient) European statesmen, while the "independent" members and civil servants of the Commission remain marked by their national origins and need to take national realities into account.

Second, in the realm of security, but also in economic affairs, institutions (such as the CSCE, the North Atlantic Treaty Organization [NATO], and the Western European Union [WEU]) and agreements (such as those that link associated states to the EC, and countries of the European Free Trade Association [EFTA] to the Community) reassure their members or signatories against fears that could, if left untended, turn a generally cooperative Europe into, once more, a continent of mutual suspicions and antagonistic precautions. The associates of the EC, left out of its decision-making process but affected by Community regulations and policies, thus, in a sense, receive compensation for being left out. And the various security organizations together reassure the Europeans about the continuing concern of the United States for their fate; reassure the Soviets about the peaceful designs of their neighbors; and reassure the Americans both about the ability and willingness of their European partners to play a major role in their own defense, and about the willingness of the Soviets to provide a fair amount of transparency, as well as to respect the agreements signed in the 1970s and 1980s. Thus, institutions can be life preservers that either save one from drowning or save one from having to drown others to survive. Even in the tragic case of Yugoslavia, the EC has—so far—played a moderating role.

Finally, even when these institutions do not play the roles described above, they can serve as magnets (or should one say: salutary mirages). The east central European states' hopes of becoming EC or NATO members, or of being somehow associated with such institutions is, for the time being, functioning as a substitute for the real thing. So are diplomatic exercises like the Pentagonale, and the negotiation of association agreements between the EC and Poland, Hungary and Czechoslovakia; so is a genuine but undernourished institution like the European Bank for Reconstruction and Development. To be sure, mirages do not last forever, and if the hopes should fade, the consequences might be grim. But precisely because the obstacles to full membership in the most significant and effective institutions are high, and the habits of cooperation among east central European states are weak, it is essential that some institutions serve as magnets, and others as first down payments.

A NEW DECADE, A NEW EUROPE

To discuss both the internal problems of Europe and the relations of Europe with the United States, one has to begin with some remarks about what happened in the year since the settlement of the "German question."

The year was one of rude awakenings. The cost of the rehabilitation of former East Germany and the dimensions of the collapse of its economy have far exceeded the expectations of political leaders—and serve as a warning of what would happen if the barriers that separate the EC from the east central European states were suddenly to disappear. In these states, economic reform has been painful: The privatization of state-owned assets has raised innumerable difficulties. Furthermore the economic turmoil of the Soviet Union, on the one hand, and the noncompetitiveness of these countries' industrial goods in the West and the agricultural protectionism of the EC on the other, block export-led growth. As happened in western Europe after the end of World War II, the political coalitions that had formed for the restoration of democracy have begun to split. Yugoslavia has erupted into civil war. The crisis in the Persian Gulf divided the Community and dampened "Europhoria" in the EC; it showed that the old barrier between economic integration and diplomatic-strategic unity is as high as ever. The sudden turn of Gorbachev to the right was another nail in the coffin of utopia.

Yet, one ought to note also that several black dogs failed to bark. Those who feared the East would hold a fatal attraction for the new Germany, pulling it away from its western moorings (largely because of the way in which Chancellor Helmut Kohl bargained all by himself with Gorbachev) have been wrong; what one has witnessed instead is the *Drang nach Westen* of the east central Europeans. German-Polish relations, which Kohl's tactics about the border issue had strained, are on the mend. Despite endless collisions and some violence, and amid general confusion, the USSR has not disintegrated, and survived a major, dangerous, and desperate attempt to restore the old order of the hard-liners. The United States, while drawing on its forces in Europe for the war in the Gulf, has not shown any sign of withdrawing militarily from Europe.

The main uncertainties for the near future result from the difficulties the three main actors in this play have experienced. The Soviet Union, whose moves have, in the past, triggered the solidarity of the United States and of western Europe—a solidarity that made possible not only the containment of the old Soviet threat, but the liquidation of the Cold War on western terms—and, in the late 1980s, led to the reunification of Europe, is obviously going through a particularly stormy phase. In 1989 and much of 1990, a common hypothesis in the United States and in Europe was the gradual integration of the Soviet Union (engaged in a process of economic and political liberalization) into the world economy, into the system of world order the West preferred, and especially into the "common European home." This—as was confirmed by the "G7 + one" London Summit—is still the common goal. But the worsening internal turbulence, the resignation of Foreign Minister Eduard Shevardnadze and the signs of a hardening as well as of a growing influence of the military, have raised unexpected problems. For even if the USSR is in no condition to cause a "clear and present danger," to pose a new military threat in Europe, the fact that it still has troops in eastern Europe (and in former East Germany), and that eastern Europe still constitutes a kind of security no-man's-land, means that a switch from a policy of deliberate cooperation and concessions to a far more suspicious and demanding one could have serious repercussions in a variety of fields. Americans and Europeans have therefore to think about not one, but two unpleasant and unfathomable contingencies—not only the effects abroad of a possible internal disintegration of the last remaining (but only nuclear) multinational empire, but also those of a shift from accommodation to obstruction. Fortunately, the failure of the attempted coup of August 19 makes the latter danger far less likely.

The second main actor is Germany, about which highly contradictory fears have been expressed. Will the new independent Germany try to reduce the burdens and constraints imposed upon the Federal Republic by the EC and NATO and behave more like a national state again—à la Britain or France—or will it now dominate these institutions, thanks to its economic and financial might in one case, its geographic position and the shrinking of the American presence in the other? Would Germany, thanks to its surplus capital, fill the economic vacuum and increase its political influence in east central Europe, or would it become excessively self-absorbed and burdened by the costs of East Germany's absorption, thus stop being the financial engine of the Community, continue to shy away from any *Weltpolitik*, and devote all its energies and available funds to the East German disaster? Equally important are the following questions: Will Germany use a fraction of its economic and financial power not only—as planned—to get the Soviets out of its territory, but also to affect events within the USSR? Will Germany agree both to devote some of this power to the rehabilitation of east central Europe and to do so not as a purely national actor, but as a participant in a Community policy? Will Germany agree to play a larger role outside Europe—even if its allergy to a *military* role continues, after so many years of attempts at repudiating a militaristic past, with the warm endorsement of all its partners!—or will its reluctance to do so doom any attempt at an effective and comprehensive common diplomacy for western Europe? An active Community policy outside the continent may become even more necessary because of what could happen to the third major actor—the United States.

Despite (or perhaps because of) its military triumph in the Gulf, will America's activism abroad remain as great as it was in the past? Much will depend on the still unsettled aftermath of that victory in the Middle East itself. If the prestige of the United States in the area does not suffice to move the Arab-Israeli conflict toward its resolution, if Saddam Hussein succeeds in consolidating his grip on power, external frustration will strengthen the arguments of those who—either because they think the United States is in relative decline or because they want to *prevent* it from declining—believe that America must give priority to its vast domestic problems and concentrate on the weakened underpinnings of U.S. power in the world. During the Gulf war, Americans showed a classic ambivalence between their determination to set the goals and means all by themselves, and their desire to get as wide a participation by others as possible. What was new was not the desire for collective legitimation, but the actual financial dependence on allied contributions, as also the wide preference, which the polls reflected, for what the hero of *A Clockwork Orange* called a "quick in-out": liberating Kuwait, punishing Saddam—and coming home as fast as possible. The decision to leave the rehabilitation of east central Europe largely to the western Europeans and to refrain from large-scale economic aid to the USSR, and the plans for a drastic reduction of American forces in NATO, had already signaled not a retreat into isolationism, but a curtailment in the scope of activism. And yet diplomatic activism remains high.

THE FEATURES OF THE NEW EUROPE

If we turn now to an analysis of what might be called the European condition, we could define it as characterized by one ambiguity and two cleavages.

The ambiguity, which has provoked almost as much theoretical speculation as the end of the Cold War and the return to multipolarity, lies in the nature of the European Community. After the old, quasi-theological debates (normative and theoretical) between supranationalists and champions of a "Europe of states," between functional federalists relying on the spillover effects of sectoral imbalances and traditionalists stressing the decisive role of interstate bargains, we now have a debate about the respective strength of the member-states and of the Community. Is the latter an emerging federation, with the old nation-states reduced to such domains as culture; atavistic political issues left over from the era of separate paths in the development of the modern state; and what William Wallace[10] calls the ability to shape the balance of national advantages within Europe and on global markets through education and social policy, training programs, research and development expenditures, partnerships with banks and firms, and direct taxation? This would obviously not be an insignificant residue: yet, it would mean that sovereignty would have been either transferred to the European level or pooled in areas as important as monetary policy, interest rates, trade, the movement of goods, people and capital, immigration, agriculture, public procurement. In other words, state autonomy and (insofar as deregulation prevails over the harmonization of existing regulations or the invention of new ones) state scope would have been sharply cut back in behalf of efficiency.[11] On the other hand, one can argue that the reinforcement of the nation-state and that of the Community continue to go together[12]—insofar as the policies and resources of the Community buttress the modern welfare state, redress regional imbalances in countries such as Italy and England, and help modernize the poorer members and provide an income to farmers (at the cost of vast surpluses); insofar as effectiveness, obtainable only at the "federal" level, is essential for the legitimacy of the national regimes; and insofar as no transfer of loyalty and allegiance from the nation-state to the Community has occurred.

Paradoxically enough, both arguments are correct. Both acknowledge the partial surrender of sovereignty. True, one chooses to stress the "federalizing process," the silent yet essential role of the European Court of Justice acting as if the Treaty of Rome were the equivalent of the Constitution of the United States for the Supreme Court, and the more recent moves away from intergovernmentalism in the political governance of the EC (qualified majority vote in the Council, dynamism of the Commission, popularly elected parliament). The other argument stresses the increasing importance of the intergovernmental European Council as the supreme body, and the continuing differences among the "formulas" for state-society relations or in the redistribution policies of the member-states—hence the absence of a single "European model," despite some visible differences between western Europe as an entity and Japan or the United States.[13] The distinction is more a matter of emphasis than a profound disagreement.[14] However, it entails, implicitly, two different forecasts.

To muddy the waters even more, I will state my own position. On the one hand, in analyzing the present, I am closer to the more "sober" view, which finds the nation-state transformed yet preserved, and does not see the relation between nation-state and EC as a zero-sum game (if only because much of what is "lost" by the states is "won" not by the Brussels embryonic state, but by the civil societies of Europe). On the other hand, I think that the federalizing process is likely to proceed, in the domain of the Single Market and in areas that—both because of the logic of sectoral integration and because of interstate bargains—are likely to become Community domains so as to help make the Single Market a reality. The two most important of these connected areas are monetary union and immigration. The former is obviously contentious, since good technical reasons justify either a *single* currency or a *common* currency added to the national ones, and sound political reasons explain why Germany's partners prefer a central bank that would, in contrast to the Bundesbank, define its policies (which affect investment, growth, and employment in their countries) from a Community point of view, whereas Germany prefers a central bank that would in effect be the Bundesbank. But it is most likely that the haggling will result in compromises and, with some delays, the establishment of European central banks and a final central bank. As for immigration, entry and naturalization policies differ profoundly by nation, but the common fears and headaches, and need to establish joint rules at the periphery as barriers within the Community fall, are enough to warrant common policies, or at least coordination of national policies.

The result is likely to be an entirely new entity in world affairs: not a traditional confederation, not a federal union, but a remarkable partnership both among states and between them and common institutions. A transfer (or rather a splitting) of loyalty might even begin if these institutions become more parliamentary and less technocratic. But as long as political life remains predominantly national, because issues of redistribution and national idiosyncrasies (such as, say, the *laïcité* issue in France or the different policies on naturalizing foreigners) dominate it, this transfer will remain limited.

The first of the two significant cleavages is that between the Single Market and its connected domains, on the one hand, and the realm of diplomacy and defense, on the other. A common EC foreign policy that would be more than a series of declarations and deplorations and a common security policy with its own effective institutions (that is, a WEU that would regain some of its original powers—for instance, in the realm of arms control—and would stop being, essentially, a debating society, but could mount common operations both within and outside Europe) seem to be as far away as ever. This is not for lack of agreement on identifying threats. The twelve Community members agree on the residual Soviet threat, caused by Soviet might, and by geography; the possible repercussions of either a disintegration of the USSR or a return to authoritarian, militaristic rule in Moscow; the threats to oil supplies from the Middle East, on which western Europe has come to rely increasingly; the threat of masses of refugees either crossing EC borders or having to be repelled, should ethnic conflicts escalate within or among east and central European countries, or should unemployment and misery drive the poor out of these countries or out of the Maghreb; the threat of terrorism; and so forth. But a multitude of threats, many of which are hypothetical, concentrates minds far less than a single, unmistakable enemy, and a new security system would not necessarily contain or prevent several of the ones listed here. Above all, the major west European partners have divergent preferences about how to cope with each of these dangers.

Let us limit ourselves to Germany, Britain, and France, the three principal actors here. The first two have a strong preference for the status quo, and the third proposes to replace it with a scheme it probably knows that nobody else truly wants, so that it could—as usual—both preserve a basically comfortable status quo and appear as a foresighted lonely champion of European reform and of the common interest. The United Kingdom continues to see in NATO—that essentially Anglo-Saxon organization—the main institution for the security of western Europe. Britain has interpreted the EC's disarray in the Gulf crisis as evidence of its impotence in world politics. While London would not object if the west European members of NATO formed a kind of caucus within it, and thus formulated plans for a rapid reaction force that would be able to operate in or outside Europe, the main purpose would be to reinforce NATO (including by extending its scope, via the WEU treaty, which is not limited to Europe). The fact that this notion was rejected by France made it possible for the United States and the United Kingdom to propose a new multinational force structure and a rapid reaction force within NATO, and thus guarantee that NATO will keep its predominance in Europe, and that "out of area" alliances will be ad hoc and interstate, as was the case in the Gulf, where Britain reestablished the "special relationship."

For Germany, the necessary and sufficient framework for its security would be a NATO that provides it with American guarantees, but also with prospects of a greater influence than it had when U.S. forces were abundant and nuclear weapons dominated NATO strategy, in combination with the CSCE. A west European security organization attached to the EC might either drive the Americans out, raise added fears of German preponderance, or put Germany under pressure for military interventions abroad. The Federal Republic has supported the idea of a common security discussion within the EC, but carefully refrained from giving it any substance.

It is France that has interpreted the Gulf crisis as evidence of the need for a diplomatic and security dimension for the Community, and the Europeans' disarray as the effect of its absence. France is now the champion of a reborn WEU linked to the EC, allied to the United States but not reduced to being a branch of or a "bridge" for NATO.[15] The French have objected to the idea of "double-hatted" European forces, at the disposal of both the WEU and NATO, because they see in such a formula a confirmation and an (out of area) extension of America's predominance. They suggest the possibility of contingency planning within an independent WEU, on the basis of a coordination of national forces. But so far, they have not indicated whether and how they would put their nuclear forces at the disposal of such an organization—a reluctance that does nothing to dispel German skepticism. To be sure, if France could get its partners to agree to a scheme that would, in effect, preserve its nuclear autonomy, coordinate west European conventional forces (thus giving France a kind of hold on Germany's), and plan out-of-area actions independently of the United States, Paris would have the best of all possible worlds. British, Dutch, and Portuguese resistance plus German indifference means the preservation of the status quo: a France protected by but not subordinated to NATO in Europe, with purely national nuclear forces and the capacity to act as a quasi–great power abroad when it deems an essential interest at stake. The French emphasize that a common foreign policy must precede a common security organization; this shows that Paris holds little expectation of an early change. Moreover, the divergences among EC members whenever they attempt to take a common diplomatic stand (as in the case of Yugoslavia, where some want above all to preserve the crumbling state's integrity, and others to stress the principle of self-determination) always tempt France to prefer acting as an independent player rather than endorsing the lowest common denominator.

Western Europe's three-way split during the Gulf crisis (with the United Kingdom and France acting as former colonial powers in the Middle East, Germany contributing only money, and the other powers participating in the blockade) and the failure to extend the EC's effectiveness into diplomacy and defense aggravate the second cleavage—between the former Europe of the free (EC and EFTA) and the former Soviet satellites (plus Yugoslavia and Albania). The contrasts are overwhelming, if one compares not only the degrees of ethnic turbulence, the economic and political institutions, the standards of living, and the fate of the environment, but also the degree of cooperation among states in each part of the continent and the amount of institutionalization. In one part, sovereignty is being dismantled and pooled; in the other, it is finally being regained. There has been no western, or west European, "Marshall Plan" for eastern and central Europe. The members of the Community have, deliberately or passively, put "deepening" ahead of "widening." (And while it is true that "widening" would oblige the Community to "deepen" in one respect—by reinforcing its central institutions—it would also dilute the EC's enterprise by introducing states that are quite incapable of accepting the rules and directives of Brussels without either committing economic and social suicide or obtaining countless special exemptions.) Thus the states of east central Europe remain—despite their preferences—outside the EC; outside the European Economic Area Brussels negotiated with the EFTA; and, deliberately, outside Mitterrand's confederation, which is still only a word, and which they dislike because—as the Prague *Assises* in June 1991 made clear—they fear that it would be no more than a "parking place" in which they would be left to linger.[16]

Many of the threats to security listed above affect the countries of the eastern half of Europe even more than the western half. But they remain a security no-man's-land, except for the valuable but limited functions entrusted to the CSCE, which is not a collective security system and has no forces at its disposal. The eastern states have come to appreciate NATO as a deterrent against a resurgent or recalcitrant USSR, and as a "container" of Germany; but they cannot become members of NATO and thus direct beneficiaries of its protection, given clear Soviet opposition to any extension of NATO eastward, and the probable reluctance of the U.S. Congress. Historical enmities or suspicions and stern Soviet warnings make military cooperation among these states doubly difficult. Indeed, one threat that hangs only over some of these states is the Soviet attempt to "sell" to them a bilateral treaty formula that would make it impossible for the signatories to join an alliance or grouping "directed against the other party." In this respect, the absence of a significant WEU, or "WETO," that could provide positive guarantees—or what François Heisbourg calls negative guarantees—to these countries[17] is as serious a hole in the tapestry as the failure to provide them with a substantial amount of public economic assistance in exchange for their mutual cooperation. But the EC suffers from overload, its members' resources are limited or otherwise engaged, and the United States suffers from untended domestic problems and costly Middle Eastern dilemmas. Here as elsewhere, the conflicting pulls of domestic political needs and external imperatives work at the expense of the latter. A revision of the EC's Common Agricultural Policy (CAP) that would allow farm products from east central Europe behind the CAP's wall would create serious troubles with French, German, and other west European farmers. A discussion of security guarantees to countries situated between the limits of NATO and the borders of the USSR would reopen, in the German body politic, some of the wounds of earlier clashes between security worriers (or warriors) and apostles or prophets of peace.

For the time being, an indispensable minimum ought to be done to soften the cleavage between east and west in Europe.[18] It is imperative that the EC devote at least as much energy and money to putting some substance into the idea (if not the controversial word) of confederation as it is putting into its relations with the Lomé countries or with the Maghreb. This would mean extending the European Economic Area beyond the EFTA, opening west European markets to the most exportable products of the east central Europeans, helping the Soviets to increase again their own imports from these countries, and promoting multinational cooperation in the East, for instance by dealing with issues not covered in (trilateral) association agreements, such as energy, transportation, and the environment.[19] And it would be useful to strengthen the still limited institutions of the CSCE, for instance—as the Czechs have suggested[20]—by extending the powers of the Vienna center for the prevention of conflicts over arms control and arms sales, and by creating peacekeeping forces that could intervene either preventively at the request of opposed parties or after a conflict. If the rule of unanimity, and the fear of some CSCE members (such as the Soviet Union and Yugoslavia) of foreign "interference" in domestic affairs, keeps reducing the CSCE's usefulness, the EC—

through the WEU—should undertake such tasks. Beyond this minimum, a commitment by the members of the Community to "widening" once certain political and economic conditions are met in Czechoslovakia, Hungary, and Poland—with a target date of, say, the year 2000 or 2002—would be indispensable, and a promise by the members of the WEU to envisage in due course a system of collective security guarantees for European states from the Atlantic to the Soviet border would be useful. (Such a system would make more sense than the European Security Organization that Richard Ullman advocates including the United States and the USSR[21] and modeled on the WEU, for Moscow's and Washington's participation in a collective security system would raise far more questions—particularly the question of credibility—than would their presence in a diplomatic and confidence-building scheme such as the CSCE.)

THE EUROPEAN POLICIES OF THE UNITED STATES

The United States, in 1989 and the first half of 1990, managed with great skill the withdrawal of Soviet power from eastern Europe and its effects. Washington succeeded in reconciling three potentially divergent concerns: preserving NATO, supporting Gorbachev (which required that the retreat not be turned into a rout), and backing Kohl (and therefore the West German drive for quick reunification). Both Kohl's concessions (on the nature and size of German forces, and on the financing of the Soviet exit from East Germany) and NATO's willingness to accommodate Soviet demands for some evidence of its "transformation" as a necessary condition for Moscow's acceptance of a unified Germany in NATO, played their part in the swift and elegant ballet. But having concentrated first on this delicate transition, then, after August 2, 1990, on the Gulf and finally on the issue of help to the Soviet Union, the U.S. government has had little time to think through the future of its relations with Europe.

In this realm, as well as in the EC, there is always the temptation of "disjointed incrementalism," especially in a period without earthquakes, with great uncertainties and diffuse issues.

Yet, one ought to be able to do better, especially if one wants to incorporate this area into a global policy of world order. American ambivalence toward west European unity remains as strong as ever. On the one hand, Washington frowns on EC policies in agriculture, or air transport, or space, or on attempts to move toward a west European security system unsubordinated to NATO: too much European unity might be a threat. On the other hand, the resonance of the Mearsheimer analysis in Washington and the belief officials or ex-officials occasionally express that the European allies of the United States, left to themselves, would be once more divided or incompetent or impotent, or all three, and thus oblige America once more to save them, at great cost, from their own mess, suggest that Washington fears European disunity even more than European integration.

Yet both attitudes indicate that the American ambition of omnipotence has not been fully overcome; recent celebrations of a post-Gulf "unipolar world" may well reinforce it. But while it is true that only the United States can mount and win a Gulf-like expedition, even the troublemakers in a world that is full of them are unlikely to provide many opportunities for such displays of mastery; certainly Europe does not appear to be a fertile ground for them. Above all, is the nagging issue of American resources for activism abroad, and the question of where the long-term interest of the United States lies: in concentrating, for a while, on internal repairs, or in more benign neglect of the domestic issues in favor of grand diplomacy. Finally, even if one believes that the latter will remain an imperative, the conditions of world politics impose on the United States a new conception and style of leadership: it will have to be multilateral, institutionalized, and in partnership with others. The analysis presented here suggests that the surest way of preventing a return to the past is to favor a continuing institutionalization of European politics, so as to provide for more cooperation, change the context and reduce the intensity of inevitable conflicts, and affect the way in which states define their interests. And this means both accepting—indeed, embracing and exploiting—the redundancy of institutions (instead of attempting to rationalize and streamline them) and trying to overcome the cleavages analyzed above.[22]

For the sake of convenience, I will examine three areas of American-European relations. The first is the traditional domain of *transatlantic relations*. Two main issues matter. One is the management of unavoidable economic friction; the main actors are the United States and the EC. A compromise over agriculture, in the current round of General Agreement on Tariffs and Trade (GATT), is necessary; it is also difficult. The initial positions of both sides were extreme and unrealistic. The Sisyphean nature of the present CAP and the policy's deleterious effects on the peasants of poor countries outside the EC make it untenable in the long run. But domestic constraints will slow down reform; a calendar of change, entailing balanced concessions on both sides, might be the best outcome. Over the issues of access of industrial goods and services from the United States into the Single Market, the general tendency of Community policy, under German and British pressure, has been toward liberalization, away from "fortress Europe." Complications may come from various European resistances to Japanese implantation, but there have also been instances of European-Japanese collaboration and compromises, and European calls for Japanese investments in Europe.[23] The trend seems to be as ambiguous as that in the relationship of the nation-state to the EC: the Community is likely to be both a formidable regional bloc (marked by a constant increase in intra-EC trade) and an international actor, inviting Japanese and American capital in.

The other traditional transatlantic issue requires a drastic turnaround by Washington. The U.S. government is clinging to the dogma of NATO's preponderance in the field of European security; it has sent three warnings in recent months to the members of the Community, telling them that the discussions on a common diplomacy and defense that President Mitterrand and Chancellor Kohl have called for should not weaken or compete with the Atlantic Alliance, but, on the contrary, should strengthen it. The United States has obtained from its partners a recognition of NATO's preeminence. Little has changed, it seems, since the "year of Europe," when Kissinger told the Europeans to subordinate their common concerns to those of the Alliance. The old American ambivalence is particularly manifest in this domain. Washington would like its partners to speak in a single voice, as long as they repeat what the United States tells them. It encourages a revival of the WEU—as long as the latter is a mere subdivision of NATO. This reaction of distrust—in an area where the convergence of interests across the Atlantic is overwhelming—is attributable in part to the fears of European inefficiency and squabbling once the American presence and guidance are removed, to the rather different fear of being unwillingly affected and committed by allied policies unless Washington can be involved in their very elaboration, and to the desire to preserve the superiority of the one common institution that the United States clearly dominates.

It is, however, a shortsighted policy. From a cynical point of view, one might argue that a less pinched American stand, one that would encourage the west Europeans to put some substance into the WEU and to link it directly to the EC, would really be cost-free, since the west Europeans—for the reasons mentioned above—are unlikely to go very far! If, on the contrary, one believes that such American encouragement might actually remove a major reason of Germany's reluctance toward the WEU (the fear of antagonizing and pushing out the United States) and propel the British toward Europe in the realm of defense just as earlier administrations had prodded it toward the Common Market, this redefinition of the security relationship ought not be feared but welcomed. This is so because, insofar as all the European governments—including, most ardently, those of east central Europe—demand the presence of American troops in western Europe (and the Soviets themselves may see it as a lesser evil than an unchecked Germany), the North Atlantic Treaty and Alliance would in no way be imperiled. Moreover, what threatens NATO is not a "rival" European entity, but the course of events: the decline of America's physical presence and of the nuclear component in NATO's strategy risk turning the integrated command into an empty shell—even if the Supreme Allied Commander in Europe (SACEUR) remains an American. And the fading away of the threat that justified so extraordinary a structure in peacetime will contribute to its erosion. It is difficult to see where, "in area," the new rapid reaction and multinational forces will be used, short of a Soviet attack, and "out of area" divisions among the allies are likely to inhibit their use as much as in the past. As a result, one may well—in the absence of a west European entity—end up with a de facto alliance between a small U.S. contingent (backed by the U.S. strategic nuclear arsenal and British-based Forward Based Systems), a conventional "NATO" under the domination of a Germany for which military-security concerns are no longer preeminent, and an autonomous France: not an optimal result. A revived WEU would entail an end of French separatism and oblige the French government to put its defense and strategy in harmony with its economic policy. It would also both *encadrer* Germany and oblige it to think seriously about defense.

Moreover, the Europeans themselves will best handle many of the threats Europe will face—not merely the nonmilitary threats represented by hordes of refugees, but also the possible fallout from interstate or intrastate conflicts in the eastern half of the continent, or threats the Soviet Union could pose to the security of states in that half. The very diffusion of threats ought to make the west Europeans the main actors in the realm of security now. The alternative to a common west European policy to deal with these problems is not a NATO policy, it is paralysis or fractured reactions; and as French officials have warned, the alternative to a west European security entity—allied with but not subordinated to the United States—is not the pre-1989 NATO, but a renationalization of defense policies. Double-hatting of national units from west European countries, assigned both to NATO and to this entity, ought to be acceptable, given a clear division of labor between the NATO and the European commands—that is, a clear division of issues between these institutions. Otherwise, the United States will soon experience the old European fear of being dragged into conflicts against its preferences, and the French (and other west Europeans) will fear American vetoes of moves that would be in the interest of the Europeans. NATO may still be "the only game in town" today, given the WEU's paleness and the CSCE's nature. But changing conditions make it wise to plan for a new game.

The second set of issues is *the relationship of the Atlantic allies to the East* (eastern Europe and the USSR). The allies need to coordinate their policies toward the Soviet Union, so as to balance the desirable pressure for democratization and for a transformation of the decaying centralized empire into a voluntary union, with the equally necessary support to a central government that is, for all its flaws, still preferable both to the old Stalinist model and to disintegration. Economic assistance should be far better planned than it has been until now: initiatives have been national and sporadic; the United States and the EC ought to prepare them jointly (this would be one way of preventing an eventually too large or autonomous role for Germany here). The same ought to be done—but on a larger scale—to help the three countries of east central Europe; the west Europeans will have to provide the main initiatives and resources, and the Marshall Plan can serve as a model. As for security assurances to these countries, it will also be easier for the west Europeans to provide them than for NATO (see above)—another reason why the United States should encourage a west European defense entity.

The third domain is that of *American-European relations outside the continent.* If we mean what we say when we talk about a new world order, this is clearly a realm of the highest importance—especially as, paradoxically, the restraints that the superpowers imposed on their clients to avoid collisions (restraints resulting not from the dubious virtues of bipolarity but from the risks of nuclear catastrophe) are not likely to be effective any longer, and the loss of influence and power of the Soviet Union reduces the benefits that the cooperation of the former chief rivals might otherwise have brought.

In some ways, the most difficult issue here is the management of out-of-area crises. One of the partners has the habit of a world role, but decreasing resources. The European "partners" have even more limited ones, because the military establishments of the west European countries are not well geared to large- or even medium-scale external engagements, or, as in Germany's case, are constitutionally prevented from committing themselves. Moreover, disagreements about goals often divide the

Americans from the west Europeans, as well as split the latter. In the short run, crisis management will remain a matter of ad hoc coalitions. In the long run, it will—again—be in America's interest to encourage the west Europeans to coordinate their foreign policies and to plan jointly, through a defense entity, possible interventions abroad. The fact that both NATO and the CSCE limit their scope to the continent contributes to the Germans' tendency to restrict their military concerns to the European theater and thus, as Heisbourg notes,[24] condemns the west Europeans, out-of-area, to purely national, low-key actions by only some of them, whereas, as he puts it, the EC's famous principle of subsidiarity would require a collective reaction at the level of the Community.

If crisis management—for many other reasons, as well—risks being unsatisfactory, prevention will have to become the key to world order. This will require a break with the past in two vital respects. The United States, the USSR, and the Europeans will have to coordinate their policies so as to put an end to their exports of advanced military technologies (or of technologies capable of receiving lethal military applications) and to reduce their exports of more traditional, but potentially just as disruptive military equipment. The immediate post-Gulf record is far from encouraging, for two powerful factors converge on "politics as usual": domestic constituencies of businesses and workers (including, for instance, in Czechoslovakia) and the traditional "game" of rewarding one's regional friends. The CSCE could serve as the framework for such an effort, inspired by Cocom. In addition, perhaps under UN auspices, the same countries ought to take part in the establishment of regional arms control and inspection regimes. But dealing with weapons is not enough. A much bigger effort will be necessary to resolve disputes before they erupt into violent crises. What can be done in eastern Europe under CSCE or, as in the Yugoslav case, EC auspices needs to be done, in other troubled parts of the world, under UN auspices, but with the United States, Japan, the USSR, and the west Europeans serving as the secular arm or steering diplomatic group for the UN. Once again, this raises the issue of the European partner.

The problem of European-American relations risks becoming not the tragedy of a return to the cataclysmic past, but the drama of a political vacuum, despite the somewhat chaotic abundance of overlapping institutions. America, the dominant partner of the recent past, may turn more inward; a European partner remains to be constructed. Just as its plate was filled by the menu of the Single Market, the EC has been assaulted by new needs and demands, both for functional and for geographic expansion. Conceived on the assumption of a stable division of Europe, with a continuing if moderated Cold War, the west European *relance* of 1984–1987 absorbs the bulk of the members' energies, just when everything else starts moving all around them. The real threat to Europe's dream of peace and democracy, vintage 1989, is not the neorealist nightmare of collisions among ambitious major actors, but economic chaos, political regression away from democracy, ethnic violence, and a void in cooperation. The real European question mark for the future is not balancing, concert, or anarchy—notions that are all conceptually inadequate—nor is it whether the nation-state in western Europe will survive. It is whether the pooled central power of the Community will be sufficiently strengthened to accomplish two goals: create effectiveness in the realms (defense and diplomacy) where either national autonomy has remained strong, but actual policies based on it have produced more illusions than results, or it has been abandoned to an extra-European big brother whose role is now far less justified; and engage and gradually absorb those countries of east central Europe that would otherwise become disaster areas.

A positive answer requires new policies everywhere: in Washington and Brussels, in London and Paris and Bonn (or Berlin). But the most decisive players—or nonplayers—will be the United States and Germany: Washington, because what is needed is, at last, a shift from primacy to world order, Bonn (or Berlin) because either the temptation of acting again as an ordinary great national power—a temptation that Germany has strenuously resisted so far—or the more likely self-indulgence in self-absorption (Germany behaving as a large Switzerland) would have fateful effects. In the first case, the patient institutional buildup would stop and unravel; in the second, the new 1992 Europe would fall far short of its global challenges and duties. In neither case would we be back in the 1910s or 1930s. But the progress toward a new kind of politics would be thwarted, and the more benign forms of traditional international politics (such as concert and balancing, which anyhow are cousins) might then reassert themselves. Presently, French officials gloomily point to an American will-to-dominate, and to signs of a new German will-to-autonomy. I am more optimistic about Germany than about the United States, whose capacity for long-term planning—manifest in 1947–1949—has suffered a long eclipse, for reasons in which government fragmentation and global complexity play a large part. Still, the time has come for a new bargain, among the leading west European states, and between them and the United States, if they want to shape the future instead of merely letting it happen.[25]

NOTES

1. John Mearsheimer, "Back to the Future: Instability in Europe after the Cold War," *International Security,* vol. 15, no. 1 (Summer 1990), pp. 5–56.
2. Stephen van Evera, "Primed for Peace: Europe after the Cold War," *International Security,* Vol. 15, no. 3 (Winter 1990/91), pp. 7–57.
3. Raymond Aron, *Peace and War* (New York: Doubleday, 1966), ch. 5.
4. See the correspondence provoked by Mearsheimer's article, in *International Security,* vol. 15, no. 2 (Fall 1990), pp. 191–199, and vol. 15, no. 3 (Winter 1990/91), pp. 216–222; Stanley Hoffmann, "The Case for Leadership," *Foreign Policy* no. 81 (Winter 1990/91), pp. 20–38; and Richard Ullman, *Securing Europe* (Princeton, N.J.: Princeton University Press, 1991), pp. 139ff.
5. Stanley Hoffmann, "A New World and Its Troubles," in Nicholas X. Rizopoulos, ed., *Sea-Changes: American Foreign Policy in a World Transformed* (New York: Council on Foreign Relations, 1990), pp. 274–291.
6. Joseph Nye, Jr., *Bound to Lead* (New York: Basic Books, 1990), ch. 6.
7. Stephen Walt, *The Origins of Alliances* (Ithaca, N.Y.: Cornell University Press, 1987).
8. See the conclusion of Louise Richardson and Celeste Wallander, "A Comparison of British and Soviet Adjustments to Structural Change in Europe" (Paper for the ISA meeting of March 1991.)
9. For instance, in the Yugoslav crises of June–July 1991, France, Britain, and Italy favored the EC, Germany—at first—the CSCE; France, on the issue of global restraints on arms sales opposes a role for the G-7 and prefers the UN Security Council; the Czechs prefer access to the EC, to Mitterrand's Confederation, etc. . . . .

10. William Wallace, "The Changing Role of the State in Western Europe." Paper presented at the seminar, "Europe in the 1990s," sponsored by the Economic and Social Research Council and the Royal Institute for International Affairs; London, March 15, 1991.

11. See Wolfgang Wessels, "The Growth of European Integration and the West European State," Bonn, March 1991.

12. Alan Milward, "Historical Elements of a Return to a Comprehensive Theory of Integration." Paper presented at the seminar, "Europe in the 1990s," sponsored by the Economic and Social Research Council and the Royal Institute for International Affairs, London, March 15, 1991.

13. See Jean-Claude Casanova, "Bourgeoise et Homogène," in Dominique Schnapper and Henri Mendras, eds., Six Manières d'être Européen (Paris: Gallimard, 1990), pp. 220–240.

14. See Robert Keohane and Stanley Hoffmann, eds., The New European Community (Boulder, Colo: Westview Press, 1991).

15. See Claire Tréan, "France–OTAN: Le Chat et la Souris," Le Monde, May 2, 1991, pp. 1 and 3.

16. Mitterrand undercut his own scheme by: a) stating just before the Assises that full membership for Poland, Hungary, and Czechoslovakia in the EC would take dozens of years, and b) proposing, at first, a Confederation that would include the Soviet Union but not the United States. Havel and his central and eastern European colleagues made it clear: a) that the United States (and Canada) should also be included, and b) that, in such a case, the CSCE sufficed!

17. François Heisbourg, "From a Common European Home to a European Security System," see Chapter 2 of this book, pp. 35–58. Heisbourg suggests that, for instance, France would promise not to use Hungarian territory for military purposes, provided no other country uses it in such a manner.

18. See the excellent suggestions of six west European foreign policy institutes in The Community and the Emerging European Democracies, by Gianni Bonvincini et al, June 1991 (published in English by RIIA).

19. See Elizabeth Guigou, "Les Européens et Leur Destin," Politique Internationale, no. 51 (Fall 1991), pp. 313–328, at p. 318.

20. Le Monde, May 5–6, 1991, p. 4.

21. Ullman, Securing Europe, ch. 4.

22. See Frédéric Bozo and Jérôme Paolini, "L'Europe entre elle-même et le Golfe," Politique étrangère, forthcoming.

23. See Michael Borrus and John Zysman, "Industrial Strength and Regional Response: Japan's Impact on European Integration" (Paper for the Council on Foreign Relations project on 1992 and the Shape of Europe, March 1991).

24. Heisbourg, Chapter 2 of this book, pp. 35–58.

25. For similar conclusions, see Helen Wallace, "Which Europe for Which Europeans?" Chapter 1 of this book, pp. 15–34; and Jenonne Walker, "Security in Post-confrontation Europe," Beyond the Cold War: Current Issues in European Security, no. 3 (Woodrow Wilson International Center for Scholars, Washington, D.C., 1990).

INDEX

Africa, 31
Aftenposten, 109–10
Agreement of Cooperation and
Friendship (1991), 162
Agricultural Producers Association,
108
Aho, C. Michael, 1
Aho, Esko, 108
Albania, 87, 147, 208
Alfa Romeo, 182
Algeria, 21
Antall, Joszef, 94, 141–42
Aron, Raymond, 195
ASEAN (Association of Southeast
Asian Nations), 103, 186
Ash, Timothy Garton, 134
Assembly of Europe, 118
Atlantic Declaration (1990), 21
Austria, 8, 9, 48, 98, 99, 130,
157; and the EFTA, 100–103;
and EPU, 101; and free trade
agreements, 95, 97; and Ger-
many, comparison of, 40; and
Liechtenstein, 107; and neu-
trality, 94, 100–103, 115, 122;
and the Pentagonale group, 155–
56; and postwar organizational
lines, 92; and regionalization,
120; and Switzerland, 106; and
the total German-speaking population in the EC, 125 n. 14; and
trade agreements, 97; and WEU,
101, 125 n. 16

Baker, James, 52, 57 n. 12
Balcerowicz, Leszek, 137
Balkan Development Bank, 156
Balkans, 26, 102–3, 134, 142–48,
156–57. *See also* Yugoslavia
Baltic states, 49, 87, 102, 109, 114;
and EFTA, 112; and separatist

and ethnic movements, 147;
Soviet crackdown in, 149, 156
Belgium, 28, 72–73, 81
Benelux countries, 103, 118, 165
Berlin Wall, fall of, 1, 2, 5, 7, 9, 10
Bildt, Carl, 104
Black Sea Zone of Economic Coop-
eration, 156–57
BMW, 176, 178
Borrus, Michael, 10, 11, 172–93
Bosch, Robert, 177
Britain, 2, 5, 12, 76, 82–84, 187,
199, 202–7, 214; and NATO,
27–38; and Sweden, 103; and the
WEU, 117
BRITE, 95
Brundtland, Gro Harlem, 109–10
Bulgaria, 46–47, 87, 134, 135, 144–
45, 150, 156–57, 161
Bulgaria Socialist Party (BSP), 144
Bundesbank, 5, 70, 199, 205

Canada, 48, 133, 152, 184
CAP (Common Agricultural Policy),
210, 11
Carlsson, Ingvar, 104
Ceausescu, Nicolae, 133, 143–44
Center Party (Finland), 108, 110
Central Bank Governors Commit-
tee, 69–70
Central Federation of Finnish
Trade Unions, 108
CFE (Conventional Forces in
Europe) treaty, 23, 28, 38, 44
Chicago Council on Foreign Rela-
tions, 65
Christian Democratic Party
(Sweden), 104
Civic Democratic Party
(Czechoslovakia), 139–40
Civic Forum, 134, 139–40, 145

221

ABOUT THE AUTHORS

Dr. Wolfgang Danspeckgruber is a lecturer in politics, on European and East European politics and security issues, Department of Politics, Princeton University. He is also Director of the Liechtenstein Colloquium on European and International Affairs, Vaduz. He has published on European foreign and security issues as well as EC and EFTA relations. An edited volume on Emerging Dimensions of European Security will be published in November 1991 by Westview Press.

François Heisbourg is Directory of the International Institute for Strategic Studies in London. He served on the Policy Planning Staff of the French Foreign Ministry and as an advisor to the French Minister of Defense. He is the author of numerous works in both French and English including *La Puce, Les Hommes et la Bombe, The Changing Strategic Landscape,* and *The Strategic Implications of Change in the Soviet Union.*

Stanley Hoffmann is Douglas Dillon Professor of the Civilization of France at Harvard University and has served as Chairman of the Center for European Studies since 1969. He is a regular contributor to scholarly journals and the author of many books, including, *Contemporary Theory in International Relations, Primacy or World Order,* and *Duties Beyond Borders.* Most recently he coauthored *The New European Community: Decision-Making and Institutional Change.*

F. Stephen Larrabee is a senior staff member in the International Policy Department at RAND in Santa Monica. From 1989–1990 he was Distinguished Scholar-in-Residence at the Institute for East-West Security Studies (IEWSS) in New York, and from 1983 to 1989 he served as Vice President and Director of the Institute. Dr. Larrabee has served as codirector of the Soviet and East European Research Program at the Johns Hopkins University School of Advanced International Studies (SAIS), taught at

Cornell University, and served on the U.S. National Security Council staff as a specialist on Soviet-East European affairs. His most recent works include *The Two German States and European Security* and (with Robert Blackwill) *Conventional Arms Control and East-West Security.*

Peter Ludlow is the current and founding Director of the Centre for European Policy Studies in Brussels. Previously he was a lecturer in history at the University of London and at the European University Institute in Florence. He has written extensively on western Europe and the European Community including *The Making of the European Monetary System, Beyond 1992: Europe and its Western Partners,* and *Setting EC Priorities.*

Gregory Treverton is Senior Fellow at the Council on Foreign Relations with responsibility for European and politico-military issues. He has worked in the U.S. government on the staff of the first Senate Select Committee on Intelligence (the Church Committee) and as staff member for Western Europe on the National Security Council during the Carter Administration. Immediately before joining the Council, he served on the faculty of the John F. Kennedy School of Government at Harvard University for six years. He is the author of numerous books and articles including: *Making the Alliance Work: The United States and Western Europe, Covert Action: The Limits of Intervention in the Postwar World,* and most recently *America, Germany and the Future of Europe.*

Helen Wallace is Director of the Western European Programme for the Royal Institute of International Affairs in London. She is also a visiting professor at the College of Europe in Bruges. She has authored numerous articles and books on the European Community and European integration including *National Governments and the European Communities, Budgetary Politics: the Finances of the European Community, Europe: the Challenge of Diversity,* and *The Wider Western Europe* (forthcoming).

John Zysman is professor of Political Science at the University of California at Berkeley and Michael Borrus teaches in the joint

School of Engineering-Business program on the Management of Technology. They are Co-Directors of the Berkeley Roundtable on the International Economy and are co-authoring *The Highest Stakes: The Economic Foundations of the New Security* (forthcoming in 1992).